WIN-WIN PERFORMANCE MANAGEMENT/APPRAISAL

WIN-WIN PERFORMANCE MANAGEMENT/APPRAISAL

A Problem Solving Approach

ERWIN RAUSCH

With assistance from
MICHAEL H. FRISCH, Ph.D.

A Wiley-Interscience Publication

JOHN WILEY & SONS

New York • Chichester • Brisbane • Toronto • Singapore

This publication is designed to provide accurate and
authoritative information in regard to the subject
matter covered. It is sold with the understanding that
the publisher is not engaged in rendering legal, accounting,
or other professional service. If legal advice or other
expert assistance is required, the services of a competent
professional person should be sought. *From a Declaration
of Principles jointly adopted by a Committee of the
American Bar Association and a Committee of Publishers.*

Library of Congress Cataloging in Publication Data:

Rausch, Erwin, 1923–
  Win-win performance management/appraisal.

  "A Wiley-Interscience publication."
  Includes index.
  1. Performance standards. 2. Employees,
Rating of. 3. Compensation management.
4. Personnel management. I. Frisch,
Michael H. II. Title.

HF5549.5.P35R38   1986   658.3'142   85-12201
ISBN 0-471-86777-2

Printed in the United States of America

10 9 8 7 6 5 4 3 2 1

PREFACE

Conceptually, performance management is a simple idea: individuals should be rewarded in the form of compensation increases, bonuses, opportunities for promotion, and other benefits in proportion to the contribution they make to the growth and health of the organization. The principle which should guide its implementation is even simpler: it can be summed up in one word: *fairness*. However, this is where simplicity ends. As one analyzes what the idea and the principle mean, they become very complicated indeed. For example, how does one measure and compare the relative contributions of a purchasing agent, a secretary, a machine operator, or a salesperson? And what does fairness mean? Two tough questions, when one tries to apply them.

In a way, these questions are behind your decision to read this book. You undoubtedly belong to one of the following groups:

1.   You are in a supervisory position.* You want to know more about performance management and about the answers to the questions so you can improve your own performance.

2.   You are in a position where you have significant responsibility for deciding how the performance management system is to operate. You either have authority to initiate changes in the system or you are consulted on changes. You

* Please note that the word supervisor is used for all levels of management. Note also that "learning supervisor" does not necessarily refer to a new supervisor but to any supervisor who endeavors to improve personal competence.

want to see what ideas you can gain from this book that
might help you improve the system.

3. You do not have the authority to make changes in the existing system, but you would like to know more about how
you can make best use of that system.

To satisfy your needs, this book is divided into five parts:

Part 1—provides a detailed overview of performance management, discusses the major components of effective systems, and provides suggestions for installing a new one

Part 2—discusses considerations in the design of a new system

Part 3—discusses problems which supervisors face who work
within an existing system

Part 4—provides a detailed discussion of skills required for
competent implementation of the various steps in a
performance management system

Appendix—provides samples of forms useful in performance
management.

If your primary reason for reading this book is described in (1),
you probably will want to read the entire book, or at least skim
thoroughly and read where it covers topics of greatest interest for
you.

If your primary reason is in (2), then Parts 1 and 2 contain the
more valuable sections for you.

However, if you are in the third group, you will gain valuable
insights from the chapters in Part 1 which explain the performance management system, and from Parts 3 and 4. These chapters
cover the steps you can take so you will gain maximum advantage
from the strengths of the system in your organization, while minimizing its disadvantages. They also provide many suggestions on
how you can work best with shortcomings of the system and on
how your appraisal interviews can be more effective and satisfying
experiences. In addition, you may want to skim very quickly
through the other sections to see whether they might contain useful ideas.

Whatever your purpose, I hope that you will find this book both

a practical source of ideas for solving problems related to performance management, and a valuable reference on management concepts and techniques which maintain and strengthen a viable performance management process.

Please note that two words are used with specific meanings that
may be somewhat different from common use:

1. *Employee* is used to describe any employee in the organization, but specifically those who report to you, or to a specific supervisor, including supervisory, managerial, and
   professional employees.

2. *Supervisor* is used to describe all managerial and supervisory employees. Thus, use of the word is different from the
   use in organizational titles where managers are usually considered to be at higher levels than supervisors. Please note
   though, that every supervisor *manages* because he or she
   must plan, organize, implement, follow-up, and also supervise. By contrast, one can manage a project by performing
   the same four managerial functions, but need not supervise
   even a single employee. Supervising means working with
   people; managing can be done well without the same close
   contact with people. For these reasons, the word supervisor
   is more appropriate than the word manager, in describing
   the individual who sets standards, and measures and analyzes performance, with and for other employees.

PERSPECTIVE ON THE HISTORY OF PERFORMANCE APPRAISAL

A few words about the history of performance management might
give some perspective before you read on. Performance management systems have a long and venerable history. Competent administration of these systems, on the other hand, has had a more
checkered past.

Ever since the Industrial Revolution brought the work from the
home into factories and offices, management has attempted to
measure and evaluate the work of employees so that tangible rewards, and disciplinary procedures if necessary, can be based on

the contribution which the employee makes toward the success of the organization.

Some form of performance management dates back to an "Imperial Rater" in the Wei Dynasty in the third century A.D. Industrial performance management approaches obviously came much later; they probably began in Robert Owen's cotton mills in the early 1800s. Fairly widespread use of performance management techniques with blue-collar employees did not start until after World War I. Appraisal of managerial and professional performance was even slower and has been used extensively only since the decade after World War II.

Earliest industrial performance evaluation and appraisal programs were simple. People were evaluated, and paid, on the basis of the amount of work they turned out, or the number of "pieces" they produced, often with provision for bonuses or other tangible rewards. It was quickly recognized, however, that in many jobs the quality also affected the contribution of the individual, and evaluation procedures as well as compensation plans were expanded to include quality consideration.

In many jobs and industries, it was not practical or effective to pay "piece rates" (payment for number of acceptable units produced), usually because only a few pieces of a kind had to be made and piece rates could not be established. The need to evaluate the output of individuals therefore brought many different systems to measure production. These systems were based on standards. In the simplest systems, these standards were established by direct observations, often with a stop watch. In more elaborate systems, minute standards were developed in advance for every small movement such as "reach 2 inches," "grasp," "release," and so forth. These standards were then combined to establish *predetermined time standards* for each job on a production line.

As work gradually shifted from directly measurable physical output to more complex activities involving the application of knowledge, more elaborate measurements were needed. At first, these were based on character and personality traits of the individuals, in addition to the supervisor's overall judgment of quantity and quality of the work produced.

Among these personality traits were items such as initiative,

Name		Position	Location	Rating as of	19
Encircle rating figure for each quality: **5** Excellent, **4** Good, **3** Average, **2** Fair, **1** Poor					
QUALIFICATION	**RATING**	RATER	—COMMENTS—	REVIEWER	

	QUALIFICATION	RATING
I S	Ambition	5 4 3 2 1
	Character	5 4 3 2 1
	Education	5 4 3 2 1
	Health	5 4 3 2 1
	Loyalty	5 4 3 2 1
	Outside Interests	5 4 3 2 1
	Personality	5 4 3 2 1
KNOWS	Present Activity	5 4 3 2 1
	Other Activities	5 4 3 2 1
	Procedure and Policy	5 4 3 2 1
D O E S	Accepts Responsibility	5 4 3 2 1
	Application	5 4 3 2 1
	Attendance	5 4 3 2 1
	Care and Exactness	5 4 3 2 1
	Cooperation	5 4 3 2 1
	Expression	5 4 3 2 1
	Follows Instructions	5 4 3 2 1
	Housekeeping	5 4 3 2 1
	Initiative	5 4 3 2 1
	Intelligence	5 4 3 2 1
	Judgment	5 4 3 2 1
	Rate of Work	5 4 3 2 1
	Sense of Economy	5 4 3 2 1

Figure 1. Performance rating form with very vague standards, using several criteria that are subjective and not work-related; simple numerical rating scale (Dale Yoder, *Personnel Management and Industrial Relations*, 4th ed., © 1956, pp. 571, 572, 574–575. Reprinted by permission of Prentice-Hall, Inc., Englewood Cliffs, N.J.)

attitude, character, loyalty, personality, intelligence, and application. These measurements were really independent of the work. They were often vague and subject to many different interpretations. Two extreme examples* are shown in Figures 1 and 2. In the first of these forms, rate of work, the only results-oriented item, is second-to-last in a list of 23 items. Of the others, very few are factually measurable. Attempts were soon made, therefore, to develop measuring techniques that were fairly precise and closely related to matters which were important to success on the job. Still, these systems were highly subjective and allowed the rating or appraising supervisors great latitude in interpretation.

As a result of continuing efforts to develop better systems, ap-

* Dale Yoder, *Personnel Management and Industrial Relations,* 3rd Ed. (Prentice-Hall, 1948), pp. 329 and 331.

FORM NO. 619 5M 6-35 ___ 8   STATE OF MINNESOTA   DEPARTMENT OF HIGHWAYS

NAME   TITLE   CLASS OF WORK   DATE

QUARTERLY RATING REPORT — EMPLOYMENT RECORD

NO.	SUBJECT	EXCEPTIONAL..10		ABOVE AVERAGES..8		AVERAGE..6		BELOW AVERAGE..4		POOR..2		Do Not Use This Column
1	HEALTH	ROBUST	___	VIGOROUS	___	GOOD	___	FRAIL	___	SICKLY	___	
2	KNOWLEDGE	COMPLETE	___	VERY GOOD	___	AVERAGE	___	MEAGER	___	INADEQUATE	___	
3	INITIATIVE	EXCELLENT	___	VERY GOOD	___	FAIR	___	POOR	___	NONE	___	
4	SPEED	VERY RAPID	___	RAPID	___	AVERAGE	___	SLOW	___	VERY SLOW	___	
5	ACCURACY	EXCEPTIONAL	___	ACCURATE	___	AVERAGE	___	INACCURATE	___	CARELESS	___	
6	RELIABILITY	EXCEPTIONAL	___	DEPENDABLE	___	SATISFACTORY	___	IRREGULAR	___	UNRELIABLE	___	
7	JUDGMENT	EXCEPTIONAL	___	VERY GOOD	___	ORDINARY	___	POOR	___	RASH	___	
8	INTEREST	ENTHUSIASTIC	___	INTERESTED	___	AVERAGE	___	INDIFFERENT	___	NOT INTERESTED	___	
9	CONDUCT	SPLENDID	___	VERY GOOD	___	AVERAGE	___	POOR	___	TROUBLESOME	___	
10	SELF-CONFIDENCE	EXCEPTIONAL	___	VERY GOOD	___	AVERAGE	___	POOR	___	TIMID	___	

OTHER QUALIFICATIONS

OTHER DEFICIENCIES

SIGNATURE ENGINEER IN CHARGE   SIGNATURE OF ANOTHER PARTY

THIS COLUMN FOR CENTRAL OFFICE USE ↓ TOTAL

SEE INSTRUCTIONS ON REVERSE SIDE

Figure 2. Performance rating form with rating scale modified with descriptions; vague standards, using several criteria that are subjective and not work-related (Dale Yoder, *Personnel Management and Industrial Relations*, 4th ed., © 1956, pp. 571, 572, 574–575. Reprinted by permission of Prentice-Hall, Inc., Englewood Cliffs, N.J.)

praisal procedures began to emphasize job-related and more easily measurable elements, such as quantity and quality of the work, attendance, cooperation, and matters related to quality of decisions. Furthermore, instead of leaving it entirely to each supervisor to define these as he or she saw them, very specific descriptions were provided for the different rating levels.

Examples of these improved approaches appear in Figures 3 and 4.* These examples provide more factual guidelines and thus help the evaluation but they still contain elements such as judgment, industry/diligence, and initiative. Note also that in Figure 3, quantity of work appears twice, in items 4 and 15, and partially in item 5.

As evaluation systems became more precise and more relevant

* Yoder, *Personnel Management,* pp. 332–335.

to the job, they also improved in usefulness. Gradually they became quite valuable for structured and repetitive work where such general characteristics could be applied fairly uniformly. They still depended heavily on the judgment of supervisors and often high ratings were given to employees toward whom the supervisors were favoraly inclined regardless of merit, or vice versa.

The concepts of quantity and quality of work, attendance, and decision quality are difficult to evaluate when the work involved professional work or supervisory activities. Therefore, the evaluation programs based on such characteristics were not considered fully satisfactory and other measures were needed. For instance, some "behavioral" systems were used in which the evaluation was based on descriptions of what the employee did or failed to do with respect to key elements of the job. These systems, too, did not satisfy the need for factual and thorough appraisals. In fact, at least one research study provided many examples of organizations where, even though fairly formal performance management procedures existed, personnel decisions on promotion and firing often ignored or even opposed the performance evaluation results.

When the concept of management by objectives became widely known in the 1950s, supervisors naturally looked to it to provide a more meaningful way to appraise the performance of employees.

Two types of performance management systems were developed. One was based on *goals*. The subordinate would accept, or commit, to achieve certain goals and he or she would understand that performance appraisal would be based on the achievement of these goals. In the other type of system, *key accountabilities* (often called key job impact areas) were identified and performance standards were set for the major activities necessary for success in these key accountabilities.

As these goal and key accountability programs came into widespread use, it became apparent that goals, and the results expected in the key accountabilities, despite their many advantages, were not as useful for performance appraisal as had first been thought. Since goals and results are primarily estimates or forecasts of what could be achieved, many external influences affect their actual achievement. Sometimes supervisors made allowance for the external events that affected achievement; at other times

GRAPHIC RATING SCALE

Efficiency Rating Form No. 8

(SEE INSTRUCTIONS ON REVERSE SIDE OF SHEET)

NON-SUPERVISORY .... □
SUPERVISORY .... □
(CHECK ONE)

CLASSIFICATION SYMBOLS		
SERVICE	GRADE	CLASS

Name _____
(Surname)　　　(Given name)　　　(Initial)

Department _____
(Bureau)　　　(Division)　　　(Section)　　　(Subsection)

NOTE: MARK ONLY ON ELEMENTS CHECKED IN LEFT-HAND MARGIN

ELEMENT NUMBER	SERVICE ELEMENTS						DO NOT USE SPACE BELOW
☐ 1	Consider accuracy; ability to produce work free from error; ability to detect errors.	Highest possible accuracy.	Very careful.	Careful. No more than reasonable time required for revision.	Careless. Time required for revision greatly excessive.	Practically worthless work.	
☐ 2	Consider reliability in the execution of assigned tasks; dependability in following instructions; accuracy of any parts of product appraisable in terms of accuracy.	Greatest possible reliability.	Very reliable.	Reliable.	Doubtful reliability.	Unreliable.	
☐ 3	Consider neatness and orderliness of work.	Greatest possible neatness and orderliness.	Very neat and orderly.	Neat and orderly.	Disorderly.	Slovenly.	
☐ 4	Consider the speed or rapidity with which work is accomplished; the quantity of work produced in a given time; the dispatch with which a task of known difficulty is completed.	Greatest possible rapidity.	Very rapid.	Good speed.	Slow.	Hopelessly slow.	
☐ 5	Consider industry; diligence; attentiveness; energy and application to duties; the degree to which the employee really concentrates on the work at hand.	Greatest possible diligence.	Very diligent.	Industrious.	Inattentive to work.	Lazy.	
☐ 6	Consider knowledge of work; present knowledge of job and of work related to it; specialized knowledge in his particular field.	Completely informed.	Unusually well informed.	Well informed.	Poorly informed.	Lacking.	
☐ 7	Consider judgment; ability to grasp a situation and draw correct conclusions; ability to profit by experience; sense of proportion or relative values; common sense.	Perfect judgment.	Excellent judgment.	Good judgment.	Poor judgment.	Neglects and misinterprets the facts.	

The form contains the following criteria (items 8–15) with rating descriptions across five levels:

8 Consider success in winning confidence and respect through his personality; courtesy and tact; control of emotions; poise.
- Inspiring.
- Pleasing.
- Weak.
- Repellent.

9 Consider cooperativeness; ability to work for and with others; readiness to give new ideas and methods a fair trial; desire to observe and conform with the policies of the management.
- Greatest possible cooperativeness.
- Unusually pleasing. / Very cooperative.
- Cooperative.
- Difficult to handle.
- Obstructive.

10 Consider initiative; resourcefulness; success in doing things in new and better ways and in adapting improved methods to his own work; constructive thinking.
- Greatest possible originality.
- Very resourceful.
- Progressive.
- Rarely suggests.
- Needs detailed instruction.

11 Consider execution; ability to pursue to the end difficult investigations or assignments.
- Completes assignments in shortest possible time.
- Completes assignments in unusually short time.
- Completes assignments in a reasonable time.
- Slow in completing assignments; or does not complete assignments.
- Takes inordinately long and accomplishes little.

12 Consider organizing ability; success in organizing the work of his section, division, or department, both by delegating authority wisely and by making certain that results are achieved; ability to plan so as to complete tasks on schedule.
- Highest possible effectiveness.
- Effective under difficult circumstances.
- Effective under normal circumstances.
- Lacks planning ability.
- Inefficient.

13 Consider leadership; success in winning the cooperation of his subordinates and in welding them into a loyal and effective working unit; decisiveness; energy; self control; tact; courage; fairness in dealing with others.
- Most capable and forceful leader possible.
- Very capable and forceful leader.
- Capable leader.
- Fails to command confidence.
- Antagonizes subordinates.

14 Consider success in improving and developing employees by imparting information, developing talent, and arousing ambition; ability to teach; ability to explain matters clearly and comprehensively.
- Develops employees of highest possible caliber.
- Develops very efficient employees.
- Develops competent employees.
- Fails to develop employees.
- Discourages and misinforms employees.

15 QUANTITY OF WORK (To be used only where accurate and comprehensive OUTPUT RECORDS are kept.)
- Highest possible output.
- High output.
- Good output.
- Low output.
- Practically no output.

On the whole, do you consider the department and attitude of this employee toward his work to be satisfactory? Answer "Yes," "No," or "Fairly so" _____

Rated by: _____   Reviewed by: _____   Total _____
(Rating officer)   (Reviewing officer)   (Date)   Final rating _____

15—218

Figure 3. Performance rating form with fairly detailed descriptions of the criteria and of the rating levels; still some purely subjective criteria (Dale Yoder, *Personnel Management and Industrial Relations*, 4th ed., © 1956, pp. 571, 572, 574–575. Reprinted by permission of Prentice-Hall, Inc., Englewood Cliffs, N.J.)

xiii

EMPLOYEE APPRAISAL

XII-11

Employee's Name _____ Classification _____

Bank _____ Department _____ Division _____

Rating Supervisor _____ Section _____

This form is designed to help you appraise accurately the value of employees to the organization. You are asked to rate the employee on each of the several traits or qualities listed here. After each trait there is a line representing various degrees of the trait. The descriptive phrases beneath the line indicate the amounts or degrees of the trait represented by five points along the line. They are guide-posts. You rate the employee by checking at any place along the line that represents your judgment of him.

In view of the importance of these ratings, you are asked to study and observe the rules printed on the other side of the sheet.

QUALITY OF WORK

| Doubtful that quality is satisfactory | While not unsatisfactory, quality is not quite up to standard. | Quality is quite satisfactory | Quality of work is superior to that of general run of employees | Exceptionally high quality | No chance to observe |

VOLUME OF WORK

| Unusually high output | Turns out more work than general run of comparable employees | Average satisfactory output | Inclined to be slow | Insufficient output | No chance to observe |

CAPACITY TO DEVELOP

| Future growth doubtful | Moderate development ahead | Shows promise | Very promising promotional material | Great future growth probable; should go far | No chance to observe |

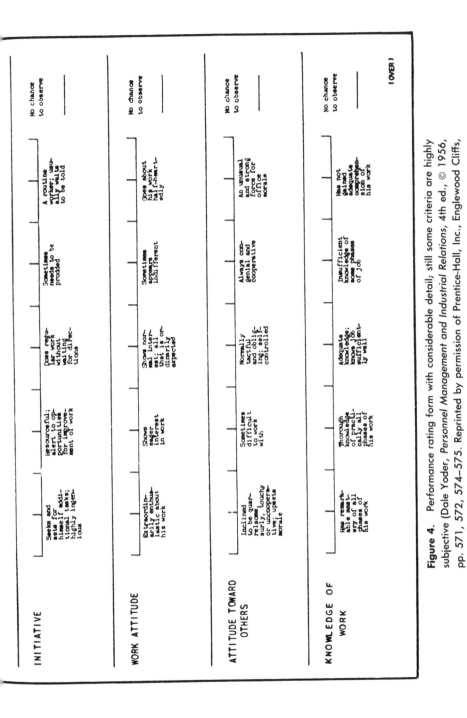

Figure 4. Performance rating form with considerable detail; still some criteria are highly subjective (Dale Yoder, *Personnel Management and Industrial Relations*, 4th ed., © 1956, pp. 571, 572, 574–575. Reprinted by permission of Prentice-Hall, Inc., Englewood Cliffs, N.J.)

people were held responsible for matters that were beyond their control. In effect, supervisors had two choices.

They could make allowances for external influences when evaluating performance of subordinates toward the achievement of goals. To do so is not easy, requires a lot of information, and can make employees feel that they are being watched closely.

Supervisors could, however, adhere strictly to the agreed-on results and ignore the requirement of a fair system which demands that people be held responsible only for matters under their control. It is easy for supervisors to convince themselves that this approach is actually quite fair. They can reason that the performance of every supervisor and professional is subject to external influences. Therefore, over time, those who achieve a higher proportion of their goals are likely to be more competent than those who miss more often. From the point of view of the employee (including professional or subordinate supervisors), however, the system appears more capricious than fair. A system that rewards luck, and disregards real effort and competence, is not likely to be respected.

When people are being evaluated on the basis of goal achievement, they quickly realize that setting low goals is a much safer strategy than to strive for difficult ones. Rather than *work* hard to achieve tough goals, they are therefore likely to *negotiate* strongly, instead, for easy-to-achieve goals.

In view of these difficulties with performance management systems based primarily on goal achievement, combination systems are becoming increasingly popular. They are intended to take advantage of the best features of those systems that are based on goals, of those that are based on character traits, and of those which emphasize key elements or key accountabilities. At the same time, wider use of peer ratings and of rating by several supervisory levels are used in the evaluation procedures to avoid the heavy subjective influence of the single evaluator.

Gradually, various approaches have emerged that place emphasis on measuring the quantity and the quality of the effort that the employee devotes to the various responsibilities of the job. These systems may be partially oriented toward goal achievement, or they might include some evaluation of personal traits and characteristics.

Most of the systems that are considered successful provide extensive involvement by the employee being rated. Often this involvement begins with a review of the tasks being performed and ends in the development of an improvement plan which is designed to lead toward more favorable evaluations in the future.

ERWIN RAUSCH

Cranford, New Jersey
August 1985

ACKNOWLEDGMENTS

One of the purposes of this acknowledgments section is to pay tribute to the many people whose contributions to society's store of knowledge have provided the foundation on which our thinking rests. I owe a considerable debt to the many management and behavioral scientists who suggested concepts discussed in this book. Indeed, there are very few thoughts that are entirely new. This book's value, it is hoped, will come from the broader perspective it provides and from the specific suggestions it makes for dealing with the various difficult situations that performance management presents.

Especially important among the managers and management scientists who have provided ideas for this book is Dr. James Hayes, previously Dean at the School of Management of Duquesne University, who, before he became president of the American Management Association and during his tenure, placed great emphasis on the importance of appropriate standards of performance as a central management tool to achieve a well coordinated and motivated organization. His contributions as well as those authors whose books have stimulated my interest in this topic have provided the foundation for many of the thoughts this book contains. The authors include Felix Lopez (*Evaluating Executive Decision Making*), Harold Koontz (*Appraising Managers as Managers*), George L. Morrissey (*Appraisal and Development Through Objectives and Results*), and a series of articles on performance appraisal which appeared in the late 1950s in the *Harvard Business Review*. They deserve considerable credit for whatever is valuable in this book.

Another, even more important purpose of this section is to recognize specific contributions to this book. I am especially indebted to Dr. Michael Frisch, who began to work with this manuscript when it was still a very rough draft and rather difficult to read. Not that it was intended to be a fun-to-read book. However, thanks to his untiring efforts and his incisive questions, the book now presents a much more appealing face to the reader.

I owe a considerable debt to John Alexander, whose lectures at the American Management Association and at the President's Association have provided many valuable insights. Similarly, I am indebted to over 2000 working managers at all organizational levels who participated in seminars in which the entire concept, or portions, were presented. The thoughtful questions, suggestions, and criticisms of these men and women helped to sharpen the ideas discussed in this book so that they can be applied more readily to the problems and opportunities which managers face daily.

The organizations where the managers attended the seminars include American Health Care Association; American Management Associations; Civilian Personnel Office of the U.S. Army; J.C. Penney, Inc.; League of Nursing; Thomas J. Lipton, Inc.; Office of Personnel Management, U.S. Government; Pennsylvania Manufacturers Association Insurance Company; Supermarkets General Corporation; U.S. Air; U.S. Department of Agriculture; U.S. Federal Bureau of Prisons; and U.S. Navy Agencies.

This book would never have reached the publication stage if it were not for the help I received from my associates at Didactic Systems, Peter Maynard, my wife, Grace, and from Dr. Helga Fagg of Paragon Associates, an affiliated organization, who contributed the section on the Civil Service Reform Act of 1978 in Appendix B. During the three years that the manuscript was in preparation, several of Didactic Systems' staff members typed and proofread the manuscripts. They include Irene Buniewski and Pat Lusardi, and also Pat Cagnassola, Geraldine Daniher, Marge De Rosa, Susan Glowacka, Barbara Richey, and Barbara Novotny.

All acknowledgments would be incomplete if I did not state clearly that any shortcomings in reasoning or elucidation as well as any errors of omission or commission are solely mine.

E.R.

CONTENTS

WIN-WIN PERFORMANCE
MANAGEMENT/APPRAISAL

Part One

THE PERFORMANCE MANAGEMENT SYSTEM

This book is about performance management:

Its purposes

Characteristics which will make it successful

Problems and challenges which must be anticipated and avoided

Skills which supervisors and managers must apply

The most visible and dramatic element of performance management is the evaluation/appraisal interview. To set the stage for our discussion, let's look in on Jim, a higher level supervisor* who is conducting a performance appraisal interview with George, one of the supervisors who reports to him.

George: Good morning, Jim. You asked to see me this morning. I think you said that we were going to have the mid-year performance review.

Jim: That's right George, and thanks for coming in on time.

---

* Please note that the word supervisor is used for all levels of management (see Preface).

As you know, I have a meeting at 11 o'clock. This should give us ample time, but we have quite a bit to discuss, so I think we may need the full two hours.

Do you have the goals with you which we set at the beginning of the year and the data on how we performed?

George: Of course I have, you asked me to bring them with me.

Jim: All right, let's take a look at them, one at a time. I also have my records and notes on what I know about your accomplishments, and about some of the problems that you have encountered. After we look at each specific goal, I will tell you how I see the situation and then you can tell me where you think I may have overlooked something or where I don't see it in proper perspective. We can then discuss everything I have not considered so that the final evaluation, which I will make, will be as fair and factual as possible. Is this procedure OK with you.

George: Certainly.

Jim: Let's get started then. Your first goal says that you would achieve a 3 percent improvement in the error rate. I know that the introduction of several new products has made that rather difficult for you because ...

(More than an hour later)

Jim: Well, we have reviewed where we stand with each of your goals and just as a brief summary, I think we agree that, overall, you have achieved most of them or are clearly on the road to doing so by year-end. There are a few goals where we did not accomplish all we set out to do and, on the error rate, we really haven't made much headway.

As far as I can see though, you did a commendable job even though there were a few places where we would have ended up better had you been able to pay more attention to those matters.

George: I guess you can say that's correct. Though I hope that you will keep in mind it was not often obvious that these matters deserved higher priorities than those we had originally assigned to them. Overall though, I guess what you are saying is basically right. We can always do better than what we have done and maybe during the second half of the year we'll have fewer problems and will accomplish more.

Jim: George, thanks very much for your efforts thus far. I hope, as you said, that we will do even better as the year progresses. In the meantime, let me know if there is any way I can help you.

George: I will, Jim.

These two brief snapshots of the beginning of a mid-year performance appraisal interview, and of the end, do not give you a complete picture of what occurred. Still, do you feel that you have captured the flavor of the discussion? What, in your opinion was done reasonably well by Jim? Where do you have doubts or concerns?

The purpose of this book is to look behind the veil of polite, cordial relations that surround a reasonably competent performance management system to see what really goes on. It will examine alternatives and steps that can, or should be taken to make the system work well. It will also take a close look at several of the most common problems which performance management can cause, and at ways to overcome them.

This book will attempt to provide a perspective so you can identify more clearly what it is that you like and do not like about the way performance management is or could be practiced in your organization. Armed with a clearer view which such a perspective brings, you will be able to minimize the disadvantages and maximize the benefits for your staff.

Chapter 1

WHAT PERFORMANCE MANAGEMENT IS— A BRIEF OVERVIEW

Performance management is a multistep process for encouraging, or stimulating performance which exists in every organization, either formally or informally. In some organizations the process is so informal that people are hardly aware of it. In other organizations, it is formalized in procedures which every supervisor must follow.

Formal or informal, performance management involves several major steps:

1. Setting of performance standards (with or without goals/objectives*) and communicating them (in advance of the period to which they apply)

2. Observation of performance while providing continuing day-to-day feedback on performance and also more formally at regular process reviews

* In this book, the words goals and objectives will be used synonymously. See pages 97 through 117 for a discussion of goals/objectives and Appendix B for a brief discussion of hierarchies of goals/objectives.

3. Simultaneous collection of performance data for appraisal and for future revision of standards

4. Evaluation of the performance of each employee periodically*

5. Conduct of evaluation/appraisal interviews during which the evaluation is communicated to the employee, discussed, and possibly revised, if an important performance aspect was overlooked by the supervisor

6. Preparation of performance improvement plans

7. Follow-up and identification of desirable revisions of the performance improvement plan and of performance standards (as required): this last step brings you right back to the first step—the setting and communicating of standards

Please note that two of these activities, the second and third, are likely to be continuous throughout the year, while all others are performed primarily at specific times (performance review dates, goals setting dates, etc.).

Supervisors†, employees, and their organizations derive benefits from performance management in proportion to the competence with which these steps are implemented. To help you follow the explanation in the following chapters, a chart of these steps is provided in skeleton form in Figure 4.1. It will then be fleshed out gradually, at the conclusion of each chapter segment.

---

* Please note that the use of the word employee includes employees at all professional, supervisory, and managerial levels (see Preface).

† Please note that the word supervisor is used for all levels of management (see Preface).

Chapter 2

WHY PERFORMANCE MANAGEMENT?

There are two reasons why you as a supervisor, use performance management:

1. The organization has a performance management system and it is part of your job to follow the prescribed procedures.

2. The organization does not have a required system and you want to gain the benefits which performance management brings.

There are many potential benefits of performance management. To what extent these benefits are realized depends on the policies and procedures (the process or system) and on the skill with which supervisors implement them.

BENEFITS OF PERFORMANCE MANAGEMENT

Performance management brings improved performance as a result of its benefits to an organization.

Higher quality of work life through greater *employee satisfaction* is probably the major benefit that an effective performance management system can bring. In addition, a performance management system contributes to:

7

EXHIBIT 2.1.   BENEFITS OF A PERFORMANCE MANAGEMENT SYSTEM

GREATER SATISFACTION OF EMPLOYEES AT ALL LEVELS
Better Control
More appropriate personnel actions
More competent employees and a valid foundation for employee development
Compliance with regulations

Better *control,* though not necessarily tighter control, over the activities of the various organizational units and individuals

More *appropriate personnel actions*

More *competent employees,** because performance management provides a sound foundation for the development of employees toward greater competence on their jobs and for future positions

Compliance with regulations pertaining to equal employment opportunity

These benefts are summarized in Exhibit 2.1 and then discussed in greater detail.

GREATER SATISFACTION OF EMPLOYEES AT ALL LEVELS

Survey after survey has shown that, at all levels, employees would like:

Their supervisors to know more about what they are contributing to the organization

More recognition for their accomplishments

To be kept better informed about how their performance is seen by their supervisors in the organization

More help with improving their performance

* Please note that the use of the word employee includes employees of all professional, supervisory, and managerial levels and the word supervisor includes all managers who supervise people (see Preface).

Guidance on how they can gain greater competence for their current jobs and to further their careers

To know and understand the criteria by which they are judged

A competently administered performance management system, whether as a formal program or administered almost intuitively as part of the organization's management style, can satisfy these needs of employees. An effective performance management system can therefore lead to enhanced job satisfaction and higher quality of work life for employees. The greater satisfaction brings higher esprit de corps and morale. In turn, these are likely to contribute to higher productivity and efficiency.

Sometimes, there seems to be the blind belief that, even without a formal system, the benefits of performance management will be obtained. In some rare organizations, where management is exceptionally sensitive to the needs of its employees, making the program more formal may indeed bring few gains.

However, in other organizations even in some where compensation and promotion decisions are made arbitrarily, it is believed by supervisors that employees will miraculously sense management's good will and that employee satisfaction, or the other benefits of performance management, will be achieved. That, of course, is only wishful thinking, most of the time.

BETTER CONTROL

Many supervisors believe that greater knowledge, in detail, about the work and progress of their subordinates, gives them better control over the activities of their organizational units. These supervisors often equate tighter controls with better control. As they see it, more mistakes will occur if they do not supervise tightly. They feel that they have to balance decisions about the time they spend watching their subordinates, against the risks of missed deadlines, quality problems, and time waste. These supervisors are committed to this style even though they are aware that their ability to keep their eyes on everything that happens is sharply limited by the time they can take away from other work. Some are even aware that they are paying little attention to the likelihood that their close supervision is resented by the more capable people and that they are doing very little to encourage development of greater competence by the others.

On the other hand, a competently administered performance management system achieves better control without tight supervision by developing a system of reviews and by providing regular feedback. It gives the individual employee greater freedom to move, but it clearly identifies the limits within which the employee is free to perform his or her work. Experienced professional employees are given wider limits than those who are less competent.

Budgets are an example of controls with formally communicated limits. Each individual is aware of the budget and the amount of resources that are available for the respective function. Procedures are another example of formal limits. Individual employees have freedom to move within those procedures. Limits, of course, should be communicated clearly.

Many less formal limits are not in writing, but rather are the result of accepted practice. Where these limits are clearly understood and adhered to, the supervisor has better control than if he or she were constantly looking over the shoulders of employees. Better control is achieved because the budgets, procedures, or other limits clearly spell out what should happen (be done or be prevented/avoided). They provide guidance but also the foundation for positive reinforcement (rewards) or disciplinary action. Nevertheless, within the limits, the employee has considerably more freedom than he or she would have in a system in which constant checking with the supervisor is required.

In establishing and revising these limits, or in setting review periods, the supervisor exercises effective control. At the same time, he or she can also make use of valuable techniques such as providing recognition and providing positive feedback to employees so they will seek higher levels of competence and performance and gain greater satisfaction.

MORE APPROPRIATE PERSONNEL ACTIONS

A good performance management system can be relied on to provide valid information about the peformance and capabilities of employees. It thus establishes a more solid foundation for personnel action such as compensation and promotion than alternative systems which are heavily based on the opinions and preferences of supervisors.

Besides its influence on compensation and promotion, a performance management system will favorably affect the number of grievances and complaints. At the same time, it will bring a better suggestion system and improve overall communications in the organization.

MORE COMPETENT EMPLOYEES AND A SOUND FOUNDATION FOR DEVELOPMENT OF EMPLOYEES

A major step in a performance management system is the development of an improvement plan for each employee. Almost every improvement plan contains developmental learning and practice assignments. This organized approach to encouraging self-development of employees leads to a more competent staff. Employees constantly enhance their skills for the positions in which they currently are serving. They also are better prepared for other positions which might become available when there is growth or when openings develop for other reasons.

COMPLIANCE WITH REGULATIONS

There are many laws and regulations which affect personnel actions. Most are intended to ensure equal employment opportunities and prevent discrimination. The more important of these are listed in Appendix B.

Furthermore, the courts have increasingly granted protection, reinstatement, and even backpay to nonunion employees who filed suit against what they considered to be arbitrary personnel actions. The need for factual data on performance is thus becoming more compelling if an organization wants to maintain a cohesive, motivated, and disciplined staff.

A thorough performance management system practically ensures that the organization complies with these laws and regulations. Unfair discrimination is impossible if personnel actions are based on factual performance data collected over time.

A CONCLUDING THOUGHT

Despite the compelling case in favor of thorough performance management, there often is resistance to setting up a formal system or to sharpening performance management skills and practices for an existing one. This resistance can be explained, in part, by failure to recognize the crucial role of performance management in enhancing productivity as well as morale. A more significant reason, however, appears to lie with lack of adequate skills on the part of supervisors for setting up and for working with a performance management approach. This inadequate skill level can bring problems which appear to outweight the benefits, at least in the eyes of those management groups who argue against making a performance management system more formal or more comprehensive.

Chapter 3

CHARACTERISTICS OF AN IDEAL PERFORMANCE MANAGEMENT SYSTEM— A SET OF PRINCIPLES

The discussions in this book will frequently refer to principles. In fact, the word principle is used widely. Not only does the book discuss the principles which a performance management system should satisfy, but it also speaks of principles for setting standards of performance, for coaching and counseling, and for providing feedback. The reasons for this wide use of "principles" are important.

Principles are behind all action; we would never have reached the moon if we had not followed principles of gravity, inertia, propulsion, and so forth. Similarly, whenever we perform a function competently, we adhere to a set of valid principles as we follow a series of action steps.

Action steps are the steps we take to complete a specific task. While we take the action steps, we apply those principles which are appropriate.

Principles and action steps apply not only at work but to activities at home as well. For instance, when we mow the lawn, we adhere to principles as much as when we train a new employee. For example:

When setting the blades on a lawn mower (an action step), we determine their height by considering a set of principles for when to cut high and when to cut low, such as the time of year

When following the action steps for on-the-job training, we keep in mind the principles of learning, such as the need to adjust the level of explanation and the learning pace to the new employee's needs

Effective performance management systems seem to adhere to four major principles all of which contribute to and provide evidence of a high degree of fairness, the ideal condition from which all principles are derived. These principles can either be part of a formal system, or they can be applied so informally that people merely sense, intuitively, that fairness is indeed satisfied. The major principles are:

1. The system should be as *thorough* as possible; it should cover all aspects of an employee's* work and all employees.

2. The system should use *measurements* of performance which are as *accurate and factual* as possible.

3. The system and the measuring techniques it uses should be *meaningful* (it should reflect *important* elements of work performance).

4. The system should satisfy the *needs of the organization and of the individual, including the shared need for effective communication.*

Fairness depends on what a supervisor does. Let's face it; you greatly influence how your employees perceive perfomance management. Consider these two examples:

1. Janet was promoted to supervise a group of 10 employees about a year ago. Until performance appraisal time, all

---

* Please note that the use of the word employee includes employees of all professional, supervisory, and managerial levels. The word supervisor is used for all levels of management (see Preface).

her people considered her a good supervisor. Janet is friendly and considerate, but she sets rather high standards which she would like her employees to achieve. She is rather shy about criticizing anyone though. She would rather pitch in and work late herself than tell an employee that she is dissatisfied. She did, however, rate the four who are not carrying their full load lower than the others, during performance appraisal. Since the employees who received the lower ratings, and lower salary increases, were not aware of Janet's dissatisfaction, they felt that Janet was grossly unfair.

2. Sue was promoted at about the same time as Janet. She also supervises a group of 10 employees. In many other ways, Sue is similar to Janet; she is friendly and considerate, and she sets rather high standards. However, Sue is gregarious, and she stimulates team work and camaraderie. Because she is well liked, even the more competent, hard working people are satisfied with their ratings, despite the fact that she gave the same rating to all her employees.

In each of these examples the supervisor's actions adhered to some of the principles, but not to all.

In the first example you have a supervisor who rates fairly but, because she does not communicate effectively, is perceived as unfair, and loses many of the benefits which performance management can bring.

The second example describes a supervisor who is more sensitive to the way employees perceive performance management. Dissatisfactions of lower ratings which are perceived as unjustified, are usually more intense than the dissatisfactions that stem from *not* getting better ratings than other members of the team. Depending on the skill of the supervisor, the latter dissatisfactions may not be damaging to team performance for some time. Sooner or later, though, it will affect the work satisfaction and the performance of the more competent or harder working employees. Ultimately the performance management system loses credibility and many of its benefits are reduced or lost entirely.

There are, of course, many ways in which the four major principles of effective performance management systems can be satisfied. Most of these ways concern standards and evaluations—*what* the standards and evaluations, cover and *how* they measure performance.

One caution: Keep in mind that, when you try to be *more than fair to one person, you are probably unfair to others.* Many supervisors believe that when they are "nice" to the person to whom they are speaking they practice good "people orientation," and when they satisfy that person they are "fair." Unfortunately, very often that is not so. In fact, seen from another person's point of view, an unfair privilege may have been granted and there may be a valid case of discrimination. In short, be prepared to do for others what you do *for one,* on the same terms, if the record shows that they deserve it.

PRINCIPLE 1—SYSTEM SHOULD BE AS THOROUGH AS POSSIBLE

Thoroughness requires that:

The peformance of *all employees* is evaluated with one or several systems, which all satisfy the four principles.

Evaluations measure *all responsibilities* (with appropriate weight). As employees, we expect due consideration of everything we do—not only of the few outstandingly good—or bad—results which the evaluator remembers.

Evaluations cover performance *for the entire period* between evaluation—not just the last few weeks which are most vivid in memory.

PRINCIPLE 2—SYSTEM SHOULD USE MEASUREMENTS OF PERFORMANCE WHICH ARE AS ACCURATE AND FACTUAL AS POSSIBLE

Closely related to the thoroughness of the system is the principle relating to accuracy and factualness of the measurements. This principle requires that:

Standards and evaluations cover *all responsibilities* and performance elements *accurately and factually* (objectively) with as few distortions from biases of the person who does the evaluating as possible. As employees we want accurate and factual evaluations—without personal feelings or favoritism. Our self-image as well as our economic self-interest are on the line.

Accuracy and factualness mean that the standards must allow *measurement of what has been accomplished, with little or no ambiguity.*

Evaluations are *comparable between evaluators.* We want assurance that the ratings will be the same, or at least very similar, regardless of who evaluates us.

An *appeals procedure* exists, of which everyone is aware. We want to feel secure that an impartial authority exists to which we can take our case if we believe the supervisor's evaluation to be unfairly biased against us. Some people consider such an appeals procedure to be somewhat extreme. In fact, enlightened managers are finding ways to provide such appeals through corporate "ombudsman" or "oversight group" arrangements, or in less formal ways where a dissatisfied employee is encouraged to request a review of the rating by a higher level supervisor.

PRINCIPLE 3—SYSTEM AND MEASURING TECHNIQUES IT USES SHOULD BE MEANINGFUL

A performance management system can best earn the respect of employees if it is perceived as meaningful and relevant to the work. This principle requires that:

Standards and evaluations consider the importance of each function to effective performance. Appropriately greater weight is given to the more important functions.

Standards and evaluations take into account only those matters which are *under the control of the employee.* As employees, we do not like to be judged by fortunate or unfortunate events over which we do not have control. We are embarrassed if we receive accolades when it was merely good luck we achieved the results. Of course, we also resent it if credit for hard, competent work is withheld because something outside of our control went wrong.

Evaluations occur *at regular intervals and/or at appropriate moments.* We want to know when we will be evaluated so we are assured that evaluations are not scheduled arbitrarily. Appropriate moments for evaluations could be the employee's anniversary with the organization or the same time each year and/or whenever compensation or other personnel action is contemplated.

Since the competence of evaluators in evaluating is so important, a good system provides for *continuing skill development of evaluators.*

Evaluation results *are used* for personnel decisions, and the process is respected by top management. We want to know that the evaluations will assist us if we are performing well.

PRINCIPLE 4—SYSTEM SHOULD SATISFY THE NEEDS OF THE ORGANIZATION AND OF THE INDIVIDUAL, INCLUDING THE SHARED NEED FOR EFFECTIVE COMMUNICATION

This fourth principle, of course, is fundamental to fairness of a system. Only when a system considers the needs of individuals as well as those of the organization can it earn the full support of employees and the respect of management. To satisfy the needs of both sides, the system should ensure that:

Standards of performance or performance expectations are *communicated in advance,* before the period begins. As employees, we want to know what the rules of the game are before we start to play, so they don't change to suit someone else's needs.

Employees are *kept informed* on the way their performance is seen by supervisors. Informal, frank discussions of progress, problems, and achievements take place whenever something occurs that deserves mention, and at regular reviews of progress on projects or agreed on goals.

Communications on performance problems and achievements are *factual, open, and honest.*

Performance *standards are high but realistic.* A system that uses standards which are too low will not meet the organization's needs, nor will it provide satisfaction of accomplishment or stimulate to high level performance. Similarly, a system that uses standards which are unrealistically high has many discouraging aspects and leads to unfair, low evaluations.

The *employee* (staff member, supervisor, or manager) *is involved* in the setting of standards and in the evaluation in a reasonable way. The organization needs a device which will provide a safeguard against a supervisor's judgment errors. We, as employees, want a chance to tell our side—as we see the standards, the facts, and our performance—so we can be sure that everything is considered—not only the matters of which the evaluator is aware. That way we have the opportunity to correct any misconceptions that may exist.

Evaluations consider the extent to which *the supervisor provided the necessary resources,* appropriate personal assistance, and other support. The organization and employees want to be sure that supervisors, as well as employees, are carrying their share of the load.

Evaluation *emphasizes the improvement plan* that should be part of the outcome of the evaluation procedure. Emphasis should be on the future, on trends, and on how we can benefit from the evaluation. Without this emphasis, the evaluation itself is likely to do little for the organization and leave us, as employees, with the unpleasant feeling that we were judged without having fully received fair consideration. An effective improvement plan greatly softens and possibly avoids such negative feelings. At the same time, it helps to ensure that the needs of the individual—for greater competence and achievement—are satisfied, as are the needs of the organization for improved results.

Language used to express the various levels of ratings will help to raise or at least *maintain self-esteem.* When we do good work, we do not want to be rated as being "average" performers or be given a "3" out of a scale of 5.

A summary of these principles is given in Exhibit 3.1.

Obviously the four principles are explained more easily than they are applied. There are many opportunities for subtle violations of each of the principles. What's worse, at least one is almost impossible to satisfy. To satisfy the needs of the organization *and* those of some individuals simultaneously may, at times, not be possible, not even with the most competently designed and administered performance management program.

EXHIBIT 3.1. PRINCIPLES FOR PERFORMANCE MANAGEMENT SYSTEMS

Fairness
The Umbrella Principle

Thorough
    Performance of *all employees* is measured similarly
    Evaluations cover *all responsibilities*
    Evaluations measure performance for the *entire period*

Accurate and Factual
    Standards and evaluations cover *all responsibilities*
    Standards and evaluations are accurate and factual
    There is little or *no ambiguity*
    Evaluations are *comparable* between evaluators
    An *appeals* procedure exists

Meaningful
    Standards and evaluations consider the importance of each function.
    Standards and evaluations measure only matters under the *control* of the employee
    Evaluations occur at regular *intervals* or at appropriate moments
    System provides for continuing *skill development* of evaluators
    Evaluation results are *used* for important personnel decisions

Satisfies Needs
    Standards are communicated in *advance*
    Employees are kept *informed* about their performance

EXHIBIT 3.1. (CONTINUED)

Communications are *factual, open, and honest*

Standards are *challenging* but realistic

Employee is *involved* in setting standards and making evaluations

Evaluations consider the extent of the *supervisor's support*

Evaluation emphasizes an *improvement plan*

Ratings maintain or enhance *self-esteem*

Chapter 4

WHAT PERFORMANCE MANAGEMENT IS

Let us return to our description of what performance management is and expand on it, by looking at its components and how they relate to each other.

From this review, we will have a broader perspective so we can decide on features of systems which would satisfy the principles and thus bring all the benefits which potentially can be obtained. Exhibit 4.1 is a skeleton chart which will gradually be fleshed out. This chart should help to provide focus and perspective as you follow the discussion of the various features of performance management.

Performance management, as it applies to a specific position, must start with knowledge of what constitutes good performance on each of the functions which the job holder is expected to perform. A measuring device is needed—some sort of standard against which actual performance can be compared—to determine *how* "good" or "bad" it was, or more important, in what way performance was good or in what areas it needed improvement.

If employees are to perform well, as measured by such standards, they clearly have to be aware of the standards at the very beginning of the period in which they are to apply. Furthermore, standards have to be accepted and respected.

Because performance standards in some organizations have

EXHIBIT 4.1.   DIAGRAM OF THE PERFORMANCE MANAGEMENT SYSTEM/PROCESS

Step I   Performance standards are set.

Step II   Performance is observed and feedback is provided instantly and informally, and at regular formal progress reviews. Data is collected for evaluation and for future standards or revisions.

Step III   Performance is evaluated.

           The performance evaluation is communicated and discussed during an appraisal interview.

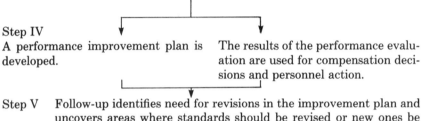

Step IV
A performance improvement plan is   The results of the performance evalu-
developed.   ation are used for compensation deci-
                                      sions and personnel action.

Step V   Follow-up identifies need for revisions in the improvement plan and uncovers areas where standards should be revised or new ones be set.

been misunderstood and incorrectly applied, they have become a controversial issue in these and other organizations. A brief discussion of pro's and con's is therefore appropriate here.

STEP I—SETTING PERFORMANCE STANDARDS AND COMMUNICATING THEM

Pros and Cons of Performance Standards

When it comes to measuring physical matters, it is usually not very difficult to find a standard—a graduated container—or an accurate yardstick to use. With performance measurement, similar standards are often more difficult to come by. Much has been written about performance standards for routine tasks. Every industrial engineering school conducted, and many still conduct, programs on stop-watch time study techniques and on methods for setting predetermined time standards for routine factory and office tasks. Still, if standards are based on the past, or past performance, they are not necessarily relevant to the future when they are to serve as guides; if they are based on what someone thinks the future will be like, they may be conjectural.

Even for repetitive tasks, where standards are easiest to set, they are often not as accurate as might be desired. Though an aura of scientific respectability surrounds standards which measure physical output (units produced), these standards have brought extensive controversy about how they should be applied. Management, employees,* and unions obviously have different views on what amount of production is the minimum acceptable level (below which disciplinary measures might be considered), what level should be considered "standard" and at what level should rewards ("incentives") be given for output that exceeds the standard. Fierce union/management battles have been fought over management rights to set standards and over the extent of the union's right to challenge them.

Part of the reasons for the different views lies with the uncertain fairness of output/results standards even for repetitive tasks. For instance, in mechanical assembly operations when a standard says that 50 parts are to be assembled in an hour, parts may fit better or worse at one time than at some other time. This would affect the amount of effort needed to achieve the standard because a factor *not* under the control of the employee affects the results.

In information processing, the raw data may vary in legibility from period to period. That too, would have a significant impact on results the employee can achieve. These variations presumably can be disregarded or accounted for, because the repetitiveness of the tasks evens out the favorable and unfavorable events, allowing much greater predictability. But, what if one person has to perform many different short repetitive tasks which are not the same from week to week, or month to month? In the end, even here the conclusion is unavoidable—judgment has to be used when inter-

---

* Please note the use of the word employee includes employees at all professional, supervisory, and managerial levels. Supervisor is used for all levels of management (see Preface).

preting the results/performances/achievements; the measuring rod cannot be completely rigid.

Where standards are used to measure work whose quality can be seen, the problems are primarly those of conflicting self-interest between management, and employees or their representatives. When quality is less easily determined, setting meaningful standards becomes a problem of a different kind.

How would you set work standards for a retail sales clerk in a busy store for instance? How important would be the total sales which the clerk rings up on the cash register? Or the number of store customers who do not buy today but will return because they appreciate the friendly helpful attitude? Or the neatness of the counter during business hours? Or the care with which the sales receipts are written? Obviously a sales clerk who is tops in all areas does an outstanding job. But what about those clerks who are somewhat less than tops in one area? In two or three? What about sales clerks who are "only" average in one, two, or three areas but outstanding in one? What about changes in layout, advertising emphasis, or merchandise the store offers, and the effect they have on the sales, customer contact, and available discretionary time? How would you adjust for these matters that are beyond the control of the sales clerks but influence their effectiveness?

The sales clerk is only one example out of legions. Teachers, supervisors, parole officers, social workers, nurses, physicians, engineers, commercial artists, computer programmers, accountants, the list is endless and growing in a world where routine work is rapidly becoming the domain of machines.

Those who champion the use of performance standards answer the doubts about their usefulness by stressing the central function of performance standards—to provide a device, albeit an imperfect one, for measuring an individual's contribution to the organization's tasks.

Performance standards, their supporters maintain, are far superior to the most widely used alternative—the subjective evaluations of performance of supervisors and others.

Without doubt, in a broad sense, performance standards do help to separate "better" performers from those who accomplish less.

Over the course of several years, most performance management systems that are based on reasonable performance standards will better satisfy the principles of fairness in evaluating accomplishment than systems based on less factual foundations. There are, however, many problems related to performance standards that do not lie with the concept itself. Instead, they are the result of inadequacies in the way standards are set and used. Standards are needed. Even if admittedly less than perfect, standards provide the guidelines and thus narrow the potential for serious inaccuracy or misjudgment. Performance management without communicated standards is likely to be capricious and largely useless.

The discussion in this chapter will shed some light on the causes of difficulties with standards-based performance management systems and provide some guidelines for holding them to a minimum.

Standards of Performance

There are two issues which must be considered in setting standards and communicating them:

1. What must a standard describe to be an effective standard?
2. What are the specifications which the *statement* of a standard must satisfy so the statement communicates clearly?

What Must a Standard Describe to Be an Effective Standard?

A standard of performance is a statement that will make it possible to determine how well the task or group of tasks, which were intended to achieve a desired result, was or were performed.

Note that the definition of a standard of performance may seem vague but is quite precise and specific. A standard which meets this definition specifies:

What is to be measured (how well the task was performed)

How it is to be measured (what the evaluator should look at, or compare, to determine the level of performance)

Note also that the standard specifies the results *and* ways for measuring. It is *based* on the results which are to be achieved, but *emphasis is on measuring* what aspects of the task have been performed competently and effectively, and where they could have been improved. In other words, the standard:

Describes, or refers to the result which a task or group of tasks is intended to achieve, and

Can be used to *determine how well* the task(s) were performed.

The first part of such a standard should be called the *description of results* segment of the standard; the second part could then be called *competence and effort* segment.

A standard which satisfies both parts of this definition provides an effective means for measuring the competence and effort that has been devoted to the accomplishment of a clearly defined function or task.

Two examples of standards of performance are:

1. Designs of fasteners will meet all design specifications as spelled out in the work order and the Design Manual. (This is the result.) Performance will be determined by the thoroughness with which the designs have considered the design specifications, the completion dates, and the budgets. (This is the competence and effort expected.)

2. Work hours used will not exceed total hours allowed to satisfy the specific production schedule. (This is the result.) Performance will be determined by the speed with which below-standard production problems are identified and by the quality, timing, and effectiveness of remedial steps. (This is the competence and effort expected.)

The first example, of course, will provide a useful measuring rod in proportion to the extent to which design specifications and the budget are clear on:

Desired performance characteristics of the design (ability of the fastener to perform its function)

How much equipment may be used for production of the fastener

Manufacturing cost of the fastener

Record keeping requirements during the design process

and so forth

Similarly, the second example will be more or less useful depending on the accuracy with which "total hours allowed" is a true indication of the effort required to produce any time segment of the production schedule. Hence, if the organization wants to measure performance well, it must first have sound procedures and records. If they are not specific and adequately thorough, performance management will be even less precise.

Note that the *what* (that which is to be measured) in the standard seems to be the *designs,* yet it is the *thoroughness* with which the designs *have considered* the specifications, completion dates, and the budgets. The *how* is determined by the way records are kept on redesigns necessary to meet specifications and on completion dates and budgets.

As another example, a standard for a college or an evening adult extension of a local school system might state:

Three new courses will be developed for the fall. Each course will be approved by the curriculum committee and bring minimum enrollment to 25 fully qualified students during the first offering. (This is the result.)

Performance will be evaluated by the *competence and effort* devoted to *course development.* Competence will be determined by adherence to established procedures and effort will be determined by the quality of the individual session outlines. (This is the competence and effort expected.)

Here too, the standard will be useful in proportion to the quality of existing procedures. For instance, its usefulness will depend on how clearly the criteria are spelled out which a course must satisfy to be approved by the curriculum committee, and how well the supervisor communicates the criteria which he or she will use for evaluating the quality of individual sessions.

These examples place *emphasis* for measurement on the way the employee *performs* the function and *works* to achieve the desired results, *not* the results themselves. However, results are the essential background. The desired results determine what tasks need to be measured and the *tasks* in turn *provide the basis for the standards.* Thus, the standards can satisfy the fairness requirement which states that evaluation should measure only matters under the control of the employee. At the same time, they help to ensure that employee effort concentrates squarely on achieving the desired results.

On first glance it would seem as though it would be easier to merely spell out the results to be achieved and to determine performance based on how thoroughly they were achieved. In fact, many managers advocate this approach (it will be discussed later in the exploration of the two major ways for setting thorough standards—from job descriptions or with management by objectives (MBO)).

Measuring results might indeed be easier, at least for highly *repetitive,* relatively *similar* tasks which have a history of previous completion so that supervisors can make forecasts reliably. For the first time a task is to be performed, however, or for tasks which are not similar, there is no reliable record of how long it takes or how "much" should be achieved. Hence, forecast by the supervisor, or even a joint forecast of supervisor and employee, of what can be accomplished has to serve as the standard. What happens to the principles of fairness in performance management if the forecast is either too high or too low? Then the standard is precise and specific—but it is neither fair, accurate, nor meaningful.

A few examples might illustrate this difficulty of using the results themselves as standards. In the simplest form, a standard for packing and sealing cases with bottles which are coming off a filling line can be very precise, such as 70 cases per hour for each operator. Should the machine break down, the operator can sign off the job and is not charged for the time. However, while the machine is running, the operator can be evaluated on the basis of the number of cases packed, the adequacy of the sealing, and possibly the thoroughness with which bottles with certain types of easily recognizable defects are rejected. At the other extreme, such as with sales of large machinery or with physical research projects, setting a dollar amount of sales, or the achievement of a specific new discovery as the basis on which performance will be measured is clearly not fair or desirable. The salesperson and the supervisor may estimate what sales will be achieved and both may be in complete agreement on the steps which the salesperson will take. Even if all are implemented with great effort and skill, the anticipated sales results may not materialize. What is the problem? Was the standard too high? Probably. But what if the salesperson's skill level was not as clearly established and the same results were achieved. In either case, how can the results be used to evaluate performance? Obviously, only by stretching the idea of using results beyond its usefulness.

Similarly, what is the benefit of a standard that states the researcher's performance will be measured by his or her success in formulating a detergent which will remove a specific type of stain from *all* types of fabrics. Can the researcher receive an outstanding evaluation if he or she discovers it within one week. Conversely, is the researcher's performance considered poor if he or she cannot achieve this result?

Most positions are somewhere between these extremes, however, the same concept applies. Far more reliable measures of performance than results alone, are the results coupled with specification of the way effort and competence will be measured.

What Are the Specifications Which the *Statement* of a Standard Must Satisfy So That It Communicates Clearly?

As the previous discussion indicated, standards must be set to communicate as clearly as possible. They must have the same or nearly the same meaning where applied to different employees, but also from one time period to the next, that is, the meaning of a standard that is set in January must be as clear in July as it was in January.

1. Description of results

The portion of a standard which describes the results could be expressed in terms such as those discussed in the following list. These terms are equally applicable for an individual employee or the supervisor of the section, department, or even larger unit. Terms which describe the description of results are:

a. Project completion

   i. Percent or number of projects completed within schedule

   ii. Percent or number of projects within budget

b. Quality

   i. Percent or number of rejects or errors (such as fewer than 2.0 errors per page)

   ii. Percent, number, or cost of warranty repairs

c. Cost control

   i. Percent or number of variation from standard cost per item

   ii. Percent rework/revision/retyping in units or dollar costs

   iii. Percent or cost of indirect labor

   iv. Percent or dollars of budget, by line

d. Case load

   i. Number or proportion of cases completed on schedule

   ii. Percent or number of cases closed satisfactorily

   iii. Audit results of case handling

e. Student Learning

   i. Percent or number of students who pass impartial board examinations

   ii. Percent or number of dropouts

   iii. Test scores

f. Market penetration

   i. Percent, unit, or dollar increase in sales by market

   ii. Percent of market share

   iii. Variance to budget

This list gives only a few examples. The specific standards would, of course, use actual numbers or specific percentages such as:

Fewer than 1.5 percent rejects or errors

No fewer than 95 percent of all cases completed on schedule

No procedure change recommendations as a result of audits

2. *Competence and effort*

Specifying how to measure competence and effort is usually a totally different matter than stating the results. It is much more difficult and usually appears to be less precise. This is another reason why it is so alluring to managers to write standards in terms of results despite the fact that such standards might be measuring outside influences (good and bad luck) instead of competence and effort.

No one would deny that results are often proportional to the competence and effort devoted to bring them about. The trouble is that, given the same competence and effort, entirely different results will appear if a competitor raids your staff, than if an important competitor folds.

Managers who rely solely on the results segment of a standard are forced to review the outside influences, at the end of the period, and then make subjective judgments based on how important these events were. A good standard must come to grips with the competence and effort component of the ways a function or task is performed.

A few examples on which competence and effort descriptions can be modeled, are:

a. Project completion

   i. Adequacy of schedules in placing emphasis on critical elements which need early attention

   ii. Appropriateness of schedule changes

   iii. Timeliness with which higher levels of supervision are informed of problems so support could be provided

   iv. Adequacy of coordination with others who affect progress of the project

b. Quality

   i. Adequacy of testing/inspection/sampling procedure

   ii. Adherence to testing/inspection/sampling procedure

iii. Adequacy of testing quality records
iv. Appropriateness and timeliness of corrective steps
c. Cost control
    i. Adequacy and currentness of records
    ii. Adequacy and timeliness of corrective actions
    iii. Methods/improvements
d. Case load
    i. Time spent on case work
    ii. Thoroughness of records
    iii. Appropriateness of handling and disposition of cases
e. Student learning
    i. Quality of lesson plans
    ii. Quality of tests and adequacy of testing
    iii. Adequacy of student counseling
    iv. Adequacy of remedial steps to overcome learning deficiencies
f. Sales/market penetration
    i. Number of calls per salesperson
    ii. Quality of presentations to prospects
    iii. Adequacy of prospecting
    iv. Appropriateness of prospects selected for calls

At first, it may seem as though it would be very difficult and require considerable time to fairly evaluate the type of activities listed. This would be true if it were necessary to constantly keep track of the way the employee performs these tasks. Judicious sampling, however, will greatly simplify the task. In fact, competence and effort can be measured quite objectively with observations at every contact during the time period. Brief discussions with the employee after each such "reading" of any problems which should be corrected, along with thorough records, establish a data base* for using the observations in the evaluation.

To make the observations easier, the standard should, of

* A more detailed discussion of the development of this data base, in conjunction with providing feedback starts in the section entitled "Step II—Providing Feedback on Performance and Collecting Data for Appraisal and for Future Revisions of Standards."

course, be as clear as possible on what you will be looking at when you make your observations. For example, in the standard "competence will be determined by adherence to established procedures and effort will be determined by the quality of individual session outlines." To evaluate performance with this standard, the supervisor would look for instances when procedures were not followed and at the session outlines to assess their quality.

Thus far, the discussion of standards has not covered the question: How does one select the tasks or functions on which to set standards? Nor has it discussed how many standards should be prepared for a single position.

Where Should Standards of Performance Be Set and How Many Standards?

There are three foundations on which performance standards can be built:

1. *The job description.* Since an up-to-date job description lists all the duties/responsibilities of a position, it can be used to prepare a list of all functions that have to be performed. Decisions can then be made on what activities and functions should receive their own specific (period or ongoing) standards and which should be covered by the umbrella standard.

2. *Key results areas.* For every position it is possible to identify those functions where accomplishments are most important. These functions then can become the foundation for standards.

3. *Goals/objectives.* Some organizations work with a system which requires that goals/objectives be set by, with, or for each employee. Goals/objectives either contain performance standards or can readily serve as the basis for standards.

Standards have also been built on personal characteristics, as was pointed out briefly during the retrospective segment in the preface.

These foundations are not mutually exclusive. Goals/objectives and job descriptions often exist happily side by side and so can job descriptions with key results areas and key results areas with goals/objectives. Some organizations use all three concepts. Even standards based on personal characteristics are often integrated with the others, despite the legal questions concerning perform- ance standards that are not clearly job related. It is not important which are used but rather *how* they are used.

These three sources are not mutually exclusive, since standards for a position could conceivably come from all three nor need they be formally derived from written documents.

In most organizations, the performance management proce- dures do not clearly specify what sources a supervisor should use to determine where to set standards. Neither is it likely that an or- ganization prescribes the number of standards which should exist for a specific job.

In many ways, setting standards from the job description and from key results areas are identical. When they are set from the job description, the supervisor and/or the employee individually or jointly determine which responsibilities or functions are suffi- ciently important so that standards should be set to allow factual performance evaluation. In essence, this is similar to determining key results areas and, in effect, is an informal way to do so, be- cause key results areas are little else but the *functions* which lead to the most important *results* expected from the jobholder. For example, among a position's duties, the job description may list: to maintain and improve the quality of the department's production.

This description is clearly important and should become the basis for a standard such as—errors found in inspection shall not exceed 1.3 percent; performance shall be judged on the basis of ad- herence to the sampling procedure, speed, and effectiveness of corrections and adjustments when needed; and the adequacy of training of new operators and of all operators when changes occur.

A similar standard would have been written from a key results area approach. With this approach when the supervisor and em- ployees set standards, they identify those functions of the position which are critical to the results that the position should achieve. Clearly, maintaining and improving quality is one such key results area, and the same standard could have been written.

Setting standards from goals/objectives or in conjunction with them is also similar to setting them with the aid of the job description or on the basis of key results areas.

A detailed discussion of the differences between using job descriptions, key results areas, or goals/objectives when setting standards would detract from the description of the performance management system. (See Chapter 2, subsection entitled Controversial Issues Concerning Standards of Performance, Goals/Objectives, and Key Results Areas.)

Types of Standards of Performance

The preceding discussion of standards of performance has treated them as though there were really only one type of standard—though mention was made of an umbrella standard. It is, however, still worthwhile to recognize that comprehensive performance management uses three types of standards for most, if not every position. The three types of standards are:

Period standards

Ongoing standards

Umbrella standards

Period standards often called project standards are for a specific period of time and are likely to be changed at the end of that time. These standards include completion dates of specific projects such as:

Project 325 is to be completed within budget, on schedule

Performance will be evaluated on the basis of conformity with the applicable standard procedures and on the basis of adherence to time schedules and to budgetary allowances.

Ongoing standards, on the other hand are not likely to change or need to be changed only at long intervals when new methods are introduced. They, therefore, continue indefinitely until there is a reason to change them. Most of the results portions of standards in the section entitled "What Are the Specifications Which the *Statement* of a Standard Must Satisfy So That It Communicates

Clearly?" are ongoing, except for those where continuing improvement is desired and the actual percentage or amount is changed
whenever new standards are set. For instance, if an organization is
working to reduce variance from standard by 5 percentage points
but could not achieve that much in one year, then the expected
results in the standard of performance on variances would then be
changed every three months, every six months, or every year until
the 5 percentage points have been achieved.

During this period of change, this standard would be a period
standard. Thereafter, the variances in this standard might be less
important than other key results and this standard would become
an ongoing standard or possibly become part of the umbrella
standard.

Umbrella Standard

All responsibilities where improvement is not needed at the time
can be placed under one standard so that they are not neglected
while the employee concentrates his or her effort on functions and
responsibilities where specific standards were set. This standard
can be called an *umbrella standard.* It is a catch-all which can
cover all functions where there are no specific period standards or
ongoing standards. Usually, most of the functions which could be
covered by ongoing standards can more conveniently be part of
the umbrella standard, while period standards, the standards that
deserve maximum emphasis at the time, remain separate. An umbrella standard could state that performance in all areas not covered by specific standards, shall be performed no less competently
than in the past, and the results shall not be any less satisfactory
than those that have been achieved in the past.

Or, more specifically, individual lines on the budget shall not be
exceeded by more than 5 percent and the entire budget shall not
be exceeded except for items specifically authorized. Competence
will be measured by the remedial steps which were taken whenever it became apparent that a budget line would be exceeded. Effort will be evaluated by the adequacy of records and of budget
analysis.

This statement is an umbrella-type standard that could cover many minor responsibilities. Another one could be, all activities not covered by specific standards of performance shall either be performed as well as in the past, or a specific standard of performance shall be set as soon as it becomes evident that one is needed to define the responsibility. In determining whether an activity is being performed as well as in the past, all aspects relating to timeliness, quantity, quality, and resources used shall be considered.

If, during the next evaluation period, performance does deteriorate significantly in one of the functions covered by the umbrella standard, then a specific standard could be added to the list to cover the problem.

Number of Standards

To prevent the performance management system from becoming a major job function/activity by itself, the number of specific period standards and ongoing standards must be strictly limited. Standards that are set should concentrate on responsibilities which are most important *at a particular time*. To paraphrase Peter Drucker, the famous management scientist/author, if 20 percent of the responsibilities achieve 80 percent of the job results then it is on those 20 percent that period standards and ongoing standards should focus.

As a general rule of thumb, no fewer than *three* nor more than about eight standards should be in force during any one time period. Emphasis and effort can thus be focused on the most important standards, and the performance management system will not deflect attention unnecessarily from the work to be done.

The use of umbrella standards makes such a limit on the number of standards realistic and drastically reduces the amount of work which performance management could otherwise require. It allows sharp cutbacks in the number of standards which have to be set for thorough coverage of all responsibilities.

Setting standards thoroughly, factually, meaningfully, and so that they satisfy needs is not enough. Standards also must be communicated properly and this means that they must be spelled out *in advance*.

Communicating—Clarifying Performance Expectations in Advance

It is important to keep in mind that, ideally, you want to perfect your performance management skills to the point where you and your subordinates can independently come up with identical appraisals of their performance. Although this is an ideal, if you see it as your goal, you will come closer to it than if you do not concentrate on it.

To be effective in explaining to people what you expect of them, performance standard setting must occur in advance. Unfortunately, a statement of expectation such as the following, is inadequate, even if it is done in advance of the evaluation period:

"You know your job description,"

"We have set our goals and I will evaluate you based on those,"

"You know how we did our last performance appraisal and that's how I intend to do future ones."

This might be all right with a job that doesn't change at all. However, even in such a case, this brief statement of expectations might be adequate only if the last performance appraisal was a very thorough one and competently conducted. The statement is not adequate if the job has changed or if it is changing in the course of the year. It certainly is inadequate if you never clarified just exactly what it is that you expect the employee to do and achieve.

In highly structured work, it is relatively easy to spell out the results segments of standards with and/or for your employee—the quantity and quality, the number of errors or rejects. These are precise and factual, and they can be communicated clearly before a major task is started or at the beginning of the evaluation period.

However, the competence and effort segment of the standard may be somewhat more difficult. As written, standards do not cover *all* aspects of the function. Therefore, it is important, when communicating standards, to state as clearly as possible what is implied by the standard, by using as many statements (see subsection entitled "What Are the Specifications Which the *Statement* of a Standard Must Satisfy So That It Communicates Clearly?") as past experience indicates to be useful. The experience level and competence of the employee must also be considered. In general, fewer words are needed with experienced employees with whom the same or similar standards have previously been set than are needed for less experienced people.

As we have already explored, in nonrepetitive work such as knowledge work, standards of performance are harder to set. Clearly communicating how you will evaluate performance is not simple, but it is every bit as necessary. Figure 4.1 the skeleton chart of performance management is the same as Exhibit 4.2, however, additional detail which summarizes what has been covered so far has been added.

STEP II—PROVIDING FEEDBACK ON PERFORMANCE AND COLLECTING DATA FOR APPRAISAL AND FOR FUTURE REVISIONS OF STANDARDS

Once standards of performance have been set and communicated, day-to-day performance management begins. It involves the second and third steps in the performance management process— tracking performance and providing feedback, and the appraisal/improvement plan interview. In fact, some supervisors have suggested that competent performance management requires only continuous review and feedback. Annual and even semi-annual review and appraisal sessons are redundant in this view.*

Some of this thinking was based on research at General Electric which indicated that comprehensive annual performance appraisals are of questionable value and that coaching (and counseling) should be a day-to-day, not a once-a-year activity. It was suggested that goal setting, not criticism, should be used to improve

* Albert W. Schrader, "Let's Abolish the Annual Performance Review", *Management of Personnel Quarterly*, Vol. 8, No. 3, Fall 1973.

EXHIBIT 4.2.   DIAGRAM OF THE PERFORMANCE MANAGEMENT SYSTEM/PROCESS—EXPANSION 1

Step I

Job description is reviewed and revised jointly

Key results areas are reviewed and/or established jointly

Performance standards are set *jointly in advance* of performance. They contain two segments:

Results Segment:	Competence and Effort Segment:
• quantity	• adherence to procedures
• quality	• adherence to budgets
• time	• adherence to time schedules
• resources	• timely notifications

Step II   Performance is observed and feedback is provided immediately or as soon as possible, and informally, and at regular formal progress reviews. Data is collected for evaluation and for future standards or revisions

Step III   Performance is evaluated

The performance evaluation is communicated and discussed during an appraisal interview

Step IV

A performance improvement plan is developed

The results of the performance evaluation are used for compensation decisions and personnel action

Step V   Follow-up identifies need for revisions in the improvement plan and uncovers areas where standards should be revised or new ones be set performance. In a similar vein, other authors* suggested that, if appraisals are needed, two separate appraisals should be conducted: (1) to help employees improve their performance, and (2) for the evaluative appraisals, which provides the basis for compensation and personnel actions. The viewpoint is that a manager cannot serve in the role of coach/counselor (helping someone improve performance) while presiding as judge over the same employee's salary decisions.

Though the suggestion to abolish the annual or semiannual performance appraisal did not take hold, the viewpoint expressed in the article has considerable validity. If you are thorough in continuous review of the performance of your subordinates, and you provide regular competent feedback, then all the appraisal will do is confirm what both you and your employee already know.

Regular Feedback and Continuous Collection of Data

The following example will illustrate the steps in the performance management process which concern the supervisor's work in collecting data and providing feedback. George, the sales manager for a small firm accompanied John, one of his salespeople, during a call to an important customer. John gave a fairly good presentation of one of the company's products but, because the product was still fairly new did not stress the benefits of the product to the particular customer on several occasions when such emphasis would have been desirable. John concentrated on showing the product's advantages over competitive products. The call resulted in a modest initial order and both George and John were quite pleased with the results.

During the rest of the morning, George and John visited several established customers, took some orders, and resolved questions and problems that existed with those accounts.

George is a competent sales manager who understands performance management principles quite well. He maintains a simple folder on each of his salespeople. The inside front jacket is used to record the compensation history and awards earned, like sales-

---

* H.H. Meyer, E. Kay, and J.R.P. French Jr., Split Roles in Performance Appraisal, *Harvard Business Review,* January-February, 1965, pp. 123.

person of the month, and Top Producer Club membership dates. Formal educational experiences such as workshops and seminars are entered on the inside of the back cover. In the folder itself, George keeps brief chronological notes on plain paper, of any discussions which he has had with the respective salesperson.

At lunch on the day when George worked with John, they reviewed the activities of the morning. George placed special emphasis on the call to the new customer. After again expressing his pleasure that John was able to open up the account, George pointed out to John that he had not stressed the product benefits for the particular customer as effectively as could have been done. He then asked John whether John would like to discuss the specific benefits for that customer of each of the product's features. John, of course, agreed.

John reviewed what he knew about the customer's needs before the call, and what additional information about the customer's needs he had obtained during the initial moments of the visit. He then listed those features of the product that were most relevant to the customer's needs. Whenever it was clear that John had overlooked something, George offered suggestions, usually in the form of questions, of possibilities that might have been considered.

After the discussion, George asked John to join him in role playing a revised presentation, this time with emphasis on benefits. Whenever John would speak of features rather than benefits, George would ask him how he could express the features more effectively, in terms of benefits to the particular customer.

At the conclusion of the role play, George pointed out that he is certain that John will emphasize product benefits with various customers the next time he visits him. He then asked John to prepare a comparison list of all the features of the product and possible benefits he might present to various types of customers. He asked John to send a copy of this list to him within two weeks and he promised to provide comments and other suggestions where relevant.

Immediately after he left John that evening, George entered the following brief notes in John's file: "6/10/84, visited ABC account—presentation showed need for greater concentration on appropriate benefits. Role played and gave learning assignment for 6/25."

In this particular instance, George had offered to provide personal coaching and on-the-job training to John. In other situations, possibly with other salespeople he might have first suggested that the salesperson read the materials the company had supplied on the product, or he might have sent the individual to a workshop if the learning needs were more serious.

In this example, George was thorough, accurate, and factual in his description of what had occurred during the call. His feedback was timely and effectively communicated, with reference to specific events during the call. When obtaining agreement to role play the call and when asking John what John thought might be useful to strengthen emphasis on benefits in his presentations, he clearly showed respect for John's competence and good judgment. He also confirmed his concern for John's needs when he discussed both positives and negatives with John right after the event, thus showing empathy for John's position.

George followed good procedures as he provided feedback and collected data. These procedures are:

1. *Feedback must be timely.* Feedback that is provided with considerable delay from the time when the respective event occurred is far less valuable and is likely to be resented. Whenever something occurs that deserves either commendation or a critique, tell the employee immediately. Thus, the feedback is prompt and, if it is provided with empathy, it is rarely resented. Rapid positive feedback is generally appreciated and helps to cement good work relationships.

If, as is desirable, you hold regular weekly, or even more frequent project or job reviews with employees who report to you, you might find it more convenient or more appropriate to provide the feedback at these job reviews. Of course, it is important that you present a balanced picture, recognizing that which has been done well as much as pointing out those actions where performance could have been better. Emphasis on *how* the employee could do the task better with specific detail is most helpful, of course, as well as suggestions for study or skill practice that might improve competence. Sometimes a simple assignment could be useful. (For elaboration, see Part Four—Essential Skills.)

2. *Feedback must be communicated effectively.* The person receiving the feedback must clearly understand what he or she has

been told. Supervisors often feel uncomfortable about providing negative feedback and therefore try to give it in such a way that it will not be taken "personally" or so it will "not hurt the recipient's feelings." In being overly cautious, they frequently provide feedback that is not cleàrly understood. Here too, refer to Part Four—Essential Skills, for techniques to ensure that you have been properly understood.

3. *Feedback must preserve, and if possible, enhance mutual respect.* Competent supervisors take the time to ensure that communications are clear. They ensure that employees understand what they are saying. They also listen carefully so they are certain that they understand what their employees are saying. They allow their employees considerable voice in the discussion, and they give appropriate weight to an employee's explanation. Consequently, they are more likely to earn comparable regard for their opinions from employees. Undoubtedly, they are more apt to achieve the change in actions and behavior that they are seeking.

4. *Feedback and collected data must be factual and accurate.* Feedback is much more effective when it concentrates on what happened and how it happened. Feedback which is heavy in advice and opinions, is rarely welcome and often inappropriate or erroneous. (See Chapter 12, Conflict avoidance and Resolution.) The data that is recorded, of course, must also be accurate and factual so that it will be of value in the future. Later on, if interpretation and conclusions during performance appraisal are based on these facts, the evaluations are more likely to be well received.

5. *The collected data must be sufficiently thorough* so that it covers all the performance aspects, including those that were performed well and those where improvement is desirable. In this regard, it is important to keep in mind that collecting and recording data takes time and effort, not to speak of the need for personal discipline which is required. Therefore, only essential data should be sought and even less should be recorded.

Therefore, files, must be simple to give you adequate factual data for your performance appraisal session and for possible future revisions of performance standards. You, therefore, need a file for each employee or supervisor who reports to you. These files should not be elaborate. Note how George used the cover of the files, for instance. A lot of paperwork rarely aids in bringing respect, or higher quality, to a performance management system. Single sheets of paper for each employee in one file folder, or separate folders for each employee are adequate. If a separate folder is used, some statistical type, nonconfidential information could be kept on the folder itself.

Entries should be made whenever a discussion with the employee takes place. In some occupations, supervisors are accustomed to keeping such records of discussions. However, most supervisors do not keep such records routinely. It usually seems as though such records are too time consuming. Making entries is therefore postponed. If the entries are not made immediately, however, much is often forgotten or the entries are not made at all. It takes a great deal of effort to develop the habit of making prompt entries, and it is not an easy habit to form especially in the beginning. Once the habit is established, it is a most rewarding practice, and it soon becomes obvious that the effort is really minimal.

Periodic Feedback and Collection of Data—Formal Progress Review

In addition to continuous on-the-job feedback and data collection, a formal progress review process is characteristic of good performance management systems. Conducted several times a year, periodic formal reviews provide further feedback to the employee and serve as a source of data which helps both employee and supervisor make more factual and thorough performance appraisals.

Progress reviews serve several useful functions:

To review progress against standards factually, and thus collect data for the evaluation

To determine what period standards and ongoing standards continue to be appropriate for the work of the employee, which should be changed, which are no longer relevant and should be dropped, and which new standards are needed

To review the umbrella standards to see whether they are adequate or need to be changed

To analyze where the employee is lacking in knowledge or skill so the supervisor can coach toward elimination of any deficiencies

To determine what additional assistance, if any, is needed from the supervisor, to help the employee improve his or her performance

When conducting a progress review session you are trying to determine whether period standards are likely to be achieved and whether ongoing standards are being met. At the same time, you are trying to determine whether the employee's knowledge and skill with respect to the necessary tasks is adequate.

During the progress review you are a coach. You are helping the employee identify how he or she could be more effective. You then work out, with him or her, what could, or should be done so that the standards will be met, or at least are more likely to be met. Your interests and those of the employee are parallel. You are not assessing performance. You are not judging but helping to find areas where support from you, a more effective approach or more learning may be beneficial.

At least four progress reviews should be conducted annually. More are desirable. Many supervisors schedule them on a monthly basis while others schedule progress reviews based on logical checkpoints for major projects, such as at the completion of specific segments of the projects. Supervisors who use progress reviews will often schedule them more frequently for their less experienced employees than for those who are more competent in the performance of their duties.

For each progress review you should follow these steps:

1. Schedule the progress reviews as the situation and the competence of the employee demands.

2. During the progress reviews, the following questions should be raised.

    a. Is the umbrella standard being met?

    b. Are period standards and ongoing standards likely to be met?

   c. Are there knowledge/skill deficiencies and what should be done about them?

   d. How is progress with respect to the improvement plan* developed at the last performance appraisal?

   e. Is additional support from you, the supervisor, required?

   f. What performance standards are still appropriate in light of the changing situation and which should be changed or added?

3. You take the steps necessary to satisfy the conclusions from the discussion of the questions in (2).

4. You make the necessary entries in the employee's performance management record.

5. You set an approximate (or specific) date for the next progress review.

In summary, progress reviews are important steps to ensure that the standards retain validity throughout the period between evaluations. They also add factual information to the day-to-day observations, thus enlarging the record on which the performance evaluation can be based to ensure that it is both factual and thorough. (The diagram of the performance management system process is once again reproduced with additional summary information, Exhibit 4.3.)

STEP III—EVALUATION OF PERFORMANCE AND CONDUCT OF THE APPRAISAL INTERVIEW

Notwithstanding those management experts who feel that an appraisal interview may be superfluous, at least one annual performance evaluation including an appraisal interview should be conducted for each employee. Even if regular feedback on performance is provided on the job, there are good reasons why an annual, formal performance appraisal is valuable, in *addition* to continuing regular feedback.

---

* For a discussion of the improvement plan, see Chapter 4, Step IV—Preparation of the Performance Improvement Plan.

EXHIBIT 4.3.   DIAGRAM OF THE PERFORMANCE MANAGEMENT
SYSTEM/PROCESS—EXPANSION 2

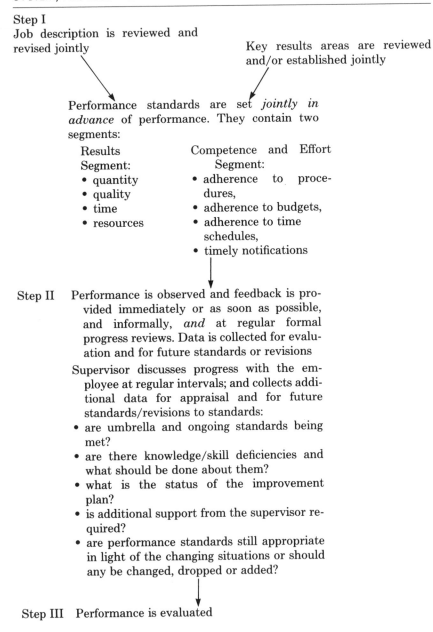

Step I
Job description is reviewed and
revised jointly

Key results areas are reviewed
and/or established jointly

Performance standards are set *jointly in
advance* of performance. They contain two
segments:

Results
Segment:
• quantity
• quality
• time
• resources

Competence and Effort
Segment:
• adherence to proce-
dures,
• adherence to budgets,
• adherence to time
schedules,
• timely notifications

Step II   Performance is observed and feedback is provided immediately or as soon as possible,
and informally, *and* at regular formal
progress reviews. Data is collected for evaluation and for future standards or revisions

Supervisor discusses progress with the employee at regular intervals; and collects additional data for appraisal and for future
standards/revisions to standards:
• are umbrella and ongoing standards being
met?
• are there knowledge/skill deficiencies and
what should be done about them?
• what is the status of the improvement
plan?
• is additional support from the supervisor required?
• are performance standards still appropriate
in light of the changing situations or should
any be changed, dropped or added?

Step III   Performance is evaluated

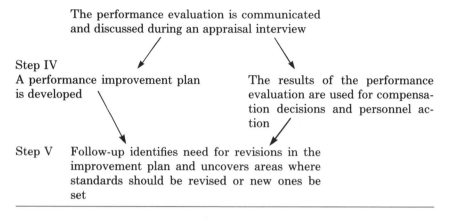

The performance evaluation is communicated
and discussed during an appraisal interview

Step IV
A performance improvement plan
is developed

The results of the performance
evaluation are used for compensation decisions and personnel action

Step V   Follow-up identifies need for revisions in the
improvement plan and uncovers areas where
standards should be revised or new ones be
set

1. To ensure that a performance management system is accurate and factual, standards have to be agreed upon and communicated. They require a somewhat broader exchange of views than that which exists at a feedback discussion on a task or at a specific project review session.

2. To satisfy the requirement that the performance management process is meaningful, personnel decisions must be based on the performance evaluations. There is the need to discuss, from time to time, how the evaluations relate to salary action and to promotion decisions. Informal feedback sessions or project review sessions just do not allow the time nor do they provide the undisturbed environment for effective discussion of these important matters.

3. Performance appraisal sessions satisfy needs by helping to ensure that performance standards are indeed communicated in advance and by involving the employee in setting standards and in the evaluation. When the review and/or the appraisal session is thorough and enough time can be devoted to it, employees can see that there is a sincere desire to work with them rather than to make independent judgments.

4. Finally, an improvement plan can be developed at the conclusion of each appraisal. It would not be possible to develop such a plan during an informal feedback session or as part of the review of a single project. It requires the com-

prehensive analysis that only a thorough performance evaluation session can provide. Without the appraisals and the
formal or semiformal progress reviews which provide much
of the supporting facts, this essential element of performance management would either fall by the wayside or require a separate program that would, in effect, resemble
performance appraisal.

For these reasons, appraisal interviews are essential and cannot be
fully replaced by continuous feedback on performance, no matter
how frequent or how carefully it is provided.

Thorough performance evaluation/appraisal sessions need not
necessarily be conducted more than once a year. However, much
can be said, for two performance evaluation/appraisal sessions per
year.

Distinction Between Progress Reviews and Performance Evaluations

1. During progress reviews, your role is that of coach (see
    Chapter 5, Periodic Feedback and Collection of Data—The
    Formal Progress Review). Your function is to help yourself
    and your employee identify what needs to be done so that
    better performance will be achieved.
2. Partly in contrast, during the performance appraisal, you
    are first an evaluator who judges the employee's perform-
    ance.
3. In performance appraisal, you determine the adequacy of
    the employee's performance and then take appropriate
    managerial actions, such as recommendations for compen-
    sation adjustments and/or readiness for promotion. Fur-
    thermore, your views on what steps should be part of an
    improvement plan will be significantly affected by your
    evaluation. Only after the evaluation has been completed
    and discussed, can you help an employee develop an im-
    provement plan. During this second segment of the evalua-
    tion/appraisal discussion, you, once again, assume a role
    that is primarily directed at coaching.*

* Skills for coaching and counseling are discussed in Part Four—Essential Skills.

In a performance appraisal your employees are, therefore, more likely to be defensive because their personal interests may be directly affected by the outcome of your appraisal. At the same time, their behavior is challenged and that too can bring a defensive reaction. In a progress review session, there is less need for such defensive reaction because your function is that of a helper rather than that of an evaluator. If you can communicate this distinction effectively, you can achieve greater cooperation in either or both types of session.

An Example

A brief case can illustrate a supervisor's functions in periodic formal progress reviews, performance evaluations, and in the conduct of appraisal interviews. It is drawn from an actual organization.

The XYZ Company, providing various services to the business community, has recently set up a performance management system. There are two separate versions of the system. One is for professional and supervisory employees. The other is for clerical and secretarial employees, the "nonexempt" personnel—those who are covered by federal wage and hour legislation.

For nonexempt positions, a committee consisting of supervisors was appointed to develop a job description, to design a performance appraisal form, and to write a supervisory instructions manual for performance appraisal for these job classifications. The committee prepared these materials, reviewed them with management and with a few employees from the nonexempt groups, updated them, and then issued them for use by all supervisors in the evaluation of people in these jobs.

Supervisors of professional employees, the "exempt" staff are expected to meet with each professional at least four times each year for progress reviews, essentially as outlined previously in this chapter (see Chapter 4, Periodic Feedback and Collection of Data—The Formal Progress Review). Supervisor and employee also meet, approximately two months before the time when the compensation decisions are made. The purpose of this meeting is to review the job functions and responsibilities and to update job descriptions. The supervisor, as well as the employee, then write brief statements about each of the major responsibilities, outlining accomplishments (including performance against standards) and areas where improvement is desirable, as well as ideas and suggestions on what could be done to bring further improvement.

The employee submits this write-up to the supervisor and, based on both write-ups, the supervisor makes a written evaluation prior to the next meeting with the employee. In addition to the narrative type evaluation about performance of job functions and responsibilities, the supervisor is expected to provide ratings on all major responsibilities of the job as well as on several characteristics which are considered requirements for all positions. These include the quality of decision making, quality of communications with peers and supervisors, and types of complaints received from customers and clients.

Evaluations are made along a five-point rating scale for each standard *and* overall job description: outstanding performance, performance significantly beyond requirements, competent performance, significant shortcomings, and inadequate performance. Every rating other than "competent," must be supported by the narrative description.

When the system was first installed, considerable effort was devoted to clarifying for all supervisors and employees, that a "competent" rating is a good rating. It is not equivalent to a general "average." A rating higher than competent indicates performance beyond that which the average *competent* person generally provides.

The organization also clarified the relationship between performance appraisal and compensation by stressing that those employees who consistently achieved evaluations above "competent" would benefit in two ways:

1. Through raises which would bring them closer to the top of the compensation range for the job than employees of similar longevity but with lower ratings
2. Greater consideration when they apply for vacant positions to which they might aspire and for which they are otherwise qualified.

After all the ratings have been completed with respect to the individual job functions and the common functions, an overall rating is established. In the overall rating, it is not adequate for a supervisor to simply add up the other ratings and come up with an average. Instead, a justification, again, must be written for all ratings other than "competent." Averaging of ratings is strongly discouraged because in every position, some job responsibilities are far more important than others. An explanation must be written by the supervisor for an overall rating other than "competent" prior to a meeting with the next higher level supervisor.

After the supervisor has completed this evaluation, he or she consults with the next higher level management to adjust the evaluation for uniformity with other supervisors. At the same time, this review ensures consideration of any additional information which the higher level supervisor may be able to contribute as well as the broader perspective of two viewpoints. The higher level supervisor then signs the form to signify his or her agreement with the ratings.

The supervisor then meets with the employee to inform the employee of the ratings, during the evaluation/appraisal interview. If the employee brings up significant information items which were overlooked during the evaluation by the supervisor, and which the employee failed to include in his or her write-up, the supervisor has the authority to make changes in a rating based on this additional information. The supervisor does not need to change the rating and supervisors are cautioned not to make changes based on relatively minor additional inputs from the employee. Supervisors are also asked to be careful so that pressure for higher ratings from highly articulate or strong-willed subordinates does not result in preferential treatment for them.

At the end of the evaluation/appraisal segment of the interview, the employee signs a statement certifying that the appraisal has been discussed with him or her. A space on the form also provides an opportunity for the employer to signify dissatisfaction with the appraisal, or with the way the supervisor conducted the appraisal interview, by writing down specific disagreements or complaints.

Shortly after the appraisal/evaluation interview segment is completed, the supervisor and the employee meet to work on an improvement plan (see Chapter 4, Step IV—Preparation of the Performance Improvement Plan).

The XYZ Company's performance management system, though not ideal, does provide a good example of the *steps* which can ensure adequate employee involvement to bring acceptance of the system. At the same time, it can ensure thorough and rigorous performance appraisals.

Steps in Performance Evaluation

Performance Evaluation required several steps:

1. Preparing for the evaluation
2. Making the evaluation
3. Review of the evaluation
4. Evaluation/appraisal interview

Preparing for the Evaluation

Before the evaluation starts, the data which has been collected since the last evaluation has to be reviewed and analyzed. This analysis should start with a review of the job functions and responsibilities even if regular progress reviews have been held and/or there is continuous contact between you and your employee. The review gives you an opportunity to check on any changes that may have occurred in the job or the key results areas, or in the goals/objectives toward which the employee was working, which may affect performance standards. Good systems usually require that this review of job responsibilities and functions is either done jointly with the employee or is reviewed with him or her to ensure accuracy and consideration of the employee's views.

Making the Evaluation

To avoid "contamination" of the supervisor's evaluation with the employee's vested interests, the first evaluation is best performed by the supervisor alone. This evaluation, including the assignment of ratings, requires substeps such as the following:

1. Reviewing the data that has been collected by observation, during on-the-job feedback and in the formal progress re-

view sessions and writing preliminary statements of events/accomplishments, relevant to the appraisal

2. Assigning a performance rating, in accordance with the organization's rating scheme, to each period standard, to each ongoing standard which is not part of the umbrella standard, and to the matters covered by the umbrella standard

3. Assigning an overall rating to the employee's performance

4. Preparing for the performance evaluation/appraisal interview with the employee by setting a time and place for it

5. Possibly asking employees to rate themselves, independently

Three particularly difficult tasks are alluded to in the substeps:

The decision of what rating to assign to the performance covered by each standard

How to develop the overall rating

Whether to ask the employee to rate himself or herself

A brief discussion of these tasks follows.

1. Assigning ratings to performance against a standard. If you look at any standard, you are looking at a guideline for rating, a verbal measuring rod which states the results which are expected from an employee's work, and how competence and effort can be measured. However, the standard does not give guidelines on the specific rating that would be most appropriate for various levels of achievement. It is up to the supervisor to decide on the manner an employee's performance should be evaluated. The task facing the supervisor is to take the information about performance and then decide whether it is outstanding or poor, or at one of three to five points in between.

Therefore, either formally, or informally, most systems, provide a series of performance characteristics, or "anchors" as they are often called, which can help supervisors decide at what level the employee performed. Anchors can be fairly specific and can make such distinctions as "always, (sometimes or rarely) checks reports (or completed pages) to ensure that they are consistent with the requirements (or free of errors)."

Or they can be rather general and refer only to comparisons with competent performance, such as "clearly better than acceptable competent performance or far beyond what is normally expected from an employee with respect to that function."

The statements in Exhibit C.6 are anchors to help with ratings, as are the statements in Exhibit 7.1. The statements can be used as anchors when assigned specific numbers that spell out different levels of performance. In chapter 4—What Performance Management Is in the section entitled What Are the Specifications Which the *Statement* of a Standard Must satisfy so that it Communicates Clearly?

2. Assigning overall ratings involves similar considerations, though the individual ratings for the various standards provide some guidance. (For a brief discussion of some specific issues in overall ratings, see Chapter 7—Other Issues in Performance Management System, section entitled "How to Label the Ratings Level.")

3. The pro's and con's of simultaneous self-ratings by employees are controversial. On balance, there are significant advantages to self-ratings but these advantages can be fully realized only by supervisors who are competent communicators and who can establish an open communication environment with their staff. (See Chapter 7—Other Issues in Performance Management System, section entitled "Employee self-Evaluation" for a brief discussion of these advantages.)

Review of the Evaluation

The next substep in the evaluation concerns the review of the evaluation with the next higher level supervisor to ensure:

1. Uniformity throughout the organization so that, as much as possible, the subjective influences of a single evaluator are reduced to a minimum, and

2. That employees are aware of the extensive effort which is being devoted to achieve fairness of ratings.

While these reviews usually involve only the next higher level of supervisors, in some cases, peers of the evaluating supervisor review the employee's evaluation either instead of, or in addition to, the next higher level supervisor or the personnel manager.

Whether to review prior to the appraisal interview, or after it, or who should do it are other controversial issues which are discussed in Part Two (see Chapter 7—Other Issues in Performance Evaluation System, section entitled "Approval of Ratings and Appeals Procedure.")

Conduct of the Evaluation Appraisal Interview or Interviews

The most complex substeps in the evaluation process are those which concern the conduct of the appraisal interview itself. (For a detailed discussion of these skills see Part IV—Essential Skills.) While in most organizations, only one performance appraisal/evaluation interview is conducted during a year, except when there are special events affecting an employee, some organizations require that supervisors conduct two such appraisals each year. Usually the first one is at mid-year and its primary purpose is to help the employee obtain a measure of the evaluation he or she would receive so that corrective steps can be taken if the evaluation does not meet the employee's expectation or is below the level which the supervisor considers acceptable.

The substeps for the performance evaluation/appraisal interviews are similar to those you take for any delicate interview. They include:

1. Setting an appropriate climate by selecting a time and place which will ensure a calm, unhurried, uninterrupted environment
2. Explaining the benefits to the employee of the performance management system, such as:
   a. Fairer compensation decisions
   b. Greater freedom to do the job

    c. Help with preparation for promotion

    d. Opportunity for desired changes in job and assignments

3. Explaining the evaluation and the ratings, and the commendation for competent and better ratings, standard by standard

4. Providing the employee an opportunity to thoroughly explain his or her viewpoint

5. Achieving agreement, as much as possible, on the validity of the ratings

6. Discussing the implications of the ratings on:

    a. Compensation

    b. Future performance (see Chapter 4, Step IV—Preparation of the Performance Improvement Plan)

7. Asking the employee to sign the form, to attest that the evaluation has been discussed with him or her and encouraging the employee to enter notes if there is dissatisfaction with the evaluation and/or ratings

These substeps related to the evaluation are added to the chart of the performance management system, Exhibit 4.4.

STEP IV—PREPARATION OF THE PERFORMANCE IMPROVEMENT PLAN

Many supervisors and managers view performance evaluation for compensation and personnel actions and the appraisal which informs the employee of the evaluation as the primary purposes of a performance management system. When this perception exists, it distorts the meaning of performance management from a comprehensive, supportive, and mutually beneficial system, to a mechanism for making or justifying compensation decisions, which in turn will—or so is the hope—"motivate" the employee to improve performance. These organizations fail to recognize that the interests of the organizations, as well as those of the employee, are best served if the supervisor helps the employee plan performance improvement.

EXHIBIT 4.4. DIAGRAM OF THE PERFORMANCE MANAGEMENT SYSTEM/PROCESS—EXPANSION 3

Step I

Job description is reviewed and revised jointly

Key results areas are reviewed and/or established jointly

Performance standards are set *jointly in advance* of performance. They contain two segments:

Results Segment:
* quantity
* quality
* time
* resources

Competence and Effort Segment:
* adherence to procedures
* adherence to budgets
* adherence to time schedules
* timely notifications

Step II

Performance is observed and feedback is provided immediately or as soon as possible, and informally, *and* at regular formal progress reviews. Data is collected for evaluation and for future standards or revisions

Supervisor discusses progress with the employee at regular intervals; and collects additional data for appraisal and for future standards/revisions to standards:
* are umbrella and specific standards being met?
* are there knowledge/skill deficiencies and what should be done about them?
* what is the status of the improvement plan?
* is additional support from the supervisor required?
* are performance standards still appropriate in light of the changing situations or should any be changed, dropped or added?

Step III

Supervisor prepares *for* performance evaluation/appraisal including review of job functions and responsibilities

Supervisor makes an evaluation and obtains a review

61

- analysis of data from observations, on-the-job feedback, and from progress review sessions
- evaluation and rating by supervisor
- possibly simultaneous evaluation and rating by employee
- review of supervisor's evaluation with next higher level of management and/or others

The appraisal interview is conducted

- appropriate climate
- explanation of employee benefits of the performance management system
- explanation of evaluations and ratings commendation for competent and better performance
- providing the employee an opportunity to express his/her viewpoint
- achieving agreement on ratings as much as possible
- discussing implications of ratings
- signing by employee and expressions of disagreements/complaints

Step IV
A performance improvement
plan is developed

The results of the performance evaluation are used for compensation decisions and personnel action

Step V   Follow-up identifies need for revisions in the improvement plan and uncovers areas where standards should be revised or new ones be set

An effective performance management system places primary emphasis on the improvement plan—on developing it and on monitoring its progress. A supervisor who understands and accepts this emphasis as a way of life, will find it far less difficult to discuss differences of opinion about ratings with the employee. Ratings can be treated more lightly because they are merely a reflection of the past. With emphasis on the improvement plan, it is the positive approach of: *How can we do it better in the future?/How can we avoid the problems we have faced in the past?* on which the discussion can be centered.

It stands to reason that the past year or half year should not have as important a place in the life of the employee and in the relationship between employee and supervisor than the future. With emphasis on the future, it is also easier for supervisors to stick with their evaluations and not to give in to friendly, but sometimes very forceful pressure, from their employees, for more favorable ratings.

If you honestly believe and adhere to this emphasis you will find yourself much more in the role of coach and counselor, as a helper to the employee, rather than as a judge. In this role, you can point out that there may have been mistakes in the past and that you may have to share some of the responsibility for these. You may not have provided as much support as might have been desirable. Therefore, the improvement plan discussion can rightfully focus on what you will do differently, not only on where the employee has to improve.

Furthermore, the improvement plan very often spells out personal development activities which will enhance the employee's competence. Therefore, achievement of the plan will enhance his or her feeling of security and provide expectation of greater satisfaction from accomplishment on the job. It may also lead to better preparation for positions which the employee would like to attain. Therefore, development of an improvement plan sometimes leads to career counseling.

By developing the plan at the time of the performance appraisal, when employees are likely to be most receptive to change, the strongest commitment to a plan can be obtained. Some organizations, for administrative purposes and possibly because they believe that the charged atmosphere of a performance appraisal is not conducive to the development of a sound improvement plan, separate these two functions and run parallel systems. By doing so, they lose a major benefit—the motivational impact which is strong at salary decision time.

To be most effective, preparation of the performance improvement plan must adhere to the same fundamental principles as

other aspects of performance management. Of particular importance are the principles of meaningfulness and need satisfaction.
The improvement plan should:

Concern only matters that are under the control of the employee

Strengthen the skills which are needed to perform at high but
realistic level

Concentrate on those aspects of the employee's performance
which will have greatest benefit to the organization as well as to
the employee

At the same time, the improvement plan should, where necessary,
contribute to continuing skill development of evaluators.

The improvement plan, therefore, involves two separate types
of activities. It specifies what the employee *will do* differently than
in the past. It also spells out steps which the employee will take to
improve competence so he or she *can do* some tasks more effectively.

It goes without saying that an improvement plan would not be a
very valuable one if it does not allow a primary voice to the employee in deciding on the steps that should be included. In setting
accomplishment milestones and goals, the improvement plan
should specify the dates by when improved performance or
greater knowledge or skill will have been achieved.

So that the performance improvement plan and the remainder
of the performance management system do not become separated
or conflict with each other the follow-up dates for the improvement plan should be made to coincide with the progress review
dates.

When setting up an improvement plan with one of your employees, the following substeps would help to ensure a successful session, regardless of whether it closely follows the performance
appraisal or is held significantly later.

1. You emphasize the objective and benefits of the improve-
    ment plan: to help the employee achieve greater compe-
    tence and better performance, but also better evaluations in
    the future.

2. You encourage the employee to suggest what elements the

improvement plan should contain and what performance improvement steps and self-development steps should be part of the improvement plan.

3. You suggest any additional behavior changes, learning, or skill practice that might be useful.

4. You and/or the employee suggest what priorities should be set for the steps in the improvement plan, and agreement is reached on these priorities.

5. In the final substep a specific timetable is set up with dates for review of accomplishments. As much as possible, the employee should be allowed to decide by when he or she will complete the various steps. A schedule which was set by the employee is more likely to be respected and accomplished, than one in which you set the specific dates.

Exhibit 4.5 is the skeleton chart of the performance management system to set the improvement plan into perspective in relation to the entire process. The final step, follow-up, requires no further expansion of the chart and it is, therefore, complete.

STEP V—FOLLOW-UP AND REVISION TO THE PERFORMANCE IMPROVEMENT PLAN AND TO THE PERFORMANCE STANDARDS (AS REQUIRED)

The major accomplishments spelled out in the performance improvement plan can be coupled with performance standards, since they are, in effect, period standards. Improvement plan items concern only matters under the control of the employee; therefore, they measure competence and effort directly.

For instance, an improvement plan item could be: By July 1, I will be prepared to answer questions about work time management on the basis of the articles I received, and I will have developed and be implementing a practical time management procedure. This item can be treated as a standard of performance because it has a results segment (a practical time management

EXHIBIT 4.5. DIAGRAM OF THE PERFORMANCE MANAGEMENT SYSTEM/PROCESS—COMPLETE

Step I

Job description is reviewed and revised jointly

Key results areas are reviewed and/or established jointly

Performance standards are set *jointly in advance* of performance. They contain two segments:

Results Segment:
- quantity
- quality
- time
- resources

Competence and Effort Segment:
- adherence to procedures
- adherence to budgets
- adherence to time schedules
- timely notifications

Step II Performance is observed and feedback is provided immediately or as soon as possible, and informally, *and* at regular formal progress reviews. Data is collected for evaluation and for future standards or revisions

Supervisor discusses progress with the employee at regular intervals; and collects additional data for appraisal and for future standards/revisions to standards:
- are umbrella and specific standards being met?
- are there knowledge/skill deficiencies and what should be done about them?
- what is the status of the improvement plan?
- is additional support from the supervisor required?
- are performance standards still appropriate in light of the changing situations or should any be changed, dropped or added?

Step III Supervisor prepares *for* performance evaluation/appraisal including review of job functions and responsibilities

Supervisor makes an evaluation and obtains a review

66

EXHIBIT 4.5. CONTINUED

- analysis of data from observations, on-the-job feedback, and from progress review sessions
- evaluation and rating by supervisor
- possibly simultaneous evaluation and rating by employee
- review of supervisor's evaluation with next higher level of management and/or others

The appraisal interview is conducted
- appropriate climate
- explanation of employee benefits of the performance management system
- explanation of evaluations and ratings
- commendation for competent and better performance
- providing the employee an opportunity to express his/her viewpoint
- achieving agreement on ratings as much as possible
- discussing implications of ratings
- signing by employee and expressions of disagreements/complaints

Step IV
A performance improvement plan is developed
- emphasis is on improved performance and better ratings in the future
- elements of the plan are identified jointly
  - performance/behavior
  - learning/development
- an implementation time table is prepared

The results of the performance evaluation are used for compensation decisions and personnel action

Step V Follow-up identifies need for revisions in the improvement plan and uncovers areas where standards should be revised or new ones be set procedure) and an effort and competence segment (as outlined in the study and development commitments).

Obviously, an improvement plan will be only as good as the commitments made to it. Therefore, you have the obligation to see to it that employees take the improvement plan as seriously as any other aspect of their work. Similarly, employees have the right to expect that you will live up to any commitments which *you* make.

Furthermore, the plan is more likely to be achieved if you follow-up thoroughly. This means that:

> You adhere reasonably closely, though not slavishly, to the follow-up dates and that you review, with each employee, the specific accomplishments that had been agreed on for those dates
>
> Any revisions to the improvement plan, that might be desirable in light of the events that have occured since the plan was set up, are discussed at each review
>
> Progress achieved by the review dates is recorded, as well as any revisions to the improvement plan that were agreed upon
>
> Employees be commended for accomplishments

At the same time, you can satisfy the purposes of the progress review which are essentially similar, only broader. They concern not only progress toward achieving the improvement plan and related standards but also accomplishments with respect to all other standards.

The progress review is where the performance management system's parts come together in a mutually reinforcing session. Achievement of the improvement plan steps is likely to have brought better performance. The review confirms the improvement and thus strengthens the resolve to continue along the improvement plan.

PERFORMANCE EVALUATION AND COMPENSATION

As defined in this book, an organization's compensation program is not directly a part of a performance management system. However, the success of the performance management system depends heavily on how it is used in compensation decisions. A few words are necessary, therefore, to clarify the relationship between the performance management and compensation systems.

There is a widespread belief that performance appraisals and compensation adjustments should be separated in time to avoid defensiveness on the part of the employee during the evaluation. Organizations which attempt this separation are often underestimating the awareness of their people on a subject of such great interest to them. They thereby merely strengthen the conviction of their employees that the organization is not fully candid. It would be much simpler to make compensation decisions promptly after the performance appraisals and to point out that the amount of the compensation increase will be affected to some extent by these reviews.

To thoroughly understand the relationship between compensation and performance management, it is important to see the three major elements of compensation in clear perspective. These elements are:

Incentive payments

Bonuses

Salary

Each of these has an appropriate role in a balanced compensation program that fully supports performance management.

Incentive payments usually are based on achievement of targets, therefore, they are likely to reflect the impact of external influences rather than the effort or competence of the individual. If business conditions become more difficult, sales in a profit-oriented organization will suffer, and salespeople understand that their commissions (incentives) will be lower. Similarly, in a factory where incentive payments are made for production, people understand that during product changes and at other times incentive payments may not be available and that their incomes may temporarily be affected in a negative way. Conversely, fortunate circumstances can bring fairly large payments even when there is little effort.

Bonuses are similar to incentives, but they are easier to adjust to valid measurements of individual performance. While the total bonus pool may fluctuate depending on the performance of the entire organizational unit and on the general political and economic conditions, an individual's share of the pool can have a direct relationship to performance. The supervisor who has established mutual trust with employees can distribute bonuses based on performance evaluation. Bonuses give supervisors a chance to tie performance evaluations directly to compensation.

The least direct relationship between performance and reward exists with *salary increases*. Various systems are used by organizations to translate evaluation results to compensation increases. These systems are basically of two kinds, based on whether:

A fixed pool of money is available for compensation changes (increases)

Funds are made available as needed to satisfy the compensation changes required by the system.

The first type is far more prevalent. As a rule an organization's top management establishes the budget for an average percentage of total compensation costs which will be available for the increases which employees will receive. The performance management system is then used to allocate the dollar amount that this average percentage increase represents to the individual employees.

Sometimes the expectation exists, in the minds of supervisors and employees alike, that everyone who turns in high performance should receive the highest possible salary increase. People often feel that high-level performance immediately deserves a large increase. For example, everyone may be aware that an organization may allow its supervisors to grant increases varying from 0 to 12 percent. At the same time, it may stipulate that each division or department may not grant more than an average increase of 8 percent. In such a situation, most employees who have earned an evaluation above competent are likely to expect increases of 12 percent.

Increases of this magnitude are probably impossible for the entire organization as a whole, and even for the employees under the jurisdiction of a particular supervisor, without unfairly low increases for employees rated as competent. The supervisor, therefore, has an obligation to explain to all staff members that salary increases are not tied directly and *immediately* to performance evaluation. High performance evaluations by large proportions of employees can, of course, bring such high organizational performance that more money will be available and everyone can enjoy larger increases. In the short run, however, this is not possible. Therefore, not only high performance but *sustained* high performance is important for the largest increases. In this example, a supervisor in the organization can, and should, evaluate all staff members in the organizational unit, and then apportion the available salary pool of 8 percent of total salaries on the basis of that evaluation and on the basis of the employee's record of above/below competent evaluations in the past.

The point is that staff members have to be made to understand that salary increases cannot immediately reflect performance evaluation. In the long run, performance evaluations affect salary decisions in two different ways:

1. Employees with the best sustained performance receive higher salary increases than those with lower merit at least until they reach the top of the salary range for the position.
2. Organizational units with excellent performance receive larger salary pools, either because the organization earned more or because that particular organizational unit relative to others, deserves a larger allotment.

Some organizations use a system that relates the salary increments more closely to performance and thus removes some of the rigidity of a fixed set of salary scales. In addition, this system uses the fixed ranges for salary grades (position levels), a variable component. Here is how this works:

1. Almost every employee receives the *"general"* increase that the organization provides to adjust for cost of living increases, or which it grants to distribute the benefits of better performance of the entire organization. In addition, supervisors can provide salary increments, for merit, to those employees whose performance rating is above competent.

2. Employees whose performance is regularly rated above competent receive larger increments (*merit* increments) than those who are rated only as competent. Those who earned exceptional evaluations receive the largest increases. Employees who consistently receive these higher ratings gradually reach the top of the entire scale.

3. Those who do not continue receiving the evaluation that they have previously achieved, (competent or above competent) gradually, over a few years, lose the extra *merit* increment and thus recede back toward the level of those employees who are consistently rated as competent. This level is usually somewhat above the center of the salary range for the position (grade level).

4. Employees who regularly receive evaluations *below competent* receive smaller increases and gradually move toward the bottom of the range for the position. Obviously, employees who consistently perform below competent, are either shifted into other positions or are separated, except where unique circumstances such as disabilities warrant their retention.

Employees should, of course, be made clearly aware of the reasons for compensation adjustments, especially how they relate to the performance appraisal, whenever the employee is informed of the adjustment. (See Chapter 9—Resolving Problems section entitled Problem 1—Relationship Between Ratings and Compensation.)

CAREER COUNSELING IN A PERFORMANCE MANAGEMENT SYSTEM

Career counseling is peripheral to the performance management system. Many organizations consider career counseling to be outside a supervisor's primary responsibilities. If it is formalized they prefer to let members of the personnel department perform this function.

However, any performance management system that does not consider the aspirations of people for growth in their careers, and for their continuing search for meaningful work, is missing a major element that can help to make the system more appealing, and thus, more useful. Furthermore, it is fairly frequent that supervisors are called on to answer an employee's question about opportunities for growth with the organization. In fact, setting up an improvement plan practically begs this question.

It is not the intention here to discuss career counseling and the supervisor's role in that function in great detail. It is, however, essential that at least a few words be said about how a supervisor should or could approach career counseling and how that relates to effective administration of the performance management system.

Competent supervisors are aware that they have a responsibility here. They should share, with the people who report to them, the perspective which their position and experience has given them, to help each individual employee gain a more realistic view of the potential career paths that exist within the organization.

Fortunately, when a supervisor accepts this limited role as part of the normal work of a supervisor, then it can make the performance management tasks considerably more pleasant. There are two major problems which career guidance can sometimes relieve:

1. In most organizations the leeway which supervisors have for providing satifactory compensation increments to employees is sharply limited. Raises have to be distributed based on the amounts available for general increases, by the compensation ranges of the individual job and by the relative position of the employee's compensation to the top of the range. Hence, there is a need to demonstrate to employees that the effort to achieve a good performance record can have benefits in addition to the immediate salary increase.

2. At the same time, an improvement plan that is geared solely to improve performance does not, on the surface, show the advantages that it provides to the employee. On the other hand, if it can be shown that the improvement plan can help to better prepare an employee who seeks career advancement or career change, for such advancement or change, then the improvement plan has considerably more meaning and appeal to the employee.

Providing career guidance has many skills in common with performance management. The coaching and counseling skills that are important for progress reviews, performance appraisals, and for setting up the improvement plan also are central to providing career guidance.

If one of your employees asks you for advice or guidance on career planning or if a situation arises when you consider it appropriate to initiate such a discussion, the following thoughts should be kept in mind.

1. Career discussions can easily raise unrealistic expectations. Your explanations of possbile career opportunities, therefore, have to be worded carefully to ensure that employees do not see you as giving advice. It often is best to explain that all you can do is to provide or obtain information about positions and to make suggestions on what the employee could do to see the picture clearly.

2. It is important for you to thoroughly understand what skills and knowledge are required for those positions for which an employee has expressed interest; or to obtain that information promptly when needed.

    When appropriate, phone or visit an incumbent in such a position to obtain the information you need, or arrange for an appointment for your employee so he or she can inquire personally about the position and what could be done to prepare for it.

3. You should also be able to discuss with employees how they can prepare themselves so they could be seen as qualified candidates when an opening occurs. Position descriptions will be helpful but, by themselves they are not sufficient. You need to sharpen your skill to translate responsibilities into competencies. You might think of the positions you are discussing in terms similar to knowledge/skill profiles. The only difference would be that, for this purpose, each item on the knowledge/skill profile can be a much larger item—even as much as a college degree, while lines on knowledge/skill profiles for coaching have to be very limited.

4. It is also important that you can explain to your employees

how better performance and greater knowledge/skill in the current positions can be of assistance to them by making them more desirable candidates for a position to which they may be aspiring.

5. Knowing how to help employees see their own strengths and weaknesses more clearly can also be of help. Working with knowledge/skill profiles, as previously suggested, will help, but knowing where to refer employees to career counseling services in your organization or in the community might even be more appropriate.

When an employee raises a career question during the development of the improvement plan or possibly at some other time, your response could include:

Pointing out that, among the benefits of an improvement plan, is the development of competencies which may make the employee a more appealing candidate for positions to which he or she might aspire.

Discussing, or offering to obtain information about competencies required for the position which the employee believes might be a step in his or her career path.

Including, in the improvement plan, where appropriate, opportunities to gain such skills either through developmental work assignments or through training experiences that help to enhance competence on the job as well as provide foundation for the other position.

Suggesting to the employee to speak to people in positions which might be of interest to him or her to clarify views about this (or these) positions.

Clarifying, to the employee, that enhancement of skills and capabilities and even demonstration of competence in these skills, does not necessarily assure that the employee will indeed be chosen for the position to which he or she aspires. All that you can do is to help the employee see more clearly what it is that he or she needs to do well, besides highly competent performance in the current job, to be considered a desirable applicant. There might, of course at any one time, be several other applicants whose qualifications might be even better for that position. Clarifying the limits, prevents raising unreasonable expectations on the part of the employee and sets the career advice into appropriate perspective.

Very often this career counseling need not be confined to positions within the organization. Forward looking supervisors will help individuals identify these requirements even for positions that do not exist in their own organization or for which no openings are expected. These supervisors recognize that competent people cannot be prevented from leaving the organization if they find better opportunities elsewhere. In helping them develop themselves for the positions which they *believe* they might like, they frequently come to see that there are opportunities within the organizations that are equal or possibly better than those which at first seemed so appealing to them.

A supervisor who is willing to provide career planning assistance to an employee does not, by any means, become a career counselor. Counseling, within the context of the performance management system should be limited. When it is appropriate, it should merely help the employee gain perspective on the knowledge, skill, and other requirements for favorable consideration, as an applicant, to those positions in which he or she may be interested.

Part Two

IMPLEMENTATION ISSUES AND PROBLEMS IN SETTING UP OR REVISING A PERFORMANCE MANAGEMENT SYSTEM

Difficult questions must be faced by:

Supervisors who have the responsibility to design a performance management system or make changes in a system, and

Supervisors who must work with an existing system.

Parts Two and Three of this book discuss a number of these problems/questions. Part II covers the questions which affect the design of a system. Questions concerning supervisory strategies within an existing system will be discussed in Part III.

This Part Two starts with a general discussion of implementation considerations and then explores seven issues.

1. **The bases for standards.** How are standards set from job descriptions, key results areas, and the MBO/goal management system, and what are the respective advantages?

2. **How to label the rating levels.** What names to give to the ratings levels and how to ensure that:

    a. Ratings are uniform between departments

    b. Raters do not gradually become more generous in assigning ratings

3. **What kind of anchors should be used for assigning ratings.** Should "anchors" be provided to help supervisors assign ratings or should supervisors use personal judgment in assigning ratings; if anchors are to be provided, what should they be like?

4. **Employee participation and employee self-ratings.** What are the benefits, if any, of asking employees to rate themselves so that such self-ratings are available during the appraisal interview, and what problems can self-ratings bring?

5. **Approvals of ratings and appeals procedure**

6. **Should more than one performance management system be used?** Should an organization have different systems for operations, sales/marketing, administrative departments, and/or different systems for different types of employees such as supervisory, professional, clerical, blue collar?

7. **Legal issues affecting performance management.** What legal issues affect the selection of standards and their use in a performance management system which serves as the basis for compensation and other personnel decisions?

In addition to the introduction and the seven issues, Part II will discuss various considerations that should be kept in mind when designing or modifying a performance management system.

IMPLEMENTATION CONSIDERATIONS

When deciding on the features of a performance management system, you will want to consider:

1. The principles discussed in Chapter 3. Performance management is like a delicate and complex machine. It is therefore important that each segment of the system is adjusted to work well with all other parts. Only if every aspect of your system comes as close as possible to satisfying *all* of the principles will the system have the coordination to successfully overcome the many problems and controversies it will undoubtedly have to face.

2. The segments and steps which were described in Chapter 4.

3. Which approaches to controversial issues, such as the ones which will be discussed in Part Two, are most appropriate for the needs of your organization.

4. How the performance management process can best be implemented so supervisors and employees* will thoroughly understand it and so they will be prepared to assist in over-

---

* Please note that the word supervisor is used for all levels of management. The word employee includes employees at all professional, supervisory, and managerial levels (see Preface).

coming problems as they develop. This subject is the first topic in this chapter.

IMPLEMENTATION STEPS

The basic soundness of a performance management program alone is no assurance for its success. How it is introduced can be of equal importance. Credibility is essential for cooperation, and credibility has to be earned.

Therefore, effective implementation of a performance management program starts during the design phase or when it is to be revised. At that time, a committee could be appointed to develop a preliminary outline of the various features of the program or of the changes that should be made, and of the implementation steps. If such a committee is made up of competent individuals, it can give credibility to the committee and to the steps or changes which are planned to make it responsive to the needs of the organization and of the employees.

A committee is not the only way to start a performance management program on the right foot. A thorough, carefully conceived system can be developed at the top, with or without the assistance of "experts," and with or without the use of a committee. No matter how it is developed, though, it must be communicated to all employees with equal care and thoroughness, first to those higher level supervisors who were not involved in the design decisions and then to successively lower organizational levels. At the first two, or possibly three levels, it could be introduced as a tentative design. Recommendations could be solicited and design changes made insofar as they have widespread support and are consistent with the fairness principles.

Once the system's tentative design has progressed to the point where it has extensive support from supervisors, it could be introduced in several steps:

1. A preparation phase
2. A three-to-four month dry run
3. Revisions based on the experience with the system during the dry-run

4. A six-month to one-year live trial of the revised system
5. A review-evaluation of the system, and possibly further revisions
6. Start of the permanent performance management system

Preparation Phase

During the preparatory phase, activities such as the following should take place if the performance management system is to receive a high degree of acceptance:

1. Preparation and training of supervisors so they are clearly aware of the benefits of the systems, their roles, and so that they are capable of accepting their responsibilities in the program
2. Expressions of firm personal support and personal participation by top management, so everyone is aware that management is fully behind the program
3. Setting up and communication of an appeals procedure
4. Orientation/education of employees so they understand their obligations and also the benefits which the program can bring to them
5. Management attitudes and actions that reduce to a minimum, some of the initially threatening aspects of a performance management system

Preparation and Training of Supervisors

An adequate training program is an essential element of a successful implementation. Supervisors must know the procedures, have clear understanding of their roles, and be skilled in discharging their responsibilities in performance management.

Some of the necessary competencies are difficult to maintain because some of the important responsibilities have to be discharged only once or possibly twice a year. Supervisory competencies for the performance management system lie along two major lines:

1. Knowledge of the system and how it should be applied by a supervisor so that it will be consistent and uniform throughout the organization

2. Skills for:

    a. Setting standards

    b. Analyzing and evaluating performance

    c. Conducting progress reviews and evaluation/appraisal interviews

    d. Developing improvement plans, and possibly

    e. Career planning and/or career counseling

To achieve the necessary supervisory competence, a procedures manual and classroom training sessions should be used.

PROCEDURES MANUAL

A thoroughly designed procedures manual which is neither excessively long nor overly brief can help greatly in achieving and maintaining awareness of the way the system works. It can thus satisfy the requirement that supervisors know the sysem and the procedures which they are expected to follow. In addition, instructions on the forms can help to ensure that supervisors will be able to adhere to the procedures and will be able to compare their evaluations with those of other supervisors. The manual and the forms can provide a foundation for those segments of classroom training which are concerned with acquainting supervisors and employees with the details of the system.

Topics that might be included in a manual to be distributed to supervisors when the performance management system is started could include:

Benefits of the performance management system

An overview of the system

Procedures for setting standards of performance or goals/objectives containing standards of performance

Description of forms that are to be used

Steps for monitoring performance, for providing feedback, and for collection of performance data

Steps and procedures for progress reviews

Steps for review of responsibilities prior to the performance evaluation and other steps to take in preparation for the performance appraisal interview.

Evaluation of performance and assigning of ratings

Approvals that are to be obtained

Procedures and suggestions for the conduct of the performance evaluation/appraisal interview

Procedures and suggestions for the development of the improvement plan

Suggestions for employee participation in each of the steps

Suggestions for the interview in which the employee is informed of compensation decisions

Suggestions for career counseling

Suggestions for follow-up

The procedures manual could provide examples for wording standards and for entries on the forms, to help supervisors prepare their own entries to support the performance rating. The manual could also give timing suggestions such as:

How much time employees should be given for their tasks, such as for the review of their job descriptions or for their self-evaluation (if these are to be used)

How much time should elapse between the review of job responsibilities (if such a review is used) and the appraisal interview

How long the intervals should be between regular progress reviews in various types of situations

CLASSROOM TRAINING SESSIONS FOR SUPERVISORS

Annual brief developmental group sessions could be scheduled in which skills are honed and where opportunities exist for exchange of views so that supervisors, in similar positions, can coordinate how they rate their respective employees, or apply the ratings to various situations. Such annual developmental sessions can be used to enhance skills of supervisors for the various tasks outlined previously. They can help the organization gradually acquire higher and higher level competence for making the performance management system work effectively.

Prior to such a developmental session or group of sessions, the performance management procedures manual should be reviewed. If changes have taken place which affect the manual, it should be updated.

At the beginning, when the performance management system is first set up, or whenever it is revised, a fairly thorough briefing session should be held to inform supervisors of their responsibilities in the new or revised system. At the same time, they can be given opportunities for exchange of ideas on how they will apply the procedures. Skill practice sessions should also be scheduled for appraisal interviews and for coaching/counseling sessions, as much as time and budget permits.

Exhibit 5.1 is an agenda that could be used for the initial training program and for the refresher program and Exhibit 5.2 is a role practice critique form for use in skill practice. This critique form can also be provided for self-critique. At the conclusion of an interview, coaching or counseling session, the supervisor can put himself or herself into the employee's shoes and do the self-rating.

EXHIBIT 5.1.   AN AGENDA FOR A SUPERVISORY TRAINING PROGRAM

Presession Assignment
If it is new or updated supervisors receive a copy of the procedures manual. They are asked to read it, or read it again, and to prepare a list of questions (or problems that have been encountered).

Program Agenda
The classroom program itself could include the following sessions:

Review of the manual and discussion of questions which supervisors raise.

Practice session on preparation of standards in which supervisors set performance standards for one or several real or hypothetical jobs which were described verbally or in writing

Practice session on the skills discussed in Part IV of this book

Practice session on conducting a review of job responsibilities

Practice session on conducting an evaluation/appraisal interview

Practice session on development of an improvement plan

Practice session on career counseling.

EXHIBIT 5.2. ROLE PRACTICE CRITIQUE FORM

	Circle Your Rating for each Question				
	Little				Much
1. To what extent did you feel your supervisor really tried to obtain your views and then discussed them with you?	1	2	3	4	5
2. To what extent did you think your supervisor really understood how you felt about the situation?	1	2	3	4	5
3. Did your supervisor *listen carefully* to what *you* had to say *first,* before giving his or her suggestions?	1	2	3	4	5
4. How thoroughly did you feel your supervisor explained his or her views and supported them with specific incidents he or she had observed, or with facts?	1	2	3	4	5
5. How carefully did the supervisor check whether you understood what he or she was saying?	1	2	3	4	5
6. How thoroughly did your supervisor discuss with you exactly what was expected and what *he or she* could do to help?	1	2	3	4	5
7. To what extent did you feel your supervisor tried to help you?	1	2	3	4	5
8. To what extent did you feel your supervisor was fair in the way he or she handled the situation?	1	2	3	4	5
9. How would you rate the discussion overall?	1	2	3	4	5
10. To what extent do you feel your performance will *actually* improve as a result of this discussion?	1	2	3	4	5

Copyright © 1983, Didactic Systems, Inc., Cranford, New Jersey 07016

As much as possible, training sessions should avoid lengthy lectures. For instance, a review of the manual could be achieved by asking various supervisors to assume the role of instructor, to outline the respective sections of the manual, and to provide leadership to a discussion of that particular section. At the end of these brief overview discussions, a panel consisting of the instructor and higher level managers and/or someone from the personnel department could field any questions about the procedures that have not been answered satisfactorily.

The various practice sessions for preparation of standards, for practicing essential skills, and for the conduct of the various interviews could be small-team discussions and role-playing sessions. In these activities, small teams of three to five supervisors could first prepare lists of points to be made in the application of the skill or conduct of the interview. They would then role play that particular skill or interview. One supervisor on each team could assume the role of the employee and another the role of the supervisor. The remaining team members could serve as observers who provide feedback, at the end of the role play, to the role players.

In organizations where many such training sessions are to be held, it is worthwhile for the person in charge of this training program to develop specific scenarios so that supervisors have more structure for the respective practice/skills sessions.

Expressions of Firm Support and Personal Participation of Top Management

It cannot be overemphasized how important it is that top management become involved extensively during the preparation phase. This participation is important in several dimensions:

Top management must clearly understand and subscribe to the elements of the design

The highest level supervisors must take performance management seriously, they must accept the personal discipline for progress reviews and performance evaluations of their own staff members, and the review of the evaluations at the next lower level, which the program demands of them.

Depending on the size of the organization, this expression of support may range from full pesonal participation in the system (the best possible support), to personal appearances at training sessions, to videotaped messages, and even to memos. It is quite important though, if memos are used, that these are not perceived as routine. They should be strong and thorough and they must clearly reflect a serious commitment.

Setting Up and Communicating an Appeals Procedure

Many performance management systems exist without appeals procedures. However, the failure to provide one deprives the system of a safety valve. At the same time, it deprives employees of the comforting assurance that they can gain another hearing without the need for confrontation with their supervisors.

Orientation/Education of Employees

If the performance management system is to achieve credibility and the respect of employees, it is important that they too are given detailed information about the process when it is first installed, and each time it is revised. A bulletin alone is not enough. In addition, there could be brief sessions annually to serve as reminders of how the system works.

All sessions with employees can be fairly brief, not exceeding one hour. During these training sessions, the memo or manual could be reviewed and employees could be given adequate opportunity to ask questions about it. These sessions for employees could be conducted either by the respective supervisors, but preferably by someone from the personnel department or by a member of the organization's supervisory development staff if such a staff exists.

Of course, new employees should be given information about the system as part of their orientation. All orientation could be based on a memo describing the system, a brief manual, or a chapter in a more comprehensive employee manual. The memo or manual would inform employees of their rights, stress the benefits, and explain the procedures so that new employees could ask their supervisor about a procedure step they did not understand.

Probably the more important part of the orientation of employees is to make them aware that the performance management program has significant benefits for them. Of course, these benefits are greater for those employees who are seriously committed to a career with the organization and who want to help the organization progress toward its goals. The list of principles is the primary list of these benefits and they should all be stressed, particularly the fact that the system will be used to help employees gain greater satisfaction from their work and maximum tangible rewards. Since a smoothly operating performance management system can bring better organizational results, frequently there are greater rewards to be shared when everyone cooperates to make it work.

Sometimes a performance management system is used to allocate bonuses to certain higher level employees. In these cases, employees who are within the bonus system and who are entitled to bonuses under the program should receive separate orientations from those who would be excluded from the bonuses.

Management Attitudes and Actions

A new system that significantly affects all employees is usually threatening until it is thoroughly understood. There is no way to explain such a system completely to employees during an orientation or training program. Even with a well-written manual and discussion of all aspects of the program, most employees are likely to be skeptical that they will indeed see benefits on balance.

For this reason it is highly desirable that top management confirm, not only its commitment to the program, but also its desire for a gradual introduction of the program. Time must be allowed for adjustments to ensure that the system will achieve what it is designed to do. This top management attitude could be expressed through brief presentations at supervisory training sessions and at employee orientation sessions, in which the following points could be stressed:

The efforts and careful thought that were devoted to the design of the system

The tentative nature of the initial design

That there will be a dry-run during which the evaluations will *not* be recorded on employee files. Furthermore, during the dry-run the system previously used will be the primary determinant of compensation decisions and other personnel actions

The intention to consider comments by employees during the dry-run of the system

The plan to analyze the results of the first year to ensure that the hoped-for benefits to employees as well as to the organization had actually been realized

The intent to make further revisions, at year end, if necessary, before the system become permanent.

Dry Run

At the beginning of this period, which is best set for three months, supervisors at all levels meet with each one of their employees to ensure that there is good mutual understanding of job responsibilities and to establish preliminary standards of performance for the trial period. During the three months, at least two progress reviews are scheduled for each employee when progress is reviewed but not evaluated. At the end of the three month period, there is a formal performance evaluation and appraisal interview, and development of an improvement plan which provides the basis for the coming period.

The best time for such a dry-run is immediately after employees receive salary adjustments so it is easy to make it clear that the dry-run will not affect compensation.

Supervisors should be requested to maintain careful records, during the dry-run, of all difficulties they encounter, of errors in manuals or forms, and of the indication they have about the views of employees. It should also be stressed to supervisors that they should emphasize the tentative nature of the dry-run to employees. Employees should be aware that the dry-run evaluations will not affect their records and that their views will be considered in any revisions to the system that might be made at the end of the dry-run.

REVISIONS BASED ON THE EXPERIENCE OF THE DRY-RUN

The dry-run will uncover minor, and possibly even some major changes that deserve serious consideration. Therefore, toward the end of the dry-run, the designers of the system should review the experience of the dry-run in meetings with supervisors and employees or with committees of employees to clearly outline the changes that the staff members consider desirable. Revisions could then be made to the system procedures and forms, prior to the live trial.

Trial

If an organization gives general increases annually, and if the dry-run is for approximately three months and started immediately after the organization's general increases, about nine months would be left for a live trial, allowing for some time for modifications. The live trial would be a full-fledged use of the performance management system as revised after the dry-run.

During the actual trial, supervisors should again be asked to keep careful records of their experiences with the system and any difficulties they encountered which could be avoided with a further design change. However, at this point, supervisors should also be informed that no extensive changes will be made in the system and that only adjustments are contemplated to help achieve smoother operation.

The impression that somehow has to be built up in the minds of the employees is that the system has been designed carefully, that it has been thoroughly tested, and that it is here to stay. Otherwise, the system will have great difficulty in achieving full acceptance. At the same time, employees have to be aware that everything will be done to implement the system in such a way that the benefits which it can bring to employees will indeed by realized.

Review and Evaluation

At the end of the live trial, another review takes place, of any difficulties which were encountered and of implementation changes that could or should be made to have the system operate even more smoothly. Many of the problems are likely to be with the skill of supervisors in implementing it, and not with the design of the system. If possible, the supervisory difficulties should be analyzed and another training program should be scheduled to help supervisors gain higher skill in administering the system so as to avoid the problems that had previously been encountered. (See Chapters 6 and 7 for a discussion on the issues that ensure that the system is one which allows for smooth administration.)

Chapter 6

BASES FOR STANDARDS— AN IMPORTANT ISSUE

There are four bases which can provide the foundation for setting performance standards, as well as combinations of these four. The foundations are:

Job description
Key job elements
Goals/objectives*
Personal characteristics

STANDARDS BASED ON JOB DESCRIPTION

If your organization has job descriptions that are reasonably well maintained, then standards can be set on the basis of these job descriptions. Setting one standard for every one of the responsibilities, or even more than one standard may lead to a large number—more than might be optimal, except if the position involved few responsibilities. With most positions it is necessary to find the most important functions and set standards for those.

If the work involves *only* activities/functions which are performed on a regular, or even continuous basis, such as clerical, so-

* The term goals and objectives will be used synonymously.

cial service, education, sales, or manufacturing work, then ongoing standards may be the only ones that are needed. These standards would specify the expected results and would measure the competence and effort being devoted by the respective employee or supervisor* to quantity and quality of the work. For project/type work such as research, design, or development, project or product management or where art is involved, period standards are needed. Often both types of standards have to be set, in addition to an umbrella standard, to obtain adequate coverage of all aspects of a position.

When job descriptions are fairly up-to-date, the advantage of using them as the basis for deciding on standards is their ready availability and the advantage of building on the work that has been done in identifying the functions and responsibilities of the position. Job descriptions usually are not as precise, however, as carefully prepared key job elements and goals/objectives in pointing to the highest priority results and tasks or functions. An example of the way a performance standard can be drawn from a job description is in the Chapter 4 section entitled "Where Should Standards of Performance Be Set and How Many Standards?"

STANDARDS BASED ON KEY RESULTS AREAS

In many organizations, job descriptions either do not exist or are so outdated that they do not lend themselves as foundations for performance standards. In these situations, standards can be based on key job elements. Such standards can be set essentially the same way as those that are set on the basis of the job description. Supervisor and employee, jointly, or first independently and then jointly,† need to identify the key job elements and then stan-

---

* Please note that the word supervisor is used for all levels of management (see Preface for explanation).

† Research has shown that creativity and accuracy can often be enhanced by individuals first working independently and then in a team. When working alone, individuals come

dards can be set. When key job elements are used, an umbrella standard is also required for all remaining job elements.

Key Results Areas

Key results areas are sometimes called *key performance areas, key impact areas,* or *key job elements.* The term *key results areas* will be used here to emphasize that, whenever possible, it is best to establish accountabilities on those outputs or results (including the activities such as assembling, report writing, monitoring, planning, communicating), that are of greatest importance to successful performance in a position.

Key results areas need not be worded in measurable terms. Some organizations use general concepts such as quality, production level, customer service, appearance of work areas, staffing levels, inquiry response time, case load, or security, to identify their key results areas. They then write one or several specific standards in each of these areas. These standards can be written with the two segments—results and competence/effort.

However, some organizations specify only the measurable *end* results, in the belief that accomplishment can be evaluated directly and clearly in this manner. They then look at processes and the steps which were taken to bring the results only when these were clearly affected by forces beyond the control of the person whose performance is being evaluated. Most of the time this is done only when performance is below standard and the employee points to the unavoidable influences. When the circumstances are fortuitous, the employee usually benefits from a better evaluation. Employees, of course, are aware of the way good or bad luck can influence their performance evaluation and their respect for the integrity of the system may be affected. Nevertheless, when key results areas are properly identified, they represent accomplishments for which the incumbent can take at least partial

---

up with more independent ideas than when they work in a group, because the thoughts expressed in a group often channel the group's thinking. In contrast, when members of a group first work independently and then meet to share their thoughts, the disadvantage of thought channeling is avoided, and the benefits of individual work and team discussion can both be realized.

credit when reached, but must also take some share of the blame if performance falls short.

Key results areas are not always easy to identify and delineate. Sometimes it may help to ask the question: What would *not* be achieved if the position were vacant? The most important answers represent the key results areas.

Key results areas can be expressed in specific, measurable terms; not only in the general, broader terms discussed. Examples of measurably worded key results areas from various occupations are:

Percent of rejects

Ratio of inventory level to production volume

Budget adherence

Ratio of warranty repairs to previous quarter shipments

Percent of approved project requests

Percent of projects completed on schedule, within budget

Percent of vacancies filled

Percent of cases closed satisfactorily

Percent of students who pass impartial board examinations

Percent of market penetration

Please note that these key results areas do not carry specific numbers. When numbers are inserted in front of the percent symbol (%) or instead of the words "ratio" or "proportion," the statement can be the results segment of a standard of performance.

At any one time, there can be key results areas among the routine responsibilities and among the special projects for which an employee may be responsible. It is useful to look at key results areas as those responsibilities where it is important to high level performance that significant effort be applied competently over an extended period of time.

Therefore, key results areas can be important routine responsibilities where deterioration or difficulties have occurred and where effort is needed to bring performance back to normal levels. Key results areas also are important projects whose competent, on-time completion is essential for high level job performance. These two types of key results areas are precisely where standards of performance are most useful and where they can best serve as measures of performance. All other job responsibilities can be lumped under the umbrella standard.

STANDARDS BASED ON GOALS/OBJECTIVES

Standards can be based on goals without regard to whether the organization:

Now has a goals or management-by-objectives (MBO) program that is working satisfactorily,*

Is setting up such a program, or

Has a goals (MBO) program that is not linked well with the performance appraisal system being used.

Relationship Between Standards of Performance and Goals/Objectives

Considerable confusion exists about the two concepts, *standards of performance* and *goals/objectives*. This is especially true in those organizations where for convenience, emphasis, or because both concepts were established and have developed inertia, they are used concurrently.

Much of the confusion is probably due to the lack of awareness that there are many definitions of standards of performance and of goals/objectives. In some of these definitions, the two concepts mean essentially the same thing, namely, results which are to be achieved and which are measurable, so it is possible to determine how well they were achieved. Sometimes, conceptional errors cause continuing difficulties with the use of the two separate approaches.

Though it is not widely recognized, goals/objectives and standards of performance can be identical because they share the

---

* For a thorough discussion of what makes a goals program successful, see Erwin Rausch, *Balancing Needs of People and Organizations,* originally published by BNA, Washington, D.C., 1978. Now published by Didactic Systems, Cranford, N.J. 07016.

statement of the results which are to be achieved. They can differ in that each one sometimes continues to a different segment:

A thorough performance standard should continue to clarify how competence and effort will be measured and evaluated

An appropriate goal/objective statement may continue by stating the resources which may be used to achieve the goal/objective; or it may stop with the results statement if it is obvious what resources are available, or if the goal/objective concerns the use of resources

Sometimes boundaries are drawn between goals/objectives and standards of performance so that there is no overlap or conflict. In such systems, goals/objectives state the results to be achieved, and are used primarily to set direction and priorities. Standards of performance are used to evaluate the competence and efforts of people.

An example may clarify these points: The goal for an assembly line states—No more than two percent defective units shall reach the test position. This goal, of course, assumes that labor costs in assembly and for inspection shall not exceed budgeted amounts. The standard of performance for the assembly line supervisor states—No more than two percent defective units shall reach the test position. Competence and effort shall be measured by the promptness with which corrective actions are taken (as determined by the number of units rejected with the same defect), by the thoroughness of operator instruction, and by adherence to inspection procedures.

The line between goal/objective and standard of performance is a thin one. When the two are that closely coordinated, it is not likely that both are needed.

However, the two are complementary if the goal is stated as the results segment in the example was, and the standard of performance states that: Performance with respect to assembly quality shall be measured by the promptness with which corrective actions are taken, by the thoroughness of operator instructions, and by adherence to inspection procedures.

Unless careful attention is given to base the standard on competence and effort, the use of goals/objectives as a foundation for performance standards can bring some difficult questions, primarly as a result of the requirement that goals/objectives are to be both achievable and challenging.

Promise and Potential Drawback of Standards Based on Goals

Goals/objectives must be challenging, so they will serve as a motivating force. If you want to set goals/objectives so that they are challenging, how can you do it? Obviously, you don't know when a standard or goal will be challenging and, yet, achievable. If you are experienced and knowledgeable, you can make some very good estimates of what will probably happen. You can set your goals/objectives higher than these estimates or you can set them lower. No matter what you do, you are only forecasting. You may achieve your goals/objectives or you may not. It all depends on the effort you devote and on the circumstances which develop as time goes by.

What are the conditions, then, under which you would be willing to set a high goal/objective even though you are not certain that you will make it? Will you do it if it is likely that you will have to explain why you didn't make it and possibly find that your performance evaluation is affected negatively? Probably not. If performance is measured on the basis of standard or goal *achievement,* chances are you will play it safe. You may still work hard to reach for high level performance, but the standard or goal you turn in will be a safe one—one that you are almost certain you can reach.

What has really happened when you do that? You have begun to play a game. Communications on goals/standards have broken down, for all practical purposes, at least partially, between you and the person to whom you report. And your supervisor's organizational unit has probably lost the chance to have a smoothly operating performance management system.

Let's take this scenario a step further. What if you were to treat your own employees somewhat differently? What if you were to say to them, in effect, that you would like them to list the areas in which goals/objectives should be set for the upcoming period and then to assign priorities to them? Assume further that you then sit down with them to discuss their priorities, so that both they and you see them the same way. There can be differences of opinion, of course, and these have to be resolved. But assume for a moment that there are no differences of opinion, that you and one of your employees see the priorities in the same light and that you are in full agreement on them.

Assume further that so far there are no numbers or dates or other specifics attached to these areas in which goals/objectives should be set. They merely are listed to indicate where the priorities should be with respect to the effort that must be devoted to improving the team's performance. What would happen if you were next to ask your employees to set specific goals/objectives with dates and numbers on high-priority items. You would ask them to set the goals/objectives so that they are challenging but still possibly within reach, which means that they should have an even chance of making them with extra effort. Suppose you were to assure them that, if they did not quite reach those goals/objectives, their performance evaluation would not suffer, that performance would be measured only on how competently and how seriously they devoted efforts to achieve the goals/standards. Not a very realistic scenario in those organizations that use goals/objectives as the foundation for performance standards.

Resolving the Contradictions

There are several questions that need to be explored if you were to follow such a scenario. In the first place, it would seem that your employees would now be free to set goals/objectives so that they are, indeed, challenging. Would they do it, though, you may ask, if there were nothing in it for them when they achieved the goals/objectives or, conversely, if there were no penalty for not achieving them? That, of course, is the key question, and the answer is very complex. It would seem that if there is, indeed, a climate that allows for maximum motivation, then there are significant rewards in goal/objective achievement for the individual—the really important satisfaction from achievement, from accomplishing something that was difficult. There also would be the recognition which you provide directly and indirectly, the greater sense of security, the higher probability of faster career advancement. In short, there would be all the benefits which highly motivated, successful people enjoy—a potential cornucopia for setting and achieving tough goals/objectives. But all this is loaded with a big "if." It will happen only "if" all employees are career-oriented people who want to achieve high level performance. Some employees probably would not respond enthusiastically, many would not exert substantial additional effort, or give up some of their free moments, or even devote significantly more thought to their goals/objectives; but they are likely to do more than they would if you handled the situation differently.

A second question concerns another "if": If only competent effort counts, but not the actual *achievement* of standards or goals, then employees are not really responsible for goal/objective achievement. If they are not, then who is?

That's easy. You are.

You know this, of course, but you probably have always felt that, while you are ultimately responsible to your supervisors, so your employees are responsible to you. In other words, you have felt that everybody, all the way up the line, is responsible or accountable for the achievement of goals/objectives.

If you were to continue exploring the scenario we previously painted, the situation would be different. As far as your employees would be concerned, they are accountable for doing everything as though they were responsible for achieving the goal/objective; but they also would be aware that, if they cannot acheve it, you would consider yourself responsible. You are undoubtedly asking yourself now whether it makes sense that you should be responsible for the goals/objectives of your employees even though you have only limited control over what they actually do. Why should the principle of fairness, which states that employees should be held responsible only for matters under the employee's control apply to your people but not to you? "Why should the buck stop with you?"

If you reflect on it for a moment, you can see that there is logic to such an arrangement because you are the one who has asked for and accepted a goal/objective from an employee that you know to be challenging. While it may appear to be realistic at the moment when you accepted it, that's not what it may turn out to be. If you accepted it, then you are the person who must help your employee achieve it. If he or she can't, even with significant and competent effort, and if you also can't do it even when you hear of difficulties as soon as they become apparent, then obviously you have no choice but to take your employee off the hook. You simply cannot expect employees to do something that you could not do yourself, given all the resources of the *entire* team which are at *your* disposal but not at theirs. Does that leave you hanging? Maybe yes, maybe no. It depends on your relationship with your supervisor and on your supervisor's competence. As far as your employees are concerned, however, the picture is clear. You have told them that you will evaluate their performance on *what they do* to achieve their goals/objectives and not on *whether* they achieve them.

If you were to establish such a relationship with your employees, that allows them to honestly submit challenging goals/objectives, do you build your own goals/objectives on these and turn them in to your supervisor? This, too, depends. Either your supervisor sees performance management as you do and has told you that you will be evaluated along the same lines as you evaluate your people, or he or she is the kind of person who believes in expecting goal/objective *achievement* from employees. If your supervisor holds the latter position, you have no choice but to continue to play the same game that you may be playing now. You remove as much of the goals/objectives that was set with your employees, as you think is wise, and then you turn in your goals/objectives based on the more conservative base.

If you are working for someone who thinks as you do, then you can set challenging goals/objectives—what you consider to be within the realm of the feasible if everyone were to put in the necessary effort. If that is what you do then you are not playing a game. If your supervisor asks you how you arrived at these goals/objectives, you can safely show the challenging, ambitious, yet realistic goals/objectives of employees and explain how you arrived at your own goals/objectives based on these. Communications are free and open and the performance management system benefits from the best knowledge that is available at each level. There is nothing under the table; nothing is hidden.

Who Is Really Responsible for Goals/Objectives Achievement

You may be wondering who is actually responsible for achievement of goals/objectives in an environment such as that previously described. Essentially, the answer is the same people as are responsible for them now. No one is really responsible for goal/objective *achievement.* If this sounds like heresy it may be worthwhile to take a look at the actual situation as it exists in the world today. On the one hand, it often happens that some people are held accountable for goals/objectives that are not achieved, and sometimes a person's head may roll even when that person devotes much time and competent effort to the achievement of the goal/objective. On the other hand, certain people are commended for achieving goals/objectives that were not worth setting as goals/objectives because they were going to be achieved even if no one payed any attention to them.

The point which many people miss is that certain goals/objectives are simply not achievable, no matter how competent and complete the effort which is devoted to them. Everyone should be aware that about 50 percent of all goals/objectives that are set as they *should* be set, namely challenging yet achievable with extra and competent effort, will not be achieved. In fact, very few will be achieved exactly and as many will be exceeded as will fall short.

Facing Reality

Although it may seem risky to hold people responsible for the quality and quantity of effort instead of the results, it is really not that different from what happens now in well-managed organizations and organizational units. Today, if a goal/objective is not achieved, the supervisor reviews what the employee has done in attempting to achieve it. If the supervisor is convinced that the effort was top notch and the reason for nonachievement was totally beyond the control of the employee, then the competent supervisor may still give the employee an excellent evaluation.

Without clear understanding of what criteria the supervisor uses for evaluation, the employee may, however, feel somewhat uneasy about being evaluated. There are, therefore, natural suspicions about the relationship between goal/objective achievement and evaluation; or at the very least, there are doubts, questions, and uncertainties that do not make it easy for employees to trust the system implicitly. As a result, performance management suffers because supervisors have to consider that some of their employees, at all levels, are building cushions into their standards.

However, to suddenly release people from the requirement to achieve goals/objectives, even if a thorough system of new criteria were substituted, could be too sudden and damaging to an organization which is accustomed to thinking of goals/objectives as targets which must be reached. The new concepts are more complex and people have to adjust to them gradually if they are to serve their purposes well.

An important aspect of a thorough performance management system that effectively deals with results-oriented standards, lies with its ability to communicate to people the fact that evaluations will not be arbitrary. They are based on criteria that everyone knows and evaluations can, therefore, be discussed—and even reviewed or challenged—in a systematic, organized way. In turn, this can lead to improved confidence by supervisors in their evaluations of the performance of their employees and in greater confidence by employees in the fairness of the evaluations.

One way to attack the problem of accountability for standards of performance which were expressed in terms of expected results, or for goals/objectives whose achievement is at least partly beyond the control of the employee, was suggested in the competence/effort segment of standards. Another approach uses a fairly standard group of steps which define competence and effort. It relies on a series of "action steps"—steps which any employee who has the necessary competence can take if he or she wants to take them. By definition, action steps are all totally under the control of the employee. One major advantage of the approach is that it is an easy one to communicate to employees in advance of the evaluation period.

One Possible System of Accountabilities

There are many activities or categories of action steps for which an employee can and should be held specifically accountable. Use of these can make it easier for supervisors to place less reliance on actual achievement of goals/objectives when deciding what to expect from employees. There are eight major activities or anchors which help to ensure that goals/objectives will be achieved. These are fully under the control of the employee and he or she can accept complete responsibility for them:

Setting or cooperating in setting challenging, but realistic goals/objectives

Setting a thorough set of action steps for working toward the goals/objectives

Maintaining continuity and consistency in planning the work needed to achieve the goals/objectives

Seeing to it that the quality of the steps taken is high

Keeping to the schedule

Solving problems as they arise

Communicating problems with goals/objectives achievement in a timely manner

Maintaining good relationships with other employees

None of these eight responsibilities are goals/objectives, yet together they can measure the competence and effort which an employee devotes to goals/objectives achievement.

Setting Challenging but Realistic Standards and Goals

As has been discussed, supervisors must keep in mind that employees will set both high and realistic goals/objectives only if they do not feel threatened when they do so. A supervisor can con-

sider, during performance evaluation, the skill and conscientious-
ness with which employees set goals/objectives in the first place,
and the extent to which they are set so that they are realistic and
yet challenging. Even though this requirement of accountability
requires forecasting and, therefore, may seem to involve matters
beyond the control of the employee, anyone in a responsible job
can learn how to forecast what can be accomplished in his or her
position. It is therefore reasonable to expect competent people to
set realistic and challenging goals/objectives or at least to contin-
uously enhance their skills for doing so.

If someone does not wish to set goals/objectives that are challenging yet realistic, this will soon be evident. The person will
generally set them too low even though it is apparent that he or
she could do better. On the other hand, someone who consistently
sets them too low because he or she does not know how to set
them at a challenging level or sets them too high so that they are
not realistic can usually be helped through training in forecasting
and estimating. High or low in this case usually refers to the dates
when a specific project will be completed, or to the quantity or
percentage which is to be achieved.

In goal/objective setting, obstacles other than competence and
desire to perform well, are involved. If employees are forced to
play a game in which they try to obtain the lowest possible goal or
objective to gain the greatest assurance that it will indeed be
achieved, then they are not likely to be cooperative. Since the employees usually know more about what can be accomplished than
their supervisors, especially if they have been trained in forecasting, their supervisors need their cooperation in helping to set
really appropriate goals/objectives.

If the supervisor wants the performance management system to
become a way of life rather than a paper program, then the supervisor cannot expect people to set challenging goals/objectives and
discipline them when they do not achieve them. Most supervisors
do make allowance for effort and do look at events or conditions
which are beyond the employee's control when reviewing the reasons why achievement fell short of expectations, or why much
more was accomplished than had been expected. But rarely do

employees know what the supervisor will consider valid or how he or she actually looks at performance. Unless they know the supervisor's standards, it is not likely that they can develop the full confidence that is needed to go out on a limb with tough goals or standards.

As supervisor you must be prepared to look at goals/objectives only as predictions of achievement. You can expect the employee to make a serious effort to attain them, but you must recognize that some may not be achieved even with the best action program and the most untiring effort. If you accept this fact, you can hold employees accountable for setting realistic goals/objectives that are quite high, and you can use the record of how they set them as a major measure of overall performance.

Setting Thorough Action Steps

Employees can also be held accountable for the thoroughness with which they develop action steps in support of their goals/objectives. Employees should be aware, at all times, of the next action steps that should be taken for all period standards and the dates by which they should be completed. Even though you would not frequently ask a competent employee what progress was being made toward the accomplishment of a goal/objective or, what actual steps were being taken, the employee should know what steps were necessary. Not all the steps need to be planned, nor need they be formalized on paper. However, should you ask an employee about the planned action steps for a specific goal/objective, he or she should have a plan or schedule and should readily be able to list and explain the next step or steps for each goal/objective.

Therefore, you can hold your employees responsible for being constantly aware of the next appropriate action steps for every goal/objective. In this, as in other areas of accountability, factual data can be obtained on performance. Not only do regular contacts with employees provide much valid data, but the records from progress reviews yield additional information on which to base a valid judgment. If the employee, at every contact and at the progress reviews, provides evidence that appropriate action steps are being taken and are planned, then that employee clearly is thorough in setting action steps.

Maintaining Continuity and Consistency in Planning

You can also hold your employees accountable for maintaining the continuity of their plans—for not allowing their plans to lapse. Competent people will think about their goals/objectives at all times. Less competent people will forget about goals/objectives during very busy periods. The least competent ones will remember goals/objectives only when they know that you will ask about them.

Continuity of effort is desirable when carrying out action steps and may be used as a measure of performance. Employees who are striving to achieve their goals/objectives will think of them every day. This will be evident by the way they approach their tasks. You can also obtain evidence of continuity in the contacts which occur between you and the employee in the period between progress reviews. Employees who regularly and voluntarily provide you with updates on progress show that they are paying continuous attention to their goals/objectives.

Assuring the Quality of Action Steps

Quality of effort is another aspect of work for which you can hold employees accountable. When looking at the action steps that the employee takes, you obviously must evaluate them to see whether they are the best that could be taken. An employee who regularly takes action steps which you consider as good as any that you would take, certainly deserves to be commended. Those who take inadequate action steps can be held accountable. When an employee's action steps are frequently less than adequate, then it is necessary to provide training. While training proceeds, the evaluation of the employee's work can reflect the fact that full competence has not yet been reached.

This requirement calls for somewhat more personal judgment by you, since there are no absolute criteria on which to base the measurement of quality. You have to judge whether the action steps are the best that could be taken and whether they are being executed competently. In making such judgments you must rely, in part, on your knowledge and experience, and in part, on the results of the action steps.

Keeping to Schedule

Completing action steps on time is also entirely under the control of employees, and therefore, they can be held accountable. If an employee agrees to complete some project by a certain time and then accomplishes it by that time, then he or she clearly has performed satisfactorily. Conversely, if an action step is not completed on time, something is wrong. For example, the quality of the action step or the amount of effort which had to be devoted to its completion may have been misjudged.

Once someone has made a commitment to a plan of action, that plan should be implemented as decided; and since by definition matters beyond his or her control are not involved, you can reasonably expect that steps will be completed as agreed.

Keeping to the schedule—timeliness—is probably the easiest requirement of accountability to measure and evaluate. It will be clear at progress reviews whether deadlines have been met. The reviews create a permanent record, in addition to your observations and informal discussions, that you can use for evaluating performance.

Solving Problems

It sometimes becomes apparent that action steps will not, in fact, lead to the achievement of the desired goal/objective. When that happens, the person working towards the goal/objective should be expected to reconsider the action steps and take any additional steps that may be necessary to reach the goal/objective.

There are many benefits in making it clear to employees that everyone is expected to be creative in solving the problem, whenever achievement of a goal/objective is threatened. When you clarify this requirement, you provide evidence of your confidence in the competence of employees, and it sets the stage for the feeling of accomplishment which comes whenever new approaches prove to be better than previous ones. It is necessary, of course, to stress that you are available to provide help when difficulties cannot be overcome.

The quality of revised action plans may be used to judge performance fairly and factually. This requirement is also fairly difficult to evaluate and must be based on your judgment, even though, as in other instances, progress reviews can provide a basis for judgment.

Communicating Problems in a Timely Manner

Once the personnel in your organizational unit understand how to work with a performance management system, everyone knows that it is essential to notify you as soon as it becomes clear that a goal/objective will not be achieved. This gives you an opportunity to decide whether to:

Provide additional resources or help in order to assure that the goal/objective can be achieved, or

Change the goal/objective if it appears that all has been done to achieve it and it still cannot be achieved, or that it does not warrant the additional resources needed for on-time achievement.

For instance, suppose one of your employees must find out what equipment should be purchased. The employee may have committed himself or herself to completion of the investigation, and trials by a certain date. He or she may find, as time progresses, that more urgent matters have come up and the tests will not be finished in time. At this point, the employee has several choices. He or she can let the goal/objective slide or inform you that it will not be achieved unless more time is allocated to investigation and trial or unless someone else will help with the task. If you are notified early enough so that the goal/objective can still be achieved, you have the opportunity to rescue it or to move its completion date back.

If everyone in an organization accepts the responsibility of providing timely notification when a goal/objective is in trouble, then there is greater likelihood that the most important ones will be achieved on time. Factually evaluating how promptly employees notify you of trouble is fairly easy. Notification must be early enough so you can still rescue the goal/objective if that is possible or desirable. About 50 percent of all goals/objectives will not be fully achieved, as discussed in the section entitled Who Is Really Responsible for Goal/Objectives Achievement. However, much data is available regarding an employee's actions when a goal/objective is in jeopardy, and a fair evaluation on this notification requirement will rarely be difficult.

Maintaining Good Relationships with Others

There is one more aspect of performance for which employees can be held accountable, and this concerns their relationships with others. Employees can be judged on the extent to which they coordinate with others who are affected by their goals/objectives, how thoroughly they communicate with these people, and possibly even on how well they obtain cooperation from others in order to achieve their own goals/objectives. Of course, employees can be judged on the basis of the cooperation they give to others.

Summary—Holding Employees Accountable

Evaluating performance is a complex responsibility which cannot be satisfied by simply checking how well employees have *achieved* their goals/objectives. Holding people accountable for the way *in which they work to achieve* their goals/objectives will bring a much better chance that they will accept the performance management system as fair and as a valid way to measure their performance.

A supervisor can therefore gain higher levels of confidence, and greater assurance that employees will be willing to set challenging goals/standards if the supervisor says something like this:

So that we do not misunderstand each other on what I expect from you, it might be well if I explain my standards. I expect you to achieve all the goals/objectives on which we have agreed and which you have accepted. However, when we review progress, and especially when we find it likely that a goal/objective will not be achieved, I will look at the following:

First, I will check whether that goal/objective was set carefully in the first place, that is, whether you had taken the responsibility for setting realistic but challenging goals/objectives which require more than routine thought and effort to achieve.

Secondly, I will look at the thoroughness with which you have laid out the action steps leading to the achievement of the goals/objectives.

Then, I will look at the extent to which you have kept these action steps in mind.

I will also look at how good these action steps were and compare them with those I might have chosen. Obviously, I do not expect you to take the same steps because many roads can be taken to reach the same result, but I will try to determine the extent to which the steps that you have taken were of high quality, and were reasonable.

I will also take a look at whether your action steps were completed as you had planned, or whether many were delayed for various reasons even though they were fully under your control.

Since we will be looking especially closely at those goals/objectives that have not yet been achieved or are not likely to be achieved, I will be checking whether you have given some thought to changing the action steps that you originally contemplated to see if better ones can be substituted for them.

If the new action steps still do not appear as though they will reach the goal/objective, I will check whether you have given me timely notification that a problem exists so that I have the chance to do something about it.

Finally, I will look at the way you have worked with others and the extent to which you have helped them and kept them informed so that they are able to help you as much as possible.

If you have done all these things and the goal/objective is still not attainable, then it is clear that I have to provide additional help or relieve you from the responsibility of achieving it on time. (See Figure 6.1, Performance Evaluation Scale, to see whether they, or similar ones, might suit your needs.)

A caution is necessary with respect to these scales. Though they carry numbers, these numbers cannot be added up to provide an evaluation total. Someone who scores a 4 on all eight criteria would score 32. That person is a very valuable staff member. Someone who scores 5's on six of the criteria but only 1's on "quality of effort" and "timeliness of results" also achieves a 32, but that person is hardly useful in any organization.

STANDARDS BASED ON PERSONAL CHARACTERISTICS

Many performance management systems set some standards on job elements which come close to being personal characteristics. Standards based on characteristics such as self-sufficiency, dependability, working with others, are sometimes built into the evaluation form, with specific brief description of levels, such as in some of the forms in Appendix C. In other systems, these characteristics are used primarily for highly routine jobs. They are thus encountered more frequently in nonexempt positions. Of course, the same personal characteristics, often described much more precisely in terms of specific improvements, do appear frequently in improvement plans.

There are legal obstacles to the use of standards based purely on personal characteristics, that cannot be precisely defined in behavioral terms, which describe what the employee does or does not do. Inevitably, the requirement of the regulations is that standards used for personnel action should be job related. With relatively few exceptions it is difficult to establish a direct relationship between the personal characteristics and job requirements

There is also some question whether standards based on personal characteristics can indeed improve performance. Usually it is also very difficult to clearly define or judge dependability (in its

I. Ambitiousness/Taking Initiative

Sets goals at exceptionally high and reasonably attainable levels   5
Sets goals at high and clearly attainable levels   4
Sets goals at acceptable levels   3
Sets goals at levels somewhat below those appropriate for the individual and position   2
Sets goals at levels considerably below or unrealistically above those appropriate for the individual and position   1

II. Thoroughness

All goals have a thorough set of action steps appropriately prepared for them   5
Most goals have a thorough set of action steps, and other goals have action steps that are fairly complete   4
All goals have a fairly complete set of action steps   3
Some goals have a fairly complete set of action steps and other goals have action steps which are not adequate   2
Very few goals, or none at all, have an adequate set of action steps   1

III. Planning

Consistently thorough at planning goals and action steps   5
Some occasional difficulties at planning goals and action steps   4
About average, when compared to others in similar positions, at planning goals and action steps   3
Fairly regular difficulties at planning goals and action steps   2
Primarily a scattered and impulsive effort at setting goals and action steps   1

IV. Quality of Effort

All action steps set are those most likely to achieve goals most rapidly   5
Most action steps set will lead to achievement of goals rapidly, but some are of lower quality   4
All action steps are of good quality and are likely to achieve the goals, although they are not the best steps that could have been taken   3
Some action steps are of good quality and are likely to achieve goals, but others are not of good quality   2
Very few action steps, if any, are of good quality; they are not likely to lead to achievement of goals without significant changes   1

V. Timeliness of Results

All action steps are achieved on time   5

Figure 6.1. Performance Evaluation Scale

full meaning) or judgment. On the other hand, some personal characteristics which are important to job performance can be defined. This is particularly true of characteristics which concern relationships to other people and which therefore may have great impact on job performance (an abrasive person, for instance, rarely can achieve what he or she could achieve with more pleasant behavior). These characteristics can therefore be made the subject of an item in an improvement plan.

Most action steps are achieved on time, with only short delays on
others   4
Many action steps are achieved on time, with a few extensive delays
on others   3
Some action steps are achieved on time, with quite a few significant
delays on others   2
Very few action steps are achieved on time; there are many signifi-
cant delays   1

VI. Problem Solving

Exceptionally imaginative action steps are added for all goals when
it appears that a goal may not be achieved   5
Highly imaginative action steps are added for most goals, and good
ones for others, where it appears that a goal may not be achieved   4
Good but not highly imaginative action steps are added for all goals
where it appears that a goal may not be achieved   3
Good but not highly imaginative action steps are added for some
goals and inadequate action steps are added for others when it
appears that a goal may not be achieved   2
Very few imaginative action steps are added for any goal which may
not be achieved   1

VII. Communications

Consistently notifies manager at earliest possible time when additional resources may be required to achieve all established goals   5
Consistently notifies manager in sufficient time when additional resources may be required to achieve most established goals   4
Generally notifies manager in sufficient time when additional resources may be required to achieve most established goals   3
Frequently fails to notify manager in sufficient time when application of additional resources may achieve established goals   2
Rarely or never notifies manager in time to apply additional re-
sources to achieve established goals   1

VIII. Inter-personal Relations

Exceptionally thorough in keeping others informed of goals and
action steps affecting them   5
Very thorough in keeping others informed of goals and action
steps affecting them   4
Average in thoroughness with respect to keeping others informed
on goals and action steps affecting them   3
Often fails in keeping others informed of goals and action steps
affecting them   2
Rarely informs others of goals and action steps affecting them   1

Figure 6.1. (*Continued*)

When performance standards based on personal characteristics
are used, it is, of course, essential that they be tied to some ob-
servable behavior by the employee. For instance, to define dependability, statements like "rarely" or "never absent without
justifiable reasons," "available for additional assignments when
necessary," and so forth could be used. Such statements ensure
that the characteristic is measurable and work/job related, and
reduce differences in interpretation by supervisors. Similarly, relations with other departments could be defined in terms of the
number of complaints, in the regularity of meetings to work on

common responsibilities, the rapidity with which problems affecting both sides are tackled and resolved and so forth.

Personal characteristics are clearly not suitable as a foundation for *all* standards of performance. They can be supplementary standards, particularly in areas where identifiable behavior by the employee obstructs the effective discharge of responsibilities.

To totally ignore personal characteristics in a series of performance standards would also be inappropriate. A good comprehensive system will therefore use standards based on personal characteristics but only in those situations where a specific characteristic of an employee creates a performance problem. An example of such a performance standard might be: Good relations shall be maintained with purchasing personnel. Performance will be measured by the absence of complaints and disputes requiring intervention by the supervisor, by the way legitimate differences of opinion with purchasing personnel are resolved, and by the way joint projects and responsibilities are approached at staff meetings and project discussion sessions.

Summary—Standards and Goals/Objectives

Performance management systems using only standards and/or goals/objectives can all be highly effective systems. Systems emphasizing goals/objectives are concerned with results and, therefore, address priorities and expected results directly. They are, therefore, probably preferable for most organizations to systems which use the standards of performance to define the results to be achieved.

However, there are great similarities between these systems and both are likely to lead to equally satisfactory results once they have been debugged and adapted to the preferences of the individuals in the organization and to the needs of the situation. In operations with highly routinized functions, standards of performance are likely to serve equally well or better, without the need to set goals. On the other hand, when most of the work is project related, the goals approach, which is more organized toward the setting of dates, is likely to be better able to meet the changing needs of the situation.

It is useful to remember that both standards and/or goals will serve an organzation best if they are used to prevent future emergencies or crises. Standards and/or goals can make an organization more proactive rather than reactive. If standards and/or goals are set on those important activities which are likely to be otherwise postponed, possibly again and again to make way for more urgent but perhaps less important matters, then the standards or goals will accomplish what no other device, except, possibly, constant supervision can achieve. But standards and goals can be highly positive and motivating while overly close supervision is demotivating and destructive.

Using a Variety of Standards

In most organizations, it is possible to use standards based on different foundations simultaneously. Performance standards that are based on results to be achieved (results oriented standards based on goals/objectives) could be used for key job elements where external influences are highly unlikely or nonexistent. This is particularly true where quantity of effort is the primary determinant of performance.

Standards that contain results statements *and* competence and effort statements could be used for those key results areas where quantity *and* quality of effort are important. Standards based on personal characteristics could be used concurrently where appropriate as previously discussed. To the extent to which these mixed sets of standards conform to the characteristics of an ideal system, they will be more or less successful in satisfying the needs of the organization and of the individuals within that organization.

Mixed or combination systems carry the respective advantages and disadvantages of the components which are used. However, carefully selected combinations can take advantage of the strength of all segments. A system that uses goals/objectives as well as some personal characteristics that are integral to work performance, can be a better system than a goals/objectives system by itself. Similarly, where job descriptions are maintained and updated regularly, they can form the foundation for either the goals/objectives or for key results areas.

Whether a system that is based solely on one type of foundation or on multiple foundations is best for an organization has to be determined by the needs of that organization. Once a system has been established, the potential for improving the system should be determined.

An Illustrative Example on Deciding on Standards

A problem that often exists when an organization attempts to decide what types of standards to set lies in the lack of a common viewpoint by managers of the implications of various types of standards. A brief example illustrates the point. Managers of a large retail organization with many stores felt that its previous method for allocating bonuses was inadequate. They decided that a performance management system should be set up to provide a more equitable base for determining these executive/managerial/supervisory bonuses.

At the meeting of the decision making group, the question was quickly raised as to what basis should be used for evaluating performance. Even though the organization did not have a smoothly operating goals program, it did have a planning system. Supervisors believed that the various steps in their plans were the goals of their respective departments.

Soon after the discussion started, the head of the personnel department suggested that the goals could become the basis for performance evaluation, together with some clearly defined personal characteristics, such as competence in working with other departments and dependability. They would provide clean, easily measurable standards. Their use would be fair because goals are set by the departments themselves and are finalized in discussion with the president and the executive vice president who usually accept them or modify them only slightly.

The operations manager accepted the idea of using some personal characteristics but immediately objected to the use of goals. She felt that it would not be fair to use goals achievement as a basis for bonuses because some goals were sometimes difficult to achieve, while other goals were sometimes very easy. She gave the example of inventory shrinkage (the losses due to damage, theft, shoplifting, and record errors) as a very difficult problem. Meaningful goals, she stated, are often difficult to set, particularly at times when there are changes in inventory procedures which lead to errors or when there are difficulties in the economy which bring a higher ratio of thefts. These problems often cannot be predicted far enough in advance, since goals are usually set for a full year. Even with most extensive effort, at times the goals might not be achievable. Similar problems existed in the operations department with overtime and these goals were subject to interferences far beyond control of the department.

The head of the public relations department then asked why the operations department, since it set its own goals, could not set them so that the department could easily accept responsibility for achieving them. At this point, the president intervened because he became concerned that the bonuses might result in goals being set too low to ensure that they would be achieved. He pointed out that it would be difficult for him to determine whether a goal was indeed realistic and still challenging, so it could be set appropriately.

The personnel and publication departments still felt that the problem was not serious, since they were able to live with their goals. They would be perfectly willing to accept judgment of their performance based on these goals. The operations manager asked for examples of personnel and public relations goals. At that point, it became apparent that their goals were not subject to extensive outside interference. They were phrased in terms such as:

Number of articles to be prepared for news releases

Advertisements to be run for recruitment

Number of invitations to be extended to local politicians for store visitations, and so forth

As this example illustrates, a lack of awareness of the differences between results-oriented standards which are subject to external interference, and standards based on effort and competence, can cause difficulties. It is also important that those members of the management team who are involved in deciding the basis for standards, understand the distinctions between the various types of standards and the implications of setting standards based on results versus setting them on matters solely under the control of the employee.

Chapter 7

OTHER ISSUES IN PERFORMANCE MANAGEMENT SYSTEMS

HOW TO LABEL THE RATING LEVELS

There are basically two types of ratings—numerical and nonnumerical. Many organizations use numerical ratings supported by descriptive statements, when desirable, for the individual evaluation lines, but then use an overall rating that is only descriptive.

Summing numerical ratings for an *overall* rating is difficult. Numeral ratings have to be very elaborate and contain weighting for each line to adjust for differences in importance, or there is a potentially serious mathematical problem in adding the ratings (or in averaging them). As the caution on page 113 indicated, if there are eight lines and on each line that can be as many as 5 points, the maximum total an employee* can receive is 40 points. An em-

---

* Please note the use of the word employee includes employees at all professional, supervisory, and managerial levels. The word supervisor is used for all levels of management (See Preface).

ployee who achieves 4 points on every one of those eight lines is a highly desirable employee and the ratings reflects that fact. An honest rating of 32, in this case, is a very good rating certainly well above normal competence.

It is also possible to achieve 32 points with six 5's and two 1's. Obviously, this is an extreme case, but an employee with two 1's in important aspects of the job could be a very undesirable employee indeed. When numerical ratings are used, supervisors have to be aware of this problem and should be given weighting to indicate importance, or should avoid making direct connections between the total (or average) numerical rating and the overall rating of the employee's performance.

The exact wording of the ratings and the decision whether to use a scale of four or five are also issues that deserve serious consideration when setting up or revising a performance management system.

A four-level system forces supervisors to choose whether an employee is somewhat above "expected/normal" competence or below that level. These systems have the advantage that most experienced and reliable employees can be given a rating that they perceive as being above "average." Since being considered "average" is detrimental to self-esteem for such employees, a rating above the average brings definite psychological benefits. The same is true of six-step systems. The disadvantage of a four-step system is that it allows only one level above that which most employees receive, while a six-level system has two such steps.

A five-step system uses the center point as the point at which most employees should be rated. However, in such a system almost every competent employee expects to be a level above the center point and few competent employees will accept that they are "average." Therefore, if a five-step system is used, it is important to set up the procedures which will ensure heavy emphasis on explaining the meaning of the five levels. Employees have to understand that the central level is not "average" but rather is a "competent" level. This is the performance level that describes experienced, reliable people. Few people exceed this level except when their education/experience and capability is significantly beyond that of other competent employees. To ensure that this level receives the respect that it deserves, supervisors should be required to justify, in writing, a rating above or below the competent level on any line. Furthermore, explanations of overall ratings other than competent should be required, in addition to the explanations of the individual lines. It should not be adequate to point to several individual ratings above competent. Similar explanations should be required in four- and six-level systems, of ratings other than the two that are closest to the center.

The names assigned to the various levels/steps of rating scales are also quite important. These labels should ensure that the central point or the points near the central point are considered good ratings, and that higher levels indicate fairly clearly that skills and effort considerably above normal competence are required to achieve those higher rating levels. On the other hand, since ratings below the central point are likely to have a discouraging effect on the employee and affect self-respect/self-esteem, the wording for levels below the center should be gentle. However, the bottom level can be clearly labeled as undesirable or inadequate, since only seriously inadequate performance would be given that label Words that are widely used to describe ratings are outstanding, exceptional, above job requirements, good, consistently beyond requirements, commendable, competent, improvement needed, below requirements, and poor or improvement required/necessary.

The need to achieve uniformity in ratings bring rather complex procedures in some organizations. Some organizations require ranking of all employees in each department by several supervisors to ensure that ratings between supervisors are fairly comparable. When this ranking takes place in a fairly large department and the supervisors must achieve consensus on those rankings. considerable time is spent on the comparisons of ratings. For instance, if supervisor Joe has rated one of his employees at a certain numerical rating and supervisor Marie has given a similar rating to an employee who is considered by most supervisors as considerably more competent, than an adjustment has to be made. A supervisor who regularly rates employees more generously to bring more favorable compensation decisions for them, comes under considerable pressure to revise his or her rating levels.

This adjusting of ratings through rankings, when used, should take place prior to the evaluation interview with the employee because greater uniformity is achieved at an earlier stage in the process. Prior adjustments sharpen supervisory skills. Furthermore, the motivation of employees of the more generous supervisors is not hurt, as would be the case when their compensation increments do not match the higher expectations which more generous ratings would stimulate.

WHAT KIND OF ANCHORS SHOULD BE USED FOR ASSIGNING RATINGS?

There are basically two types of anchors which can be used by supervisors to assign ratings when evaluating performance against a function or standard:

Anchors which represent scales and provide brief statements to identify each performance level.

Anchors which describe *incidents* that are characteristic of employee behavior, and, therefore, can be used to identify performance level.

Anchors Which Are Scales

Most performance evaluation procedures include statements to help a supervisor decide how to rate performance with respect to a particular standard, responsibility, or function. Most of the sample forms in Appendix C contain anchors that are of this type. Figure 6.1 Performance Evaluation Scale is of this nature. As well as the examples in Figures 3 and 4 in the Preface.

The widespread use of anchors that provide brief descriptions ranging from best performance to poorest performance attests to their basic usefulness in helping to achieve relatively uniform ratings between supervisors. However, because they attempt to bridge the entire gap between poor performance and outstanding performance with respect to an entire function, they are necessarily vague and still allow wide individual interpretation on the part of the supervisor.

Obviously, considerable work is required to develop anchors, and therefore, anchors are rarely set on project or period standards but are primarily on ongoing standards and possibly on the umbrella standard where one exists.

For many years, there was a strong belief that the more precise anchors could be written, the more accurate and more reliable the performance evaluation system would be. This was particularly true when positions were less complex than they are today and where there were greater similarities between similar jobs. See Figure 3 in the Preface which shows some attempts to achieve more precise descriptions.

Nevertheless, the hope that more precise descriptions would indeed lead to fairer and more meaningful evaluations did not fully materialize. In the current knowledge worker era, precise descriptions become more complex and less useful as accurate guides for evaluators.

Behavioral Incidents

To overcome the inadequacies inherent in the general nature of anchors which provide a range from excellent to poor, various attempts have been made to write descriptions of specific behaviors that are characteristic of various levels of perfomance. When such behavioral anchors are prepared, the levels of performance are usually identified with words such as: outstanding, good, competent, improvement needed, and poor. For each of these levels, specific behaviors are identified and brief descriptions are written, such as the ones shown in Exhibit 7.1. These are intended to provide "anchors" for the evaluator to use when evaluating performance.

In concept, the idea is excellent. If realistic, specific behaviors are listed, it should be easy for a supervisor to select the appropriate performance level and his or her choice should closely match that of another supervisor. However, in practice, the behavioral anchors have proven to be partially effective because each function or each standard involves so many possible different behaviors that a system of anchors based on behavioral incidents becomes unwieldy. Very often it still does not provide an accurate description of the behaivor of an individual. Supervisors find that any individual will match specific behavorial incidents from several of the ratings. For instance, it is very likely that an individual employee would exhibit behavior that is illustrated by incidents in all three ratings; outstanding, good, and competent. When that occurs, what finally happens is that the supervisor has to use his or her judgment to decide what level to assign to that particular employee's performance. Such a rating then is quite similar to one in which the supervisor attempts to evaluate performance with the aid of the general descriptions that cover the entire range of the work involved in the function. Examples of these descriptions are: almost always meet deadlines, usually meet deadlines, rarely

EXHIBIT 7.1.   INCOMPLETE LIST OF EXAMPLES OF INCIDENTS AS ANCHORS FOR ONE SUPERVISORY COMPETENCE

Competence: Ability to Recruit and Select Sales Representatives

Outstanding

Maintains a backlog of candidates for future needs by being alert and on the lookout at all times for qualified candidates.

Evaluates each territory individually, to determine the specific strengths and attributes a representative must have to succeed in that territory.

Uses large variety of appropriate sources (employment agencies, newspaper ads, customer referrals, employee recommendations, etc.) thus securing large number of qualified applicants from which to select.

Searches for and hires qualified minority and female candidates in accordance with Affirmative Action programs, by utilizing all possible sources specializing in recruiting protected groups.

Regularly fills territorial vacancies within 60 days.

Very Good

Evaluates recruiting sources of personnel (agencies, ads, referrals) to establish most effective ones.

Maintains good and continuous relationship with limited number of selected recruiting sources, including college placement centers.

Demonstrates ability to use such above-average interviewing skills as establishing benign interview climate, assisting applicant to talk spontaneously, using open and reflective questions, probes, problem questions, etc.

Keeps recruiting time to a minimum by carefully screening all resumes and referrals before arranging personal interviews.

Gives feedback to employment agencies as to adequacy of their screening.

Encourages employees to recommend outstanding candidates.

Good

Follows company policies during the recruitment/selection process.

Checks references and other elements of candidates' work and educational background with efficiency and care.

Maintains adequate resume file; studies and reviews resumes prior to arranging interviews.

Places ads in accordance with company policy.

Makes final decision regarding candidates promptly.

Maintains and forwards to superior, records of job applicants and disposition to prove Affirmative Action activity.

Gives applicant complete job description from sales manual, reviews sales territory from geographic standpoint and discusses additional policies and procedures at time of hiring.

Improvement Needed

Similar incidents are used for this rating level.

Unsatisfactory

Similar incidents are used for this rating level.

meets deadlines, or seldom meets deadlines. The latter require far less work to prepare than the difficult procedure of identifying, writing, and evaluating incidents.

On balance, therefore, reasonably well prepared anchors that represent a range are more likely to become established and gain acceptance within an organization. Any particularly important aspects of the work that should be considered when assigning a rating, can receive such a range statement. For instance, if numerical errors in reports are of importance, then within the specific standard, a range can be established which assigns "outstanding" when errors represent no more than a given proportion, and different ratings for higher proportions of errors.

When there are several supervisors whose employees perform the same or very similar work, the principles of fairness are undoubtedly served better if the organization provides anchors. These could be set by a committee of the supervisors, or by a higher level supervisor or someone from the personnel department, with reviews by supervisors.

On the other hand, when there are only a few employees and one supervisor in each function and there is little similarity in the work, then it is best to provide training and/or guidance so supervisors can, themselves, set appropriate anchors for standards. Involvement of subordinates in anchors, as much as possible, should be encouraged with the caveat, that supervisors should not allow strong-willed, articulate employees to establish preferential anchors.

EMPLOYEE PARTICIPATION AND EMPLOYEE SELF-RATINGS

Employee Participation*

Using procedures to achieve the right kind of participative leadership style is like legislating morality. Leadership style is a matter of individual supervisory personality and competence. When supervisory training is provided, when the atmosphere (as set by the example at higher supervisory levels) favors participation, and when there is a meaningful appeals process, then procedures can support and strengthen a favorable climate for participative leadership. Specific procedures in a performance management system that can help to ensure participation are:

A requirement that employee *responsibilities* be reviewed jointly by supervisor and employee prior to evaluation

Space on the evaluation form which requires the employee to certify that the supervisor has discussed the evaluation with him or her

Another space on the form which asks for confirmation that the employee has had an opportunity to express his or her views

Possibly a space where the employee expresses how he or she feels about the evaluation interview; to what extent his or her views were taken seriously and considered by the supervisor

An opportunity for employees to rate or to rank the evaluation on the basis of how fair they consider it to be

---

* A detailed discussion of management theory on participation is in Appendix A.

A space on the improvement plan on which employees certify their agreement with the plan, or can express concerns

Devices such as these can help to ensure that supervisors do more than allow superficial participation by the employee.

In the United States, it is almost universally accepted that greater employee participation will bring better acceptance of a new system, especially one that has such significant impact on quality of work life, and potentially on compensation. Still, most companies rely most heavily on procedures for guiding supervisory implementation of performance management systems rather than on a combination of procedures, leadership development, and participative leadership example from the top.

Employee Self-Evaluation

The most important aspect of employee participation can be completion of a self-evaluation form, using the same form as the supervisor, while the supervisor independently performs his or her evaluation.

There are significant advantages to asking or requiring supervisors to provide for *voluntary* self-evaluation by employees. The advantages to the organization are in addition to those which stem from greater employee satisfaction. Self-evaluations by employees provides a rich source of data to show how they feel about their work and how they believe their supervisors treat them. They also provide considerable information about the general attitudes of employees toward the organization. In effect they can represent an informal attitude survey. As a result, the higher level supervisors can obtain considerable feedback about the various ways in which their respective supervisors and lower level supervisors rate employees. Management thus has access to another tool which helps to bring about more uniform and more meaningful evaluations.

Requiring simultaneous evaluations and comparing those evaluations also can bring the benefit of pointing to ways in which the evaluation system can slowly be improved. It is obvious that, if employee self-evaluations are very similar to those of their supervisors, the system is indeed an exceptionally good one. Exposing differences between supervisor and employee evaluations helps to identify ways in which the system or communication between supervisor and employee could be improved.

Many supervisors believe that it is worthwhile to let the employees evaluate their own performance independently, at the same time that the supervisors make the evaluations, so they can be better prepared for the interview. These supervisors feel that both sides can gain from the procedure. They point out that employees have access to the same performance data and, therefore, can be given the opportunity to evaluate their own performance using the same forms as those which their supervisor uses.

Nevertheless, many supervisors are reluctant to allow their subordinates to rate themselves and to then discuss the ratings. This reluctance is understandable, because the discussion of ratings has high emotional impact and, therefore, is not easy to conduct. Supervisors are often concerned that, if employees first rate themselves, many will become convinced of the validity of the self-assessment and be less willing to accept the supervisor's performance assessment.

Still, as a supervisor, you will gain if your employees rate themselves independently before you meet with them to conduct the performance appraisal interviews. The benefits will be there regardless of how the employee sees himself or herself. Consider the four possibilities:

The employee's self-rating is very similar to yours. This allows you to discuss those individual ratings that were different and, thus, ensures the employee that you have a genuine interest in fair ratings. The similar ratings create a climate in which you have many opportunities to provide recognition for your subordinate. At the same time, you develop an excellent foundation for a performance improvement plan, since the areas where improvement is desirable are seen in very similar light.

The employee's ratings are lower than those which you have assigned. This highlights the fact that the employee has somewhat lower self-perception than is realistic. Under these circumstances you have an opportunity to help the employee make more valid evaluations. At the same time, it places you in the highly desirable situation where you are proving to your subordinate that you are holding him or her in higher regard than he or she expected.

The employee rates some performance elements significantly higher and others significantly lower than you did. This situation identifies either inaccurate perceptions on your part or on the employee's part. Careful discussion of those elements can provide you with a better picture. At the same time, it ensures the employee of your sincerity in trying to obtain all the information that is necessary for an honest, fair evaluation. It also highlights those areas where there is lack of understanding on the part of the subordinate and you can then help the subordinate overcome these.

The subordinate rates all, or most lines significantly higher. In this situation, the problem is far more serious than just the performance evaluation. It is important that you recognize the employee's distorted perception so that he or she, and you, can gradually work on making him or her a more useful member of the team.

APPROVAL OF RATINGS AND APPEALS PROCEDURE

Approval of the evaluation by higher level supervisors or a review with other supervisors can either be required before the appraisal interview, or afterwards. If the performance appraisal results are used directly for compensation decisions, it is usually considered more desirable to require approvals prior to communicating the evaluation to the employee. If on the other hand, the relationship is less direct, then sometimes higher level supervisors need not see evaluation results until after the appraisal interview has taken place. In these instances, the approval is more or less automatic because it is very difficult for a higher level supervisor to intercede in the evaluation of an employee that has already been discussed with the employee. In these cases, the review at the next higher level serves primarily as a way to inform that supervisor of the status of the employee's performance. It provides an opportunity for him or her to help ensure, indirectly, that evaluations by different supervisors will be reasonably comparable to each other in the future.

Of course, there is a drawback. If approval has to be obtained before the appraisal interview, then employees may perceive the appraisal interview to be strictly one-sided. The evaluation has already been approved further up the ladder. They do not believe that they can obtain a change in their favor even if they present significant information that was overlooked. This drawback can be partially eliminated by joint review of responsibilities, by employee and supervisor, before the evaluations by the supervisor (see section entitled Forms for Performance Management).

Nevertheless, advance review of ratings, prior to the discussion of the evaluation with the employee, have a much better chance for ensuring equal or very similar ratings between supervisors, than ratings that are reviewed only afterwards. As a result, over the long run, they are more likely to enhance acceptance of the system—especially if supervisors continue to improve their professionalism in working with the system.

Appeals

An appeals procedure that is perceived as reasonably impartial by employees, can help considerably in ensuring that the performance management system is not perceived as one-sided by those who are rated in the system. (This is especially true if ratings are reviewed by higher level supervisors in advance of the discussion with the employee). It is, of course, difficult to find an individual or group who is perceived as sufficiently impartial to effectively provide a single level of review.

It is even more difficult to set up two levels of reviews. However, whenever possible, two levels of appeal can help to bring important evidence of fairness to a system. The first level of review could be the higher level supervisor who may have signed off on the evaluation without detailed knowledge of the employee's performance at the time of signing. If that supervisor is indeed the first level of review then a second level is almost essential. The second level could be in the personnel department or could be a high level supervisor without very significant responsibilities for the output of the organization, such as the person in charge of public communications. The second level also could be a committee of supervisors or a committee of peers and supervisors.

SHOULD MORE THAN ONE PERFORMANCE MANAGEMENT SYSTEM BE USED AND WHAT FORMS?

The question really is whether it is wise to attempt to cover, with one system, all the diverse types of positions. Can a system that is appropriate for fairly routine tasks be useful at the other extreme, with highly professional tasks where uncertainty and many professional judgments are the rule? There are positions in which a close proximity of supervisor and employee is essential, and there are others where supervisor and employee are geographically separated by extensive distances. Can one system serve both types of supervisory requirements, if they exist in the same organization?

Very likely the answers to these questions is *No;* for all practical purposes, it is impossible, to design one performance management system that will satisfy all these differences. Therefore, most organizations use more than one system. Factory production workers will be covered by one system while office, clerical, and administrative staff who are not exempt from the wage and hour laws might have another system. Still other systems might apply to sales personnel in the field, to supervisory employees, and to the research facility.

Of course, to achieve a high degree of fairness and comparability, these respective systems must have equal validity to the constituencies to which they apply, and they must respect the fairness principles which are a fundamental requirement for success.

The systems must also have valid relationships to each other so that high level performance in one type of position results in benefits which are similar to a parallel level of performance in a different type of position in one of the other systems.

The challenge is to design systems that will meet these requirements. Of course, the easiest systems are those for positions that are very similar. For that reason, in the example in Chapter 4, the subsection entitled An Example, the nonexempt staff which consisted primarily of clerical and secretarial employees, were separated from the others who perform supervisory or professional functions. Job descriptions emphasizing duties and responsibilities which are common to the nonexempt positions were used to define most of the standards which would apply to the positions. Some of the positions required additional standards for unique duties.

When appropriate, the procedure used for setting standards for professional employees was applied. Obviously, it is necessary to provide safeguards and restrictions on preparation of specific standards or on modified job descriptions for individual positions. Without safeguards, a deterioration of the system is likely because each supervisor would attempt to exempt preferred employees from the system which covers most employees in a classification, on the basis of insignificant differences in the positions.

A committee of supervisors, the supervisory hierarchy, or the personnel department should serve as watchdog. Before a specialized description or standard can be used, approval has to be obtained.

Obviously, if a position does not receive a special pay scale, then there is little advantage for writing a special job description or standard. For that reason, within the performance management system a position would qualify for special standards only if the position can be assigned a compensation level different from the level that applies to all others within the classification.

Forms for Performance Management

Each system needs its own forms or variations of a basic form to ensure more uniform evaluation in the positions covered by the specific evaluation forms and by the procedures applicable to those forms.

The forms, and the procedure manuals which provide instructions on the use of the forms, have to be designed and should be tested thoroughly before actual use. Examples of evaluation forms and of instructions for the use of forms are provided in Appendix C. (A sample of a form for progress reviews will be discussed in this section.) The forms in the appendix are from several different organizations, including governmental organizations and businesses. One set is in use at the headquarters of a professional association.

Evaluations forms should provide for:

1. A segment for review of responsibilities. It would help to achieve a common view, between supervisor and employee, on the responsibilities of the position. In addition, it could provide spaces for the employee to enter:

   a. Thoughts on exceptional achievements during the period to which the evaluation applies

   b. Any particular difficulties which he or she has encountered in attempting to discharge the responsibilities

   c. Suggestions for changes in responsibilities, in supervisory support, or in working conditions, which would make it easier to achieve higher level performance

   If such a form is completed independently by the employee and by the supervisor, prior to the time when the supervisor works on the evaluation itself, it can provide valuable information for the performance evaluation. It will sharpen the supervisor's view of the responsibilities of the position. It will help to ensure that those accomplishments of which the employee is proud are all considered, and it will provide perspective for problems which the employee has encountered. Review of responsibilities prior to evaluation and reviews of evaluations with a higher level supervisor also ensure a better review by that supervisor. What may be even more important, is the assurance it gives the employee that his or her accomplishments will be considered during the evaluation review.

   In addition, the form can provide suggestions for the types of entries that might be appropriate for the various segments of the form.

2. A segment for the evaluation itself. The evaluation segment can be prepared or designed with various degrees of structure.

The examples in the appendixes show some forms where very little or no structure has been provided. The supervisor enters a rating and thoughts on the reasons for the rating along several dimensions such as:

a. Standards or major responsibilities outlined in the job description, or key results area

b. Unique accomplishments and unique shortcomings, that are not specifically related to any other items listed

A more structured form could provide spaces for entry of thoughts along very specific job responsibilities that are common to all positions in the classifications for which the form is used, such as those shown in one of forms:

a. Improving operations

b. Planning and organizing

c. Responding to change

d. Communicating

e. Working with others

If the form is fully structured with specific standards or key job elements defined this way, it would also, of course, have to give prominent position to items such as quantity of work, quality of work, adherence to schedule or priorities, cooperation with procedures and supervisor, work organization, working independently without supervision and so forth.

All these dimensions are subject to various interpretations by supervisors. Either a scale has to be provided or, as some of the sample forms show, specific descriptions for various points along the scale to help achieve a high level of uniformity.

Combination forms also exist, as shown by at least one of the samples, where part of the form is unstructured, allowing for entry of thoughts on performance with respect to specific standards or responsibilities of the position. In addition, a few important characteristics are specifically listed with structured scales.

3. A segment for the improvement plan. As much as possible, the form should encourage entry of very specific items in

the improvement plan, either as goals, specific standards or projects. It should provide dates by when the employee will complete the assignment or will achieve the higher level of competence or behavior specified.

The improvement plan segment of the form should specifically recognize the importance of supervisory support in achieving significant performance improvement by allowing space for entry of actions that will be taken by the supervisor to support the efforts of the employee. The improvement plan segment should also require entries to indicate when progress will be reviewed.

4. Spaces for signatures, approvals, and other comments. Several form segments, particularly the evaluation segment itself and the improvement plan should have specific spaces for signature by the supervisor, the next higher level supervisor, and the employee.

The signature spaces should clarify that signatures by the next higher level of supervision merely signify that the completed evaluation has been seen prior to the actual evaluation/appraisal interview, or after the development of the improvement plan, respectively. The form might also state that the signature provides some assurance that the evaluation appears to be reasonable in relation to the evaluations of other employees.

Similarly, there should be spaces for the employee's signature, again with a printed statement which indicates that the employee's signature does not necessarily indicate agreement with the review. It merely acknowledges that its content have been discussed. In addition, the evaluation form and the improvement plan form should allow space for the employee to enter any disagreements with the statements in these two forms.

One other space can sometimes be useful on evaluation and improvement plan forms. In effect, this space provides some information about the quality of the rating by supervisors. In this space, several questions could be asked of the employee, such as:

a. Was the feedback which the supervisor provided you about your performance of such a nature that it is possible for you to take action based on it and so you can improve your performance?

b. Do you feel that your supervisor was thorough in explaining your evaluation to you?

c. How thoroughly do you think your supervisor understood your point of view?

LEGAL ISSUES AFFECTING PERFORMANCE MANAGEMENT

Appendix B is a brief discussion covering the major pieces of private sector legislation which can have an impact on the performance management system. These are:

National Labor Relations Act

Labor Management Relations Act of 1947

Labor Management Reporting and Disclosure Act (Landrum-Griffin Act)

Equal Pay Act of 1963

Title VII of the Civil Rights Act of 1964

Age Discrimination in Employment Act of 1967

Equal Employment Opportunity Act of 1972

In addition, Appendix B contains a discussion of the Civil Service Reform Act of 1978, which affirmed the civil rights legislation as applied to employees of the federal government and further extends it specifically to performance evaluation of employees in the federal government.

These laws represent two major groups of legislation. The first group concerns the right of employees to organize and join unions and the second group concerns equal opportunity without regard to sex, race, color, religion, or national origin.

With respect to the first group of laws, the important point is that the courts have held that, in unionized shops, all aspects of the performance management system are legitimate bargaining issues. The second group is intended to ensure equally fair treatment of all groups of employees. It has been used successfully by female, older, and minority employees to obtain redress against discrimation when they were injustly passed over for promotion or when they did not receive compensation increases which were due them.

Civil rights legislation has also given employees the right to see the information in their records and has established the principle that the only information that can be used for personnel action, favorable or unfavorable, must be information that pertains to job- or work-related matters.

A thorough performance management system that satisfies the principles outlined in Part 1 and follows procedures similar to those outlined in Parts I and II can help to ensure that all personnel actions meet the requirements and the spirit of the legislation. Still, there are some specific steps which you can take to help ensure that neither compensation, nor favorable or unfavorable personnel actions are successfully challenged by employees.

1. *Document discussions with employees, about performance.*
   One good approach is to have a file jacket for each employee,* in addition to the permanent file, in which you insert:

   a. Notes from each progress review

   b. Notes about instances when you had occasion to either command or correct the employee

   c. Last one or two performance evaluation forms

   d. Last one or two improvement plans and the notes on progress (follow-up)

   e. Compensation adjustments you recommended and those actually received by the employee

2. *Maintain an open communications climate.* Ensure that

---

* Such a file jacket is also discussed in Chapter 8—Considerations for Designing or Modifying a Performance Management System section entitled Observing Performance and Providing Feedback Informally and at Regular Reviews; Collecting of Data for Performance Evaluation/Appraisal and for Future Standards, or Revisions to Standards.

the employee knows what is in his or her jacket and file. Whenever possible give him or her a copy, or obtain a signature or initials to a line on the paper which merely says: was discussed on (*date*), or even just: seen (*date*).

3. *Observe the fairness principles.* Nothing succeeds like success, they say. Similarly nothing is as fair as fairness. Except, that fairness is in the eye of the beholder. If you do not ensure that your people know how you judge performance, then they don't know that you are indeed fair. Talk about the principles, show how you follow them, and your people will become aware that you are doing your best.

4. As has been pointed out previously, Chapter 3—Characteristics of an Ideal Performance Management System, *Keep in mind that, when you try to be "more than fair to one person, you are probably unfair to others."* Many supervisors believe that when they are "nice" to the person to whom they are speaking, they practice good "people orientation" and when they satisfy that person, they are "fair." Unfortunately that is not so, very often. In fact, seen from another person's point of view, an unfair privilege may have been granted and there may be a valid case of discrimination. In short, *be prepared to do for others, what you do for one,* on the same terms, if the record shows that they deserve it.

Chapter 8

CONSIDERATIONS FOR DESIGNING OR MODIFYING A PERFORMANCE MANAGEMENT SYSTEM

If you accept the validity of the principles which are characteristic of an ideal system, then these principles become guidelines for setting up a performance management system or for revising an existing system that falls short of being fully satisfactory. Obviously, there are many ways to satisfy these principles, usually allowing several of the options from which you can choose those which are most appropriate for your organization. The discussion here provides additional thoughts on the five steps of a comprehensive performance management system in those sections where such detailed discussion would have been distractive in Part I. For a quick review, these steps are:

1. Setting performance standards and communicating them in advance of the period to which they apply.

2. Observing performance and providing feedback informally and at regular progress reviews. Collecting of data for per-

formance evaluation/appraisal and for future standards or revisions to standards.

3. Evaluating the performance of each employee* and communicating the performance evaluation during an appraisal interview with each employee.

4. Preparing an improvement plan jointly with the employee.

5. Following-up to identify possible need for revision of the performance improvement plan and to uncover areas where performance standards should be revised or new ones set.

SETTING PERFORMANCE STANDARDS AND COMMUNICATING STANDARDS IN ADVANCE

When designing a new performance management system or revising an existing one, provisions should be made to ensure that supervisors are thorough in setting standards and equally thorough in communicating them. That is not an easy requirement and has already been discussed. Though, with adequate training and coaching from higher level supervisors, thorough advance communications on standards can become accepted procedure.

If standards are carefully communicated in advance employees will be aware of what their supervisors expect from them. Supervisors cannot assume that employees know the standards because it is rare that there is full concurrence with respect to *all* standards or responsibilities.

With simple or repetitive work, it would seem that standards can clearly communicate expectations. It is true that, over time they can allow for fairly clear measurement of performance. However, even in rather routine work, the conflicts between quantity and quality can make it difficult for supervisors to communicate specific standards. The example of a reservations agent for an airline might be a typical example. Standards for a reservation agent

---

* Please note that the use of the word employee in this book includes employees of all professional, supervisory, and managerial levels. The word supervisor is used for all levels of management. (see Preface).

or a part of the standards for a supervisor of reservation agents could be for reservation agents:

To accept at least a given number of calls in an average hour,

To be sure to ask where the ticket should be mailed after reservations have been completed, and

To avoid errors when booking reservations.

These and similar standards could be very precise and easy to communicate. However, if courtesy and willingness to provide service to callers, such as checking alternative routing possibilities, or checking for least-cost alternatives are made part of the standards, then there is clear conflict between the number of calls that can be completed and the quality of service that will be provided. If the calls are completed more quickly, then the reservation agent can show a high number of calls accepted but is likely to be perceived as being somewhat abrupt.

How can supervisors be trained for specifying expectations so that these needs are satisfied and so that the best possible balance is achieved? That is a major challenge, when setting up or revising the performance management system. The following suggestion and example might provide ideas for an approach.

1. Supervisors can be given specific data for time and/or cost per operation as achieved by competent employees.

2. With this data, either referred to in the standard or clearly implied, standards can then be set on the quality aspects of the tasks.

3. For example, a standard might read: While achieving (a specific number) average calls per hour, reservation agents shall (1) offer to check alternate routings if the caller does not make a reservation, (2) offer to check least-cost alternative if the caller does not make a reservation, (3) ask where the ticket should be mailed if the reservation is made, and so forth. Actual average call time and reports from call monitors (employees who sample/spot check by listening in), can provide information on how well the standard is being met.

The difficulty in communicating standards in advance, however, makes it imperative that supervisors are trained and provided other assistance so they will become effective in performing this crucial task.

Probably one of the most pernicious traps in communicating performance expectations is the belief that a good understanding has been achieved. Therefore, higher level supervisors must monitor supervisory practices at lower levels if communications are indeed to be thorough.

OBSERVING PERFORMANCE AND PROVIDING FEEDBACK INFORMALLY AND AT REGULAR PROGRESS REVIEWS; COLLECTING OF DATA FOR PERFORMANCE EVALUATION/APPRAISAL AND FOR FUTURE STANDARDS, OR REVISIONS TO STANDARDS

Skills and methods for providing feedback by supervisors are discussed in Part Four. Providing the informal, instant feedback is solely at the discretion of the direct supervisor. When setting up or revising a performance management system, however, decision makers can affect the more formal procedure for providing feedback and collecting data, including:

1. Allowing each supervisor the freedom to decide what approach for providing feedback, and for collecting and recording data he or she wishes to use, as long as it satisfies the principles and provides information for valid compensation decisions

2. Prescribing a minimum of four to six fairly formal process reviews in addition to informal feedback, but leaving it up to the supervisors when such reviews should be held, and how the data should be recorded.

3. Providing specific procedures with required timing of reviews and specific forms, possibly including a jacket (folder)

for recording relevant and permanent data. An example of a form is Exhibit 8.1. Possible jackets are discussed in Chapter 7—Other Issues in Performance Management System section entitled forms for Performance Management and in the following. One copy of the form could be completed at each progress review and kept in the folder for one to two years. In addition, the folder could contain one or several copies of a knowledge/skill profile for the job with the incumbent's strengths and weaknesses from the last review. The folder would also contain a copy of the last performance evaluation and, of course, a copy of the latest improvement plan. On the outside, the jacket could have space for name, address, and telephone humber. The inside of the jacket could have spaces for positions held with the organization, complete with dates, previous performance appraisal ratings, compensation history, awards earned, possibly names of family members and hobbies (as reminders for the supervisor), and so forth. This list, of course, is only provided as an example.

Maintaining the integrity of the performance management system should be at least one of the performance standards for supervisors. Standard setting/communicating, feedback, and data collection activities could even be made a preprinted or a required item on the supervisory progress review form (Exhibit 8.1) and/or on the performance evaluation form, so that adherence can be monitored and, when necessary, encouraged or enforced by higher level supervisors.

Data Collection

Procedures for data collection can be left to supervisors. However, if uniformity of data is desirable, forms can be used to provide guidance. In effect, forms become procedures if all levels of supervison makes full use of them. Forms can outline what information to collect, how frequently to collect it, and how to record it.

EXHIBIT 8.1.   PROGRESS REVIEW FORM

Standards/goals/objectives which are being achieved: either list without comment, or enter notes on:	Standards/goals/objectives not being met, or not yet achieved; enter notes on:
1. How well is the standard being met?	1. Will the standard be met? If not, what is the problem and what should be done about it?
2. How difficult/easy was it/is it to meet the standard?	2. What is needed from you, as supervisor, to help your subordinate achieve the standard?
3. How adequate/extensive, was your support in helping your subordinate meet the standard?	3. How adequate are communications so far in all directions?
	4. How appropriate is the involvement of those people who are affected by this standard?
	5. Is the standard still appropriate in light of changes in environment?

Summary of Standard	Priority	Review Comments

EVALUATING THE PERFORMANCE OF EACH EMPLOYEE

Evaluation procedures cover a wide range of matters including:

Timing and frequency of performance evaluations/appraisals

Relationship of performance evaluations to salary/compensation actions

Rating scale to be used

Approvals required

Employee participation in decisions

Appeals procedure

All but the first of these have been discussed in considerable detail either in Part I, or as one of the issues in this Part.

Timing and Frequency of Performance Evaluations/Appraisals

By far, annual appraisals are the most common procedure. The major advantage is obvious—careful performance evaluation takes time. Supervisors have many pressing duties, in addition to performance evaluation/appraisal and the less frequently these are conducted, the less the burden on supervisors, and the more time can be devoted to other duties.

There are disadvantages, too, to single annual performance appraisals. These stem primarily from the benefits that can be gained if employees are informed more often than once a year of how their performance is viewed by management. For instance, a mid-year evaluation provides notice so that employees can still improve their performance for the year-end evaluation.

When two appraisals are standard procedure, the mid-year evaluation also brings greater meaning to the improvement plan. Some organizations who review compensation once a year either allow supervisors the option to conduct two appraisals a year or require them to do so. When an organziation grants more than one general increase, a performance evaluation may be advisable prior to each one. Some organzations require additional evaluation for employees who are entitled to more than one salary increase (such as new employees) and/or for employees who apply for promotion or transfer.

Dating of performance evaluations usually depends on compensation policy. Organizations with formal performance appraisals, who do not follow a practice of annual compensation increases for all employees at the same time, are likely to schedule performance appraisals a few weeks before the anniversary date of the employee, or whenever the employee is entitled to consideration for an increase.

It is advisable to explain to supervisors the reasons for timing of performance appraisal and compensation decisions. There is a widespread belief that performance evaluations can be more factual, and proceed without emotion-charged atmosphere if they are not tied directly to compensation decisions. Obviously, an attempt to make such separation removes, from the performance management process, an essential justification. It violates the major principle that the system should make direct use of the performance evaluation. Furthermore, there is hardly an employee in an organization today who is not aware that, in one way or another, the results of the performance evaluation will be used for compensation decisions. Organziations who attempt to separate the formal performance appraisal session from the compensation decisions are not likely to enhance the respect with which the performance management system is held in the minds of employees.

A far more rational approach to the separation of performance reviews and compensation appears to be the approach taken by those companies who require fairly frequent progress reviews. In these fairly formal progress reviews, the situation, including progress toward achievement of standards or goals/objectives and any additional support that may be required from the supervisor, are discussed thoroughly. Progress toward achievement of the improvement plan is also reviewed on these occasions. The reviews thus provide a thorough separation between compensation and progress analysis. The supervisor can be totally supportive, provide suggestions, review whether his or her support is adequate, and be updated on all important matters relating to the employee's job. At the reviews, standards can be changed if they are no longer appropriate or goals can be revised.

The review sessions provide considerable data for the annual performance and yet help to establish a very positive climate between employee and supervisor. In effect, they assure that the supervisor is indeed aware of the employee's contribution and of the employee's work, in a comprehensive sense. The reviews also allow for a discussion of priorities and thus for revising them, as well as ensuring that both the employee and the supervior see them the same way.

If regular reviews of this type take place, then the supervisor can safely change roles from coach to evaluator at one or two annual performance evaluation/appraisal sessions without causing any damage to the relationship.

When setting up or changing a system, procedures should be decided on, for recommended or mandated timing of:

Progress reviews (such as at least four times annually, every other month, last week of every quarter, etc.)

Evaluations (all at the same time, at anniversary date of employee, prior to any compensation action, prior to application by employee for promotion, etc.)

Development of the improvement plan

EVALUATING PERFORMANCE AND EVALUATION/APPRAISAL INTERVIEWS WITH EACH EMPLOYEE

Procedures should be provided as guidelines for *what* should be covered in each of these steps, and *how* it should be covered. All procedures could be part of a special procedures manual and could cover:

1. Progress reviews:
   a. The importance of handling progress reviews as coaching sessions and not as evaluation sessions

    b. The forms to be used in conjunction with the progress review (such as specific progess review forms, knowledge/skill profiles, use of folders/jackets)

2. Function of the various evaluations, if there is to be more than one (the purpose of a mid-year review for instance, as a pilot or dry run)

3. Steps for each specific evaluation including:

    a. Independent review by employee and supervisor of job responsibilities, accomplishments and lack of accomplishments, and a joint review of the responsibilities

    b. Forms to be used for those reviews

    c. Suggestions for entries which supervisors and employees might make on these forms.

    d. Number of different forms to be used (for exempt and nonexempt employees; possibly different ones for certain specific occupations)

    e. Evaluation of performance on each responsibility, including the ratings to be used and the way they should be applied, with anchors and/or examples

    f. Whether employee self-evaluations are to be optional or required

    g. Reviews of the evaluations that are to be required (with next higher level supervision or others, whether prior to the meeting with the employee)

    h. Procedure for meeting with the employee including specific recommendations for required steps in the interview (such as review of employee self-evaluation, signatures, specific explanations of benefits of performance management, etc.)

    i. Signatures required from the employee at the end of the interview

    j. Timing of implementation plan development in relation to the evaluation

    k. Forms and required steps for development of the implementation plan (such as personal development steps, priorities, review dates, and steps to be taken by the supervisor for the improvement plan)

1. Use of improvement plan steps in the next progress reviews (whether they become standards or goals/objectives to be achieved)

The procedure should give heavy emphasis to the process which is to be used to help ensure that evaluation will be fair and comparable between supervisors.

A very important element in the acceptance by employees of procedures for the conduct of performance evaluations is the personal support and example which senior management provides. Possible evidence of such support could be that:

The highest level supervisors also conduct performance evaluations along the same procedures, using the same forms as other levels

It be made clear that it is the responsibility of higher level supervisors to ensure uniformity of evaluation and adherence to the principles of fairness, during reviews of evaluations by lower level supervisors

It be made a standard of performance of lower level supervisor to follow the procedures of the performance management system in such a way as to help ensure uniformity of ratings*

The previously discussed steps for performance evaluation interviews could also become part of the procedure for the conduct of the evaluation.

PREPARING THE IMPROVEMENT PLAN

Improvement plans are developed in a formal way only with fairly comprehensive performance management systems. However, very often they consist only of goals/objectives, or projects that employees are expected to meet or complete, and thus employees have difficulty separating the improvement plan from their other

---

* While on first sight, this requirement appears to be difficult to measure, and thus violate the principles of factual and accurate measurability, various methods can be used to factually evaluate supervisory performance. Most widely used is one that involves ranking of all employees in a department with several supervisors.

assignments. Effective improvement plans concentrate on *self-development* steps. Therefore, they address the primary cause of performance—the employee's competencies and behaviors.

When a formal performance management system is to be set up, or when one is being revised, supervisors should be provided with suggestions or procedures to guide them, as they develop improvement plans with their employees. Improvement plans can become rather comprehensive and thereby partially defeat their purpose. They can confuse employees about the relative priorities of items on the improvement plan as compared to items on their goals/objectives lists or other work schedules. The improvement plan goals/objectives or projects should be integrated into all other work an employee has to perform, so that they can be given appropriate priorities in relation to the other work.

Supervisors have to assume the responsibility to see to it that these priorities are set and understood. If they fail to do so, they have failed to clarify expectations in advance and they have imposed on their employees the task of setting priorities which they were either unwilling, or unable to set themselves. Weak indeed is such a supervisor's complaint when employees work on projects or responsibilities with low priority instead of on high priority items.

When a meaningful goal system is in operation, the items on the improvement plan can either become goals/objectives for the upcoming review period of one to three months, or be deferred for later periods. In either case priorities relative to other goals have to be clearly established.

Procedures for the improvement plan could specify:

Minimum and maximum number of items to be in a plan

Whether and how the improvement plan should be approved or reviewed at higher levels

What minimum records should be maintained

Specific procedures pertaining to the improvement plan could also communicate the resources that are available for learning experiences and for traning programs. These could include funds for outside programs, specific training programs being offered by the training department of the organization, and authorizations for developmental job assignments.

To acknowledge the fact that performance improvement is not solely dependent on the subordinate, the improvement plan form should allow space for entering the steps which supervisors will take to provide support to their people.

There are three types of steps that a supervisor can take to help employees improve their performance, and thereby their ratings:

1. Supervisors can *remove obstacles* that stand in the way of improved performance by the employee. They can see to it that machines are repaired more quickly, that the work layout is changed where necessary, or that procedural obstacles are removed.

2. Supervisors can *provide or arrange for training* that will lead to better performance by reducing or eliminating knowledge/skill deficiencies.

3. Supervisors can *help with the relationship between staff members.* Sometimes, work relationships and/or personal relationships interfere with optimum performance. If there is an open climate, a supervisor is usually aware of such problems. Nevertheless, a performance management procedure which requires development of improvement plans will bring many new ideas for helping employees remove such obstacles to higher achievement. At the same time it is even possible, if not likely, that procedural obstacles to efficient work flow are discussed and eliminated.

Often supervisors do not know specifically what they can do to provide effective support to their people. Those who establish an open climate during the regular review sessions and during the appraisal interview can get feedback on what they can personally do which will help the respective employee perform his or her work more effectively.

Sometimes, even if the climate is not open, supervisors may hear things they may not like—such as "give me more freedom to do the work," "don't change signals so often," or "let me know more about what's going on." Supervisors may have to admit that employees have good justification for these requests but they may find it difficult to satisfy them. The risks may appear to great, or the supervisor may feel that he or she has the same problems with higher levels, or may not receive enough information himself or herself. Nevertheless, these are areas where employees feel that more help may be useful to them.

A supervisor who is reluctant to allow an employee greater leeway in his or her work can use an improvement plan to set conditions of employee performance which would first have to be achieved before the employee can be given the greater freedom. For instance, a supervisor may have been accustomed to weekly checks on status of all projects. The same supervisor may be willing to forego the checks after the employee has satisfactorily completed a few steps in the improvement plan which provide greater assurance to the supervisor that projects will be completed on time and correctly.

Thus, the improvement plan can become a vehicle to initiate changes which will lead to more productive relationships between supervisors and their people.

FOLLOW-UP

Procedures also should be included in a performance management system on the follow-up steps that supervisors are expected to take. With most employees, follow-up to ensure achievement of the improvement plan is all that is necessary. However, for employees whose evaluations are below competent, especially for those who are consistently below competent, procedures should suggest or mandate the steps that supervisors should take. Suggestions for steps could include:

1. Procedures for more thorough competency analysis to see whether the employee is able to perform the work appropriately (Whether he or she *can* do what's expected)
2. Training where the employee is lacking in knowledge or skill
3. Developmental work assignments
4. Changes in work assignments to adapt the position to the employee, where that is possible and where the employee has sufficient potential to make this worthwhile

5. Disciplinary steps (which steps, in what sequence, and under what conditions they are warranted)

6. More appropriate tangible and/or psychological rewards if the reward system is inconsisent or inappropriate

7. Approvals that may be required for job redesigns, for major training, and for disciplinary steps

A FEW CONCLUDING THOUGHTS

Setting up or revising a performance management system with features that are consistent with each other is not an easy task. Many management professionals consider it the most complex part of establishing a cohesive, comprehensive management system. In many ways, performance management is so difficult because there is no other management function where employees feel that they must exert influence over the system for personal protection and possibly for personal gain. To gain the voice they seek, employees are often successful in enticing their supervisors to undermine the system to obtain favorable personnel/compensation actions for them. Supervisors frequently see no other alternative except to accede to employee demands because to do otherwise might make it impossible to achieve the goals which their supervisors expect them to achieve.

In short, only when the system is a sound one will it assist supervisors so they can honestly work the system as intended, follow the procedures, and adhere to the intent. With run of the mill systems they often are forced to face controversy on a regular basis, thus making a difficult task even more unpleasant.

Only when a system satisfies, as much as humany possibly, the fairness criteria and supervisors have the skills to administer it effectively does the system have a chance to gradually gain thorough acceptance. Under those conditions, it can establish its integrity and gain the respect of management and employees so that "game playing" will be reduced to a minimum or avoided entirely.

Part Three

WORKING EFFECTIVELY WITHIN AN EXISTING SYSTEM

After a general discussion of your role in ensuring smooth administration of a performance management system, Part III will provide suggestions on problems you may face when working within an existing system. These problems concern:

Problem 1. Relationship between ratings and compensation

How to answer employees who ask why their improved ratings do not bring significantly greater compensation increments

Problem 2. Defending the "competent" rating level

How to respond to competent employees who want to know why they did not receive a better rating than other employees who are less effective, to varying degrees

Problem 3. Employees with exaggerated views of personal performance

How to conduct appraisal interviews with employees with erroneously high perception of their own performance.

Problem 4. Claims of more generous ratings in other departments

How to respond when employees claim that other supervisors rate more reasonably/fairer/leniently/generously

Problem 5. Is there enough time for performance management?

How to answer a supervisory employee who reports to you and who claims that there is not sufficient time for the performance management functions

Problem 6. Difficulties with performance standards

What to do when you find that standards often are not set on the most important responsibilities, are not sufficiently clear, or are perceived as too difficult to achieve

First, some general thoughts on your role as supervisor. You have two types of obligations as a supervisor in an organization that has a performance management system. You have obligations toward the organization and you have obligations toward your staff. They are very similar, whether the system is reasonably effective or whether it is considered rather ineffective. These responsibilities are there even when it is difficult to determine whether a performance management system exists. It may be hidden behind a management by objectives process or in personnel procedures which merely require you to fill out forms once a year, where you provide information about the performance of each of the employees* who report to you.

To the organization, you owe a leadership style that ensures

---

* Please note: The use of the word employee in this book includes employees of all professional, supervisory, and managerial levels. The word supervisor is used for all levels of management (see Preface).

high and achievable standards of performance for your staff. To the employees, you owe *maximum* adherence to the principles of fairness within the limits which the environment in which you have to supervise, imposes on you.

Also so the system will be as fair as possible, you owe an honest effort to do the best you can with existing procedures to the organization. This means that your organization has the right to expect that, in addition to your concern for the individual employee and for the needs of the group, you will keep the organization's short- and long-term interests in mind, and that you will follow the procedures at least as conscientiously as any other supervisor.

The organization also has the right to expect from you that you give some thought to the advantages and shortcomings of the procedures or systems with which you are asked to work, and that you provide suggestions on how those procedures could be made more effective and fair.

Toward your staff, you have similar set of obligations. First, you owe them administration of the system with as much adherence to the principles of fairness as your system permits. Second, just as you owe the organization feedback on how the system works and suggestions on improving it, you owe your staff a commitment to work toward gradually changing those aspects of the system which prevent it from being as fair as it could be.

Fairness to the organization and to the employees also means that you have to administer performance management so that it helps the organization develop its human resources in such a way that those human resources contribute most effectively to the organization's short- and long-term goals/objectives, no matter how that organization chooses to define them. These are the thoughts you want to keep in mind as you work on administering performance management concepts.

When you comply with an existing system and its procedures, you may be facing one of the following situations:

1. The system may have procedures which restrict your freedom to administer a performance management approach in accordance with the principles of fairness as outlined in Part One.

2. There may not be any procedural obstacle to your imple-

menting a performance management approach that is in keeping with the suggestions embodied in the principles of fairness but, since other supervisors do not adhere to any uniform approach, you feel inhibited in speaking about performance management. At the same time, you see little gain to yourself, and possibly some disadvantages, to devoting greater effort to performance management than other supervisors.

3. The organization may have a formal performance management program that is working reasonably well, but you are facing difficulties with respect to some aspects of the program.

Obviously, your approach to working within the system is determined by the situation in the organization. However, if there are serious defects in the system itself, then whatever you do about operating more effectively within your department should be in addition to your efforts to gradually achieve an improvement in the system itself. (Improvements you would seek could be patterned along the suggestions in Parts One and Two.)

BRINGING CHANGE IN AN EXISTING SYSTEM

Many supervisors at all levels believe that systems which are set up at higher levels of the organization cannot be influenced by them to any significant extent. While this is true in many organizations, it is also possible that a supervisor may have much more influence than appears to him or her. This is particularly true in small organizations and in those larger organizations where the particular system is also being quesioned by other supervisors.

Every organization has procedures for suggestions and for initiating change that slowly can bring a reevaluation, or a start in the change process. Sometimes, the formal suggestion system is appropriate for that purpose, but at other times departmental meetings are a better forum. At still other times, letters or memos to people charged with primary responsibility for a program or system are the best way to go.

Of course, there is momentum, and considerable inertia against change but the point is that it is better to have tried and failed, especially at the first try, than never to have tried at all. Sometimes the attempt to bring change is worth more than one try. Sometimes such attempts to bring change are recognized *if they are submitted competently,* even if there is no response at all at first, or even if there is never a direct response. Favorable visibility of the initiator may be the result and his or her reputation may be enhanced.

Changes may involve various aspects of performance management:

The organization's or your supervisor's requirements as he or she has spelled them out to you

The way your employees perceive the needs which you are expected to satisfy so that you can acheive the best possibly atmosphere within your organizational unit

The pressures that develop because of the way your peers in the department and in other departments interpret their procedures

Your own personal needs, your personal style, and the way you assess what will best further your career and your interests

In all these, change can be initiated by you.

INFORMAL APPROACHES FOR WORKING WITHIN A SYSTEM

Much more, of course, can be done within your own department with the employees who report to you. Here you can gradually establish the atmosphere of fair and effective performance management. This can be done informally without any dramatic changes or formal announcements. It can be done gradually so that your employees slowly begin to realize that you consider performance management to be a two-way street which must provide benefits to employees as well as to the organization.

Specifically you have to insulate your people from any aspects of performance management system, or lack of system, which acts to treat them unfairly. When you do that you have to establish ground rules and you have to communicate them. Your employees should know where you stand and how you see your obligations toward them as individuals and as a group. They should know your feelings, such as:

> You owe them information about the standards by which they will be judged in advance of the period when you will apply those standards
>
> You owe them as much information about where they stand as you can possibly provide
>
> You owe them guidance in working toward the competence which will allow them to achieve higher levels of performance
>
> You owe them strong representation in comparisons with other sections or departments, and maximum effort to achieve as much in the way of remuneration and job opportunities as employees in other departments
>
> You do *not* owe them overly *generous* treatment as individuals, however, because that would undermine the entire system.

It is the extent to which you are able to hold your ground in fair and uniform evaluations within your department that you will develop and protect an equitabl system. Internally, within your department, you have to ensure an open, just, and equitable system. External to your department you have to strive, as hard as any other supervisor, to obtain at least as large a pool of benefits for your people as others are gaining for theirs.

Within your department, as much as you deem them appropriate for the way your employees perform their functions, you can adapt the procedures outlined in this book. In effect, you could set up as much of a performance management system internally as you feel is reasonable in your situation. You can personally conduct progress reviews, collect and maintain data, evaluate performance, conduct performance assessment interviews and establish improvement plans along most of the lines discussed. If you are so inclined, you can thus set up your own miniature performance management system, with little regard to other units outside of your own organizational unit. However, you must be careful, to watch the principles of fairness and to avoid any situation that may be interpreted as conflict with the procedures of the larger organization.

When you set up your own performance management approach in line with the principles outlined here, you will undoubtedly accrue many of the benefits of the performance management system for your employees as well as for yourself. You will not, however, avoid the problems and questions discussed in the remainder of this Part.

Chapter 9

RESOLVING PROBLEMS

PROBLEM 1—RELATIONSHIP BETWEEN RATINGS AND COMPENSATION

In addition to the discussion of performance evaluation and compensation in Chapter 4, Performance Evaluation and Compensation, the following ideas may help you to better articulate the complex relationships between compensation and performance appraisal ratings when you inform your employees of their salary increases or other compensation decisions. They may also be useful when you explain the benefits or fairness of the performance management system during the evaluation/appraisal interview or when you have to answer questions from employees on compensation.

Particularly when responding to competent, reliable employees who ask why their efforts to achieve higher ratings do not bring significantly greater compensation increments, it is important that you understand the many considerations which determine salary sales. Some of these are in conflict with each other. Still, all have to be balanced in an effective compensation system. They include:

Equal pay for equal work

Appropriate pay differentials for work requiring different levels of knowledge, skills, and physical exertion

Reasonable pay level, in comparison to pay for similar work in other organizations

Pay ranges wide enough to allow for differentials based on merit

Capabilities of the incumbent which are beyond the requirements of the position are not given great weight

Differentials based on longevity become very small, or disappear, after several year

In some way, total earnings reflect the individual's contribution to the task of the organization

As much as possible, pay scales are known to employees

Some of these requirements ask for comparison with the outside world, others ask for comparisons internally, and still others refer to the relationship of the employee's loyalty/reliability to the level of the employee's performance. Obviously, there are no factual standards on which an organization's compensation system can be based. Judgment has to be applied which must take into consideration the particular situation within and outside the organization.

It is, of course, only natural that employees expect good evaluations to result in significant compensation adjustments. Often these expectations cannot be met and the supervisor is faced with the difficult task of explaining why a "good" rating did not bring a "good" salary increase.

For instance, an employee may complain that another organization pays more for a specific skill. It may be important to point out that when an organization depends heavily on a particular skill and has only very few people in a position requiring that skill, it can afford to pay a fairly high price for people with that skill. Another organization that either uses many people with that skill or where the skill is not as important, may find it difficult to be competitive, especially since higher compensation in that skill could require raising the total compensation level.

Other questions may concern differentials between locations in different geographical areas. Here it may be important to point out that the requirement that equal pay be given for equal work, has to be balanced with the equally important requirement that differences in cost of living or in the employment market may require pay differentials.

Fairness in compensation decisions therefore cannot be proven on an absolute scale. Through good communications and significant effort, you can, however, achieve a balance or provide explanations that most employees will consider to be reasonable and fair.

When responding to questions about compensation, it is useful to point out the factors that are being weighed when decisions on salary are made that is:

The actual evaluations relative to competent performance

The trend in performance (whether there is improvement and how extensive)

The money available for increases

Current compensation in relation to the top of the position's range

Within any one job grade, the difference in the increase between competent performance and excellent performance usually is fairly small. It is the job that has the greatest influence on salary level and not the quality of the performance. That fact should probably be emphasized more extensively than is done in most organizations, most of the time. Of course, at the same time, you have to set the salary implications of good ratings into perspective, in relation to the other benefits of the position.

Summary of the Relationship of Performance Management and Compensation Programs

1. Contrary to widespread beliefs, performance evaluation and salary/bonus discussions *do* belong together.

2. Whenever appropriate, career guidance should also be included in the discussion which surrounds notification of compensation adjustments.

3. Employees should be made fully aware of the three influences on their compensation:

    a. Their performance relative to competent performance

    b. The available pool of money, and

    c. The overall salary structure which places limits on the compensation for each position.

4. Employees should understand the considerations which affect compensation decisions (equal pay for equal work, appropriate differentials, etc.).

5. Incentives/bonuses should have a direct relationship to performance evaluation in each position/job level. (This topic is appropriate only if compensation includes bonuses.)

6. ·Salary increases depend on immediate performance evaluation *and* on continuity of performance.

7. Continuity in high ratings will lead to higher competence and possibly to better positions.

8. Continuity in low ratings will lead to lower increments or no increments, and possibily to demotions or separation.

Suggested Steps for a Response to an Employee*

The following suggestions are merely intended to provide ideas as you plan meetings with employees that may involve compensation complaints related to performance management.

1. Establish rapport (encourage the employee to tell his or her side of the story and listen carefully).

2. Attempt to summarize the employee's point of view to ensure that you understood, and to provide assurance to him or her that you do understand.

3. Express empathy if the employee's point is valid.

4. Provide perspective; thoroughly discuss the considerations

---

* As a rule, it is best not to hold discussions on such sensitive topics as quickly as possible after the employee approaches you. He or she may be upset at that time and a brief time for cooling-off is likely to be beneficial. However, do not delay. Make an appointment immediately. Set a time and place where the environment will be proper, and where the employee's concern can be given the attention it deserves. The delay will also give you the necessary time to plan for the meeting.

which must be balanced in an effective compensation system and/or the factors which influence compensation adjustments (see Chapter 9, Summary of the Relationship of Performance Management and Compensation Programs),

5. Explain additional benefits, to the employee, of continuing to achieve high and/or improving performance ratings.

   a. Greater consideration when requesting privileges

   b. Greater consideration for positions to which he or she may aspire

   c. Greater job satisfaction from knowing that he or she is doing a competent job

   d. Enhanced feeling of security which comes from greater personal confidence and knowledge that the supervisor is aware of his or her contribution to the organization

6. Ask a few open questions to ensure that the employee understands your point of view.

7. Provide as much evidence as possible that you respect the employee's efforts and that you acknowledge his or her contribution.

8. Express your support to the employee—that you are available to help him or her in any way you can, without showing preferential treatment by granting privileges that you cannot grant to others.

PROBLEM 2—DEFENDING THE "COMPETENT" RATING LEVEL

If your system has five levels for rating performance, then it is important that the middle level be considered the appropriate rating for the fairly wide range of actual performance exhibited by competent employees. The *competent* level, or whatever the central level is called, must reflect the *overall* performance of most employees, as well as their performance on most of the individual job functions. If this level is not used to represent the broad range of performance of competent employees, then the system will gradually deteriorate. Most employees will receive ratings above the competent level and possibly at the highest level. When that happens, the performance management system has lost its ability to discriminate between the various performance levels. For all practical purposes, it has become useless except possibly to discipline those employees whose performance falls *far* short of acceptable levels.

It may be difficult to explain to an employee that the same competent rating is indeed correct and fair if his or her output has increased year after year partly as a result of improving competence. Still, as an organization improves its technique and tools for its tasks, and as employees gain the competence to effectively apply these methods, it is quite possible for the individual output and performance of most employees to continue to go up, as measured by any absolute standard of output. This is true whether the organization is manufacturing products or whether it is performing services.

Not only is it possible for performance to improve steadily, but it is likely that the improvement is necessary for the organization to maintain its position relative to other organizations. Improving performance is also a necessary ingredient for an organization's ability to offer increasing level of compensation year after year and to maintain some assurance of job security for its employees. The competent employee whose performance improves is therefore doing his or her share to help the organization remain vibrant, and possibly even alive.

A rising level of output in some functions is possible to achieve and, in fact, must be achieved in order to maintain an overall rating of competent by most employees. Furthermore, each person must perform above the central-competent level in *some* functions because most people are naturally weaker in some areas than they are in others. Above-competent performance is therefore necessary to balance performance levels in those other functions where the individual employee is less proficient.

While maintaining the integrity of the central level, you do have the responsibility to also recognize and acknowledge when an employee is performing beyond this competent level. That may sometimes be difficult. Really outstanding performance is easy to recognize. When many employees perform the same task, it may also be fairly easy to determine who is clearly doing more than is expected of competent people.

But, what about the situation when there are only a few employees in the same work, or only one? Is it that the employee performs above the competent level or are the standards too low? If standards are set so that they are fairly easy to achieve with normal effort level, then most standards will be achieved or exceeded by the employee.

If a large proportion of standards are exceeded by several such employees then the standards must be evaluated to determine whether they were set too low or whether the employees are indeed of superior competence. This question can best be resolved by comparison with output/performance of employees in other organizations. Every organization hires such people from time to time. If the new hire is quickly able to achieve the same level of performance, then there is reason to believe that the standards of performance are set somewhat low for competent individuals. Of course, it is possible that the new employee is also an outstanding person whose performance is well above the competent level. If that is the case, however, why was he or she willing to change jobs and forfeit any longevity benefits that had accrued? The answer to this question together with information on how his or her performance compared with others could provide considerable insights which would help determine whether standards are low or whether the new employee's performance is also above the competent level.

During a discussion of an individual employee's rating in which an employee points to what he or she believes to be superior performance he or she is likely to point to strength or specifically the areas where performance is better than that of *one other* employee. If you are faced with such a situation, you might find it worthwhile to ask whether that particular employee is more competent or performs better than a third employee who is also rated as competent. Should that employee, too, be given the higher rating since he or she is also performing better than still other employees? This question is likely to dramatize to the employee what would happen if you adjusted ratings based on comparisons with other employees.

Beyond that, comparisons to other employees should be

avoided because otherwise it would appear as though you are following a quota system in which you allow a certain number of employees to achieve above competent level while the others have to
stay at that level or at one even lower. Still, an acknowledgement
that statistics do apply to the way employees perform in any one
function is in order. Everyone probably knows the bell-shaped
curve which statisticians use to draw conclusions about data from
a series of similar events. With respect to most functions, the performance of employees with respect to any one function can fall
into some form of that bell-shaped curve. It is likely that the curve
will not have a pronounced low end but is cut off there, since employees who cannot rise above that lowest level, even in one important job function, are likely to be removed from that function
or separated entirely. However, inexperienced new employees can
sometimes perform at that level temporarily and thus validate the
curve. Usually, with respect to one function, most employees are
within an acceptable range. Usually one or a few employees are
performing clearly better than the others, with respect to any one
function.

If you look at any single function that way, an employee could
fall into the upper segment of the curve and therefore deserve consideration for above-competent rating in that function. An employee who, with respect to most functions, is outside the major
section of the curve, clearly deserves consideration for a rating
above competent on an overall basis.

What is the practical implication here? If you find it difficult to
assign ratings, use the bell curve. In general, according to the statistical table, without getting involved in details of statistics, you
could arbitrarily rank all your employees on the basis of performance with respect to those specific functions that all or a large
proportion of them perform. If many employees report to you, you
could then assign the highest rating to the top 5 percent or so, and
the intermediate level to the next 10 percent or so. Similarly, the
lowest 5 percent or 10 percent could be considered to perform
below the competent level. But if you were to do that with respect
to every function, you would not be applying any numerical quota,
but you would rather be saying to each employee something like
this: If with respect to most functions, you are either in the top

group or in the one just below it, then you are entitled to consideration for an above-competent *overall* rating. The same would apply to those who are in the lower segment.

If with respect to each function, there are only very few, or possibly only one person, then this approach obviously is not a practical one. You will have to rely heavily on ensuring that the standards you set are indeed achievable yet challenging. You can then evaluate the employee on the basis of the extent to which he or she achieves or exceeds the standards.

Suggested Steps for a Response to an Employee*

The following suggestions are merely intended to provide ideas as you plan meeting with employees which may require defending the competent rating level.

1. Establish rapport (encourage the employee to tell his or her side of the story and listen carefully).

2. Attempt to summarize the employee's point of view to ensure that you have properly understood, and to provide assurance to him or her that you do understand.

3. Express empathy if the employee's point of view is valid.

4. Provide perspective by carefully explaining your position, including the procedure you used to arrive at the ratings you assigned.

5. Discuss the problems which would come if you were to give credit for a performance *in the upper range of the competent level* by granting higher ratings. Show how that would slowly cause the entire system to deteriorate

6. Provide as much evidence as possible that you respect the employee's efforts and that you acknowledge his or her contribution.

* As a rule, it is best not to hold discussions on such sensitive topics as quickly as possible after the employee approaches you. He or she may be upset at that time and a brief time for cooling-off is likely to be beneficial. However, do not delay. Make an appointment immediately. Set a time and place where the environment will be proper, and where the employee's concern can be given the attention it deserves. The delay will also give you the necessary time to plan for the meeting.

7. Ask a few open questions to ensure that the employee understands your point of view.

8. Express your support to the employee—that you are available to help him or her in any way you can, without showing preferential treatment by granting privileges that you cannot grant to others.

PROBLEM 3—EMPLOYEES WITH EXAGGERATED VIEWS OF PERSONAL PERFORMANCE

Most supervisors do not look forward to conducting a performance appraisal session with an employee whose view of his or her performance is significantly better than the supervisor's. Such employees usually are fairly competent but difficult to work with and the prospect of conducting an appraisal interview is not an appealing one.

When the employee is *not* particularly competent, the problem is considerably less serious. It is essential that the employee understands that the performance must be improved and the performance appraisal interview is an opportunity to ensure that awareness.

There are a number of considerations that influence how you plan to conduct the interview with a *competent* employee who, you believe, will insist on a better rating. Consciously or not, the employee attempts to place you in a somewhat defensive position by an aggressive demand and thus makes it difficult for you to maintain control over the interview. The employee undoubtedly believes, rightly or wrongly, that he or she can obtain better compensation in a different organization. Failure on your part to meet his or her demand may have a significant demotivating effect.

Obviously, there are no easy solutions or approaches to such an employee. Nor is there any assurance that whatever you do will have the effect you are hoping to achieve. If you can help this employee gain a more balanced perspective on his or her personal performance, however, then you will have achieved your goal. You will at least partially satisfy his or her need, and at the same time you will have opened up the potential to have him or her make a meaningful contribution to the organization. With somewhat more realistic view of what it takes to be better than competent, the employee may even strive to achieve superior performance.

Emphasis in your discussion must always be on the positive, to come close to such a result. The future is positive. Reassurance that you feel that he or she does indeed have the potential or competence to achieve above-competent performance can be a rewarding thought.

Assuring the employee that you are interested in helping him or her achieve his or her goals can also be an important element in bringing about such a positive direction for the interview. If appropriate, the meeting may be a good time to initiate a career counseling—career direction discussion.

Suggested Steps for a Response to an Employee*

The following suggestions are merely intended to provide ideas as you plan meetings with employees who have an exaggerated view of personal performance.

1. Establish rapport (encourage the employee to tell his or her side of the story and listen carefully).

2. Attempt to summarize the employee's point of view to ensure that you have properly understood, and to provide assurance to him or her that you do understand.

3. Express empathy with those aspects of the employee's point of view that are valid.

4. Provide perspective by carefully explaining what procedures you use to ensure that your ratings are as factual/objective as you can make them.

5. Be open and firm in explaining that you feel what are you

---

* As a rule, it is best not to hold discussions on such sensitive topics as quickly as possible when the employee approaches you. He or she may be upset at that time and a brief time for cooling-off is likely to be beneficial. However, do not delay. Make an appointment immediately. Set a time and place where the environment will be proper, and where the employee's concern can be given the attention it deserves. The delay will also give you the necessary time to plan for the meeting.

doing is correct and that you do not intend to change the ratings unless the employee provides important and significant information about something that would affect ratings and which was not considered during the evaluation.

6. Explain the problems you would create if you gave in to requests for higher ratings. Show how giving into requests for higher ratings would slowly cause the entire system to deteriorate.

7. Provide as much evidence as possible that you respect the employee's efforts and that you acknowledge his or her contribution.

8. Ask a few open questions to ensure that the employee understands your point of view.

9. Express your support to the employee—that you are available to help him or her in any way you can without showing preferential treatment by granting privileges that you cannot grant to others.

PROBLEM 4—CLAIMS OF MORE GENEROUS RATINGS IN OTHER DEPARTMENTS

Depending on the leadership style of the person to whom you report, he or she may demand that you adhere to the procedures rather rigidly. If other supervisors at his or her level also expect fairly rigid interpretation of the rules, then the performance management system and the appraisal procedures probably present little conflict for you.

If on the other hand, other supervisors at your supervisor's level are much more lenient than your supervisor, then you and the other supervisors who also report to him or her face some difficult decisions. Should you protect the people who report to you by being considerably more lenient in the ratings and then defend these ratings with your supervisor, or should you defend a tougher interpretation of standards when you hold the performance appraisal interviews with your people.

If rather lenient interpretation of standards is the rule in other departments, then what can you do to answer a high-achieving employee who reports to you and who asks: "Why should I continue to devote considerably more effort than others, if the system gives everyone high ratings and reward for those who devote greater effort are slim indeed?"

What you can do in this situation, depends greatly on the specifics. It is influenced by the respect your supervisor enjoys, by the level of compensation in your department as compared to other departments, by any privileges your employees enjoy that are not available to other employees, and by other differences between departments. Also important is the relationship between you and the person to whom you report, and the extent to which other supervisors who report to the same person, and you, work together as a team.

You can adhere to the "tougher" approach required by the person to whom you report if the more rigorous ratings will not bring lower compensation levels to your people. Some supervisors are quite successful in achieving favorable consideration for their people even though the ratings are more rigorous and less lenient than the ratings of other supervisors. More frequently this is the case when the higher level supervisor insists on rigorous ratings only as a spur to greater selfimprovement by the employees in the department.

To balance the negative psychological impact of lower ratings than in other departments, you can be more generous in providing evidence of recognition to your people. You can do this by making use of the bulletin board, through taking advantage of any opportunities that your organization offers to give recognition to employees, and so forth.

The great benefit of an approach which combines firm ratings with competent protection of employees' needs is that it allows you to maintain the integrity of the performance management system in your department while at the same time ensuring that the treatment which your employees receive is equal to that enjoyed by employees in other departments.

Good communications are essential for this approach so that your employees receive the recognition that they deserve. It is also the key to help them see that you are doing your best to obtain for them the highest possible compensation and the greatest consideration when they apply for positions in other areas of the organization.

Another benefit of this approach is that those employees who do receive high ratings in your department are likely to receive especially favorable consideration when they apply for a position elsewhere. When doing so, you are setting an example, either together with your supervisor or alone, of fair but tough ratings. Gradually, your department will gain the reputation of a tight ship equivalent to the kind of reputation that the Ivy League schools enjoy. Your department will be perceived as being staffed with individuals of significant competence. This not only effects your department but you, too, will enjoy the respect of supervisors at all levels.

On the other hand, you may be working for a supervisor who insists on rigorous ratings, not because he or she wants to enhance motivation for self-improvement, but solely to obtain a higher output from the department. He or she may not be willing to reciprocate with additional effort to ensure that the employees in the department receive equal treatment with other departments where ratings are more lenient.

In that situation, you have no choice but to seek to provide the highest possible rating for your employees which you can justify with your conscience and to defend those ratings as much as possible until the atmosphere in your department changes. It may seem that what is advocated here is the playing of games with the performance evaluation system and that is tantamount to heresy in management. However, if the system is really not fair, then fairness to the employees should take precedence over protection of the integrity of an unfair system.

Suggested Steps for a Response to an Employee*

The following suggestions are merely intended to provide ideas as you plan meetings with an employee who claims Performance ratings are more *Generous in Other Deparments*. These steps would apply only when your ratings are rigorous.

---

* As a rule, it is best not to hold discussions on such sensitive topics as quickly as possible when the employee approaches you. He or she may be upset at that time and a brief

1. Establish rapport (encourage the employee to tell his or her side of the story and listen carefully).

2. Attempt to summarize the employee's point of view to ensure that you understand and to provide assurance to him or her, that you do understand.

3. Express empathy if the employee's point is valid.

4. Explain to the employee the reasons why it is important that ratings are objective, fair, and rigorous and that, otherwise, the pressure of generous ratings would gradually force supervisors to provide higher ratings to all employees, until the system becomes useless. If that were the case, competent employees such as the employee who is complaining, would not benefit but rather would suffer because they would be treated no better than employees who are not performing nearly as well.

5. Provide as much evidence as possible, or as you have available that, despite the difference in ratings between your department and the department to which the employee refers, salary and other compensation adjustments have been as favorable to the employees in your department as they have been to employees in other departments.

6. Provide assurance to the employee that you are doing all you can to gradually bring about awareness of the need for greater uniformity in ratings throughout the organization.

7. Ask a few open questions to ensure that the employee understands your point of view.

8. Provide as much evidence as possible that you respect the employee's efforts and that you acknowledge his or her contribution.

9. Express your support to the employee—that you are available to help him or her in any way you can without showing preferential treatment by granting privileges that you cannot grant to others.

---

time for cooling-off is likely to be beneficial. However, do not delay. Make an appointment immediately. Set a time and place where the environment will be proper, and where the employee's concern can be given the attention it deserves. The delay will also give you the necessary time to plan for the meeting.

PROBLEM 5—IS THERE ENOUGH TIME FOR PERFORMANCE MANAGEMENT?

Maintaining records on employee performance, conducting regular progress reviews, reviewing data on employee performance, evaluating their performance, and conducting appraisal interviews are all activities that take time. Therefore, supervisors sometimes question whether there is enough time to perform this function properly, so that it will be effective and bring the benefits which it potentially can bring. They are rarely aware that competent performance management can actually save time because the improved communications it brings can and usually does lead to fewer crises and to reduced need for frequent meetings and supervisory follow-up activities.

Of course, as a supervisor, you have to be convinced that performance management is worth this effort. You also may be called on to speak to a supervisor who reports to you and who feels that he or she does not have the time to do justice to performance management.

At these occasions, knowledge of good time management techniques can be useful. First and foremost, time management is a matter of priorities. Secondly, it concerns realistic delegating, avoiding interruptions, not allowing outright time-wasters to steal too much of the workday. When it comes right down to it, the time we spend at work should be spent on those things which are most important—the key elements of the job first and other elements later and that requires good time management. A brief discussion on setting priorities may be helpful.

Setting Priorities

The best approach that can be used to set priorities involves relative urgency and importance of the task when compared to other tasks that have to be done. Figure 9.1 shows how priorities can be set based on their relative urgency and importance. It suggests that tasks regularly be grouped into four categories. They should then be classified relative to other tasks. For example:

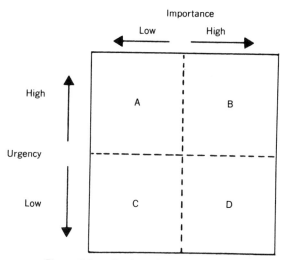

Figure 9.1. Guide to Setting Priorities

C—It is obvious how to handle items in cell C. These low urgency/low importance items can be postponed, ignored, avoided completely, or perhaps referred to someone else, such as a secretarial or clerical employee. For example, a cell C item might be straightening out the contents of your desk drawers. This task can be postponed or ignored for quite some time, since it is possibly of low urgency and low importance relative to other projects you have to complete.

A—Cell A, the high urgency/low importance items should be delegated or handled immediately by you, if importance is not so low they should be ignored. An example of an A item, might be the task of answering a call from a client who's leaving town soon and needs some of your literature for the trip. Such a task may need your immediate action if you cannot get someone else to do it for you.

B—High urgency/high importance items, those in cell B, should be best handled by you with assistance from others as necessary. If your budget for next year is due tomorrow and if you have only today received a summary of last year's expenditure which must accompany the presentation, such a matter will obviously get your immediate attention and probably become your top priority.

D—Low urgency/high importance items are the ones where you lay the foundation for good time management in the future. These are the items which will become crises and timewasters if they are ignored now. Most people do not assign tasks in this cell a very high priority and unfortunately, as a result, these tasks which today are not particularly urgent become the crises of tomorrow. Such tasks may involve a newly hired employee who requires training but, because there is work that must be accomplished today, no training is given. Suddenly, at some future time, a rush period arises and a crises develops when the individual cannot do the work because of inadequate training. A low urgency/high importance matter has suddenly become quite urgent.

Consequently, work on cell D items should be started as soon as possible, and some time be set aside regularly. This will aid in preventing them from becoming crisis situations later on.

It is important to remember that the tasks and projects that are inserted in Figure 9.1 are always considered relative to others. (Taken alone, priority decisions concerning them are sometimes difficult to explain.)

If you review once more the benefits of performance management on which appear in the section entitled Problem 2—Defending the "Competent" Rating Level, you will undoubtedly agree that performance management is one of these cell D items. You may conclude that is one of *the* most important functions which a supervisor has to perform. In a way, that settles the question. Performance management does deserve the time.

Suggested Steps in Response to a Supervisory Employee Who Feels That Not Enough Time Is Available to Do Justice to Performance Management

The following suggestions are merely intended to provide ideas as you plan meeting with employees on this subject.

1. Establish rapport (encourage the supervisory employee to explain his or her reasons for feeling that not enough time is available for thorough performance management).

2. Attempt to summarize the employee's point-of-view to ensure and provide assurance to him or her that you do understand.

3. Express empathy if the supervisory employee indeed has many urgent tasks to perform.

4. Discuss the importance of careful prioritizing to ensure that the most important things receive the attention they deserve. If appropriate, explain Figure 9.1.

5. Ask a few questions to ensure that the employee understands your point of view.

6. Explore with the supervisory employee to what extent you can provide assistance during performance evaluation, so that he or she would be under less pressure in the event that too many urgent demands are made on his or her time. (For instance, could an earlier start with performance evaluation alleviate the problem? Could assistance be provided with urgent tasks that could be delegated if someone were available? Could you provide resources for that possibly in the form of a "loan" of an employee during exceptionally busy periods?)

PROBLEM 6—DIFFICULTIES WITH PERFORMANCE STANDARDS

There are four major problems that are generally encountered by supervisors in performing the action steps for setting standards of performance. These are:

a. Standards of performance do not concentrate on the most important responsibilities

b. Too many standards and therefore too much paperwork

c. Standards not clear enough

Standards do not concentrate on the most important responsibilities. You can reduce the impact of this problem if you follow the suggestions about key results areas or goals/objectives provided in Part Two. You could also assure concentration on the most important matters if you base the standards on the major responsibilities outlined in the job description. First, though, you have to review the job description, jointly with the employee to see whether the major responsibilities are still the same and whether they cover the same activities.

Another way to ensure that standards are on the most important responsibilities is to ask yourself the following questions:

If I were to fill this job myself would I be able to perform it better?

What changes would I make to improve the results that are achieved on this job?

What would an ideal job holder do on this job?

Any one of these questions is likely to point to these crucial areas on the job where standards might be possible.

There are too many standards and too much paperwork. Paperwork, too, can be reduced to a minimum if standards for a particular position concentrate on those responsibilities where performance improvement will do most to achieve better results. By emphasizing only these matters, and lumping all others together in an umbrella standard which ties performance and results to the past, the remaining standards can concentrate on the essential. At the same time, paperwork is reduced and explanations are minimal. When standards are set on that basis, however, it is important for you to remain alert to spot performance problems as they begin to develop in important functions covered by the umbrella standard. As soon as a performance problem is suspected, a separate standard should be set for that function.

Possibly the major benefit of emphasis on a limited number of standards during any one period, is the lack of confusion. Employees can concentrate their creativity on those specific responsibilities where improvement is most useful without wondering what is really expected of them.

Unclear standards can be avoided by reviewing that the standards meet the criteria for clarity. If standards spell out or clearly imply in the results section quantity

quality, and

time

and if resources are also spelled out or clearly implied, then the standards are specific, and results can be measured against them.

The competence and effort section, of course, has to be just as clear. One way to ensure such clarity is to reread the section several days after it was written. If it still means the same to you, check it by envisioning some hypothetical performance incidents to see how you would evaluate them.

It is, of course, important to keep in mind that clear and concise standards should also be standards that are in some way reasonable. At the same time, they should not be exceptionally easy to achieve or they are not worth setting.

A FEW CONCLUDING THOUGHTS

Long gone are the days when people thought that excellence in management and supervision merely required the appropriate application of a few simple concepts. We are becoming increasingly aware of the complexity of the supervisory/management function and of the difficulty of raising the level of supervisory competence. There is a growing need for supervisors to pay close attention to sharpening their skills in supervising, in addition to the skills which their particular function requires. You can therefore come close to achieving excellence as a supervisor only if you accept this self-developmental responsibility. Fortunately, there are similarities between most supervisory functions, so that practice in the skills which bring improved competence in one function, can make it easier to apply *these* particular skills elsewhere. Skills important for performance management are outlined in Part Four.

If you apply these skills effectively, with close attention to the subtle distinctions which bring excellence, your organization's performance management system can be a lever for reaching higher levels of supervisory performance in all functions. This is the case because performance management is both the core of effective management and a major cornerstone. It is the core because performance is what organizational life is all about. It is a major cornerstone because it supports all supervisory/managerial activities.

Whether you look at management/supervision as planning, organizing, implementing/leading and adjusting or as goal setting and leading toward goal achievement, performance management is the function which ensures that employees understand what you expect from them. It provides the vehicle to let them know how they can best assist you in getting to where you are going, and it tells them "what's in it for them." These are the reasons why close attention to sharpening your skills in working with performance management can be the key to excellence in supervisory/managerial performance.

Part Four

ESSENTIAL SKILLS

Effective performance management requires a number of skills. If you are in a supervisory position, you already possess most of these skills. Nevertheless, the discussion in this Part can provide you with useful ideas. It can help you decide where sharpening of your skills or those of your supervisory employees might be desirable and how you could go about doing so.

The major skills needed in performance management are all skills of effective coaching and counseling. They are:

Critical observation

Maintaining constant awareness of process

Applying transactional analysis (T/A) concepts

Conflict avoidance and resolution

Understanding the Johari window

Using questions effectively

Providing information and feedback

Leading a discussion toward agreement

Providing recognition and evidence of support

Chapter 10

COACHING AND COUNSELING SKILLS

Many supervisors are confused about the two words coaching and counseling, they are often used interchangeably. However, there is a clear distinction between the two.

Coaching involves helping employees gain greater competence by guiding them toward acquiring more knowledge and sharpening of skills.

Counseling involves helping employees* change inappropriate behavior on the job, solve performance problems, or personal problems which affect their work and to provide career guidance.

In addition, counseling applies to other areas that are not related to work and therefore are not supervisory responsibilities, such as family problems or coping with illness.

Also note that progress reviews often involve coaching discussions, as does the development of the improvement plan. Similarly, the analysis of knowledge/skill strengths and weaknesses which is an essential prerequisite for effective competence development and discussed in Chapter 8—Considerations for Designing

---

* Please note that the use of the word employee in this book includes employees of all professional, supervisory, and managerial levels. The word supervisor is used for all levels of management (see Preface).

or Modifying a Performance Management System under the section entitled Observing Performance and Providing Feedback Informally and at Regular Progress Reviews, collecting of Data for Performance Evaluation/Appraisal and for Future Standards, or Revisions to standards can be considered to be a step in the coaching process.

The skills/principles which you apply in both coaching and counseling are so similar that they can be summarized in a single list. These principles are:

Keep motivation to learn and/or to change in mind

Show empathy

Keep the interview process in mind

Listen and provide evidence of full attention

Use questions appropriately to *solicit* information and feedback

Provide information and feedback that is

    Relevant

    Timely

    Factual

Provide recognition and evidence of confidence and support

MOTIVATION

Motivation to Learn and/or to Change—A Key Element in Coaching and Counseling

Coaching and counseling are difficult processes. You are attempting to make the employee aware of those knowledge and skill deficiencies or of attitudes/behaviors which prevent him or her from reaching full competence and best performance. You want to help the employee become more effective. At the same time, you are attempting to instill a desire to change, learn, and to practice. These are activities which, to most people, involve some joy. They also often bring a considerable amount of inconvenience and possibly even some pain. Therefore, the key to successful counseling or coaching, is the motivation to change and to learn.

Motivation applies to you, the supervisor, too. No supervisor is as good a coach or counselor as he or she could be. Like all other personal improvements, it takes effort and critical self-observation—the most difficult kind of observation. If you can muster the motivation to work steadily on sharpening these skills, you will undoubtedly find that your employees will respond most favorably. The key to achievement of learning objectives or to lasting behavior change lies with stimulating motivation to learn and motivation to change.

Motivation to Learn

Motivated learners will accept a larger share of the responsibility for acquiring competence than less motivated learners. The more the responsibility for learning or for skill enhancement is accepted by the learner, the more likely the learner will actually achieve the desired level of competence and not be satisfied with just completing a learning assignment. Similarly, employees who are motivated to change their behavior will do so sooner, and more thoroughly, than employees who are responding to initiatives from their supervisor.

PRINCIPALS OF EFFECTIVE LEARNING FOR ADULTS

To provide an environment which permits the highest possible level of motivation, *several principles for effective learning by adults* have to be considered. These principles are:

1. The topic must be *relevant* so that the learner can see the benefits which greater knowledge and competence will bring. Do not assign a lot of theoretical reading but provide for immediate application, if possible. Whenever possible, be sure your employee clearly understands why the topic is important to competent performance.

2. A *voice in decisions* on what to learn, how much, and when, will increase motivation and commitment to achieve the agreed-on competence.

3. The learning program must *involve the learner* and be suf-

ficiently varied to maintain high level interest. As much as possible, provide varied developmental work assignments, some reading/studying, some specific practice, role playing with you where applicable, and so forth.

4. The learning experience must *adapt itself* to the particular needs of the individual learner (in pace, medium, complexity, structure, etc.). In short, keep the capabilities of your employee in mind, when you assign topics to study, during on-the-job training, or when you make developmental assignments.

5. Effective learning experiences provide for:

   a. Acquisition of new knowledge,

   b. Demonstration of how the new knowledge is applied in the work environment. This is the step that is often overlooked, and the ability of the employee to apply new learning or even to take the next step (step c), may be significantly impaired,

   c. Personal application for reinforcement of learning and for skill practice, and

   d. Feedback and remedial assignments where learning was inadequate.

6. Regular process checks provide reinforcement and feedback on topics not adequately mastered. There is a wise old quality control supervisor who used to say: "You get what you inspect," meaning that employees will pay greater attention to that which they know to be important enough for the supervisor to check.

7. Recognition for learning achievement enhances motivation to learn.

8. A framework for relating facts and information can assist in retention and recall. For this reason, checklists and diagrams for some learners can greatly assist the learning process.

9. Learning with challenges such as developmental assignments to new tasks are desirable but should be held within reasonable limits. If the task or the topic to be learned is too

challenging, it will discourage the employee. If it is not challenging enough, it will not stimulate interest or hold his or her attention.

Motivation to Change

What is true of motivation to learn is similarly true of motivation to change.

1. The employee must be aware that the behavior change will benefit him or her. During the discussion which identifies the need for a change, you, as a supervisor, need to make appropriate use of questions so you can ensure, that the employee agrees with the need for change or, at the very least, that you are aware of his or her lack of acceptance of the need to change.

2. If you allow your employee a major voice (though not necessarily the determining voice) for deciding what segment of the planned change will receive priority, and when the various aspects of the change will be achieved, you will undoubtedly see much higher levels of motivation than if you dictate these matters.

3. Regular progress checks to provide reinforcement and feedback and appropriate recognition are as important to enhance motivation for change as they are in bringing greater desire to learn.

4. Subtle challenges can also add to a motivational climate for change. Asking a employee whether he or she can conquer a habit or can avoid getting angry at unreasonably requests from members of the public, and to follow the procedures for these situations, is such a subtle challenge that it can add to motivation.

Empathy

Empathy is not really a skill. It is more in the nature of an attitude. You have a high degree of empathy when you can clearly understand your employee's point of view and feelings. You reflect that understanding in the way you hold your discussion with him or her.

Since you once undoubtedly were in the same or a similar position as your employee, you have the knowledge necessary to put yourself into the employee's shoes. However, your employees will not automatically know that you are tuned in to their point of view and feelings. You prove it to them by the way you explain a point which they have difficulty learning on their own, and by the patience you show when they are struggling to sharpen a skill or develop a change in behavior.

Keeping Process in Mind*

Process in progress reviews or performance appraisal interviews refers to the principles of coaching and counseling. It is easy to keep a sharp focus on what you want to tell your employee. It is more difficult however, to constantly keep in mind *how* that information can be transmitted most effectively. yet, it is this *how* that will determine how thoroughly and how effectively you communicate with him or her. It is in this area where every supervisor can further improve skills through practice and attention to detail.

This coaching and counseling process suggests that you will be most effective if you keep the principles constantly in mind as you follow your action steps during the coaching or counseling interview.

Other major principles/skills in addition to motivation, empathy, and keeping process in mind involve:

Listening and providing evidence of full attention (see section entitled Listening and Providing Full Attention)

Using questions appropriately to solicit information and feedback (see Chapter 12—Conflict Avoidance and Resolution in the section entitled Using Questions Appropriately)

Providing information and feedback (See Chapter 12—Conflict Avoidance and Resolution in the section entitled Providing Information Feedback)

* For a more detailed discussion of *process* see section entitled Process and Content.

Preventing undesirable conflict (see Chapter 12—Conflict Avoidance and Resolution)

Listening and Providing Evidence of Full Attention

Your employees expect you to give them your full attention when you discuss an important topic. If your words are to carry the weight which you expect them to have, your employees need evidence that they, too, have your full attention.

How can you make your employee aware that you are indeed listening carefully? Obviously, you must appear to be attentive. More important, however, are the type of questions you ask to obtain clarification. It is through adroit questions that you show how well you have listened and how thoroughly you understand all that your employee is saying.

A more extensive discussion of listening is in Chapter 12—Conflict Avoidance and Resolution in the section entitled Listening.

ACTION STEPS FOR COACHING AND COUNSELING

Though principles are the same for coaching and counseling, the action steps are different. The action steps for *coaching* are:

1. Identification and analysis of knowledge/skill strengths and weaknesses

2. Possibly a coaching interview or informal discussion leading to commendation on strengths and decisions on study and skill practice assignments, developmental work assignments, or on-the-job training to overcome the weaknesses

3. Implementation of remedial steps and monitoring of progress

4. Evaluation of progress and further coaching or possibly supervisory actions such as changes in job assignments

You perform coaching steps during progress reviews, and during the development of the improvement plan whenever your analysis of knowledge/skill strengths and weaknesses shows opportunities for improving performance through training/learning. If other obstacles to performance improvement exist, such as attitudes, personal problems which interfere with the work, or disagreements on how the work should be done, then you may have to hold a counseling interview.

To clarify these distinctions, during *progress reviews,* you perform:

Coaching functions when you identify knowledge/skill (competence) strengths and deficiencies, and lead toward decisions on a course of action to remedy them.

Counseling functions when you identify performance obstacles in the employee's behavior such as inappropriate ways in relating to other people, or personal problems that interfere with performance. You also perform counseling functions when you lead toward decisions to overcome a problem.

During *performance evaluation/appraisal,* you perform:

Coaching functions when you lead the employee toward commitments on improvement plan steps which involve elimination of competency weaknesses.

Counseling functions when you lead to commitments on improvement plan steps which require behavior change by the employee.

The steps for a *counseling session* are somewhat different than those for coaching session. They are:

1. Identification and analysis of problems which interfere with performance of tasks or job functions.

2. The counseling interview which results in agreements on job environment (work hours, work assignments, etc.) and/or behavior change on the part of the employee and the supervisor.

3. Implementation of the decisions reached during the interview and commendation for improvement, where applicable.

4. Evaluation of the situation and further counseling or possi-

bly managerial actions such as changes in job assignments or disciplinary steps.

The fundamental distinction between performance evaluation on the one hand, and coaching sessions on the other, which was referred to before cannot be stressed enough. When you are coaching your employees, you are helping them to strengthen their desire to learn and you are helping them to gain higher levels of competence. This is not the time to evaluate performance.

When you conduct a performance evaluation, you are in a different role. You are informing the employee how his or her performance is seen. You are accepting comments about the evaluation, particularly those that concern matters you may not have considered, or of which you may not be aware. However, your role here is more of a judgmental one than in a coaching session. You are informing the employee of the performance strengths and weaknesses *as you see them*. You are commending for good performance and you are stating where you see performance to be less than what *you* expect. The final portion of the performance appraisal interview, the development of the improvement plan, places you again into a position where you are helping your employees rather than evaluating them.

Many counseling interviews are similar to performance evaluation interviews because they concern problems that affect performance. Therefore, in those counseling interviews, you are also in the role of evaluator who informs the employee of performance problems. In other counseling interviews, though, you are helping the employee overcome a problem which is primarly of concern to him or her and secondarily affects performance.

Action Steps for Coaching and Counseling Interviews

Despite the extensive differences between coaching and counseling, the specific steps which you have to follow during the respective *interviews* are remarkably similar. These steps are:

1. Ensure a calm environment
2. Explain the purpose of the session and the benefits to the employee if the objectives are reached

198 COACHING AND COUNSELING SKILLS

3. Explore views on knowledge/skill strengths and weaknesses, performance problems, and/or other problems

4. Gain agreement on ways to solve the competency or performance problem

5. Jointly establish priorities and obtain agreement

6. Explore alternative courses of action for each competency weakness and/or performance problem

7. Obtain agreement on a course of action and on follow up dates

8. Summarize and confirm common understanding

The specific discussion of coaching and counseling in this chapter segment should help to firmly establish the distinction between principles and action steps. Note that each of the principles that were discussed, is used in most if not all of the action steps. For instance, the principle "keep motivation to change and/or learn in mind" would apply in every action step. Similarly, "showing empathy" would apply to all of them. On the other hand, listening and providing evidence of full attention would apply to all except the first action step.

ENSURING A CALM ENVIRONMENT

In coaching sessions and in counseling interviews, the environment can have profound effects on attitudes, and through them on the success of the discussion. The same is true of progress reviews and performance evaluation/appraisal sessions which, as previously discussed, may combine both types of interview formats.

There are some supervisors who believe that coaching and counseling interviews are so important that only serious emergencies should interrupt them. Other supervisors make little or no attempts to avoid interruptions.

However, most experts on interviewing do agree that even in highly informal organizations and in situations where the relationship between supervisor and employee is excellent, it is better to avoid interruptions as much as possible.

If you want to avoid interruptions and you do not have a secretary who can screen calls, and prevent other people from disturbing you, you could use a small conference room or a vacant office and leave word to call you there only for emergencies.

Other steps that help to ensure a calm environment are:

Planning the interview so it will take place at a time convenient for your employee, as well as for you

Notifying the employee well in advance of the purpose of the session so he or she can prepare for it

Preparing yourself thoroughly so you have all the data you may need

Discussing matters factually and observing the rules for providing feedback (see Chapter 12—Conflict Avoidance and Resolutions in section entitled Providing Information and Feedback

Remaining calm and adult, in the transactional analysis sense (see Chapter 11—Transactional Analysis) throughout the session, even if the employee becomes excited or even hostile

Observing the principles for effective coaching/counseling sessions (see Chapter 10—Coaching and Counseling Skills)

Keeping a positive viewpoint by looking for ways, to solve the problem, that are mutually acceptable, that are win-win solutions (see Chapter 12—Conflict Avoidance and Resolution)

Exploring Views on Knowledge/Skill Strengths and Weaknesses or on the Performance Problem

In coaching as well as in counseling interviews it is essential that a common understanding is reached of knowledge/skill strengths and weaknesses and/or the performance problem, before the various alternate possible solutions are explored.

It is unlikely that a satisfactory result can be obtained from an interview if this common view is not first achieved. At the very least, it is critical for both sides to understand how the other person perceives the performance problem or the strengths and weaknesses in the employee's competency (knowledge/skill profile). Early in the coaching or counseling discussion, these views should therefore be stated, by you, as clearly and as factually as possible and then the employee should have a chance to explain his or her views. If the employee, as well as you, the supervisor, can then raise clarifying questions about the other's views, a solid foundation is created for the discussion of competency or performance weaknesses.

GAINING AGREEMENT ON WAYS TO SOLVE THE COMPETENCY OR PERFORMANCE PROBLEMS

Once the views on these matters have been discussed, then alternative courses of action (possibly solutions) have to be explored. Whether or not there is complete agreement on the existence or type of competency or performance problems, differences may arise over the best approaches to correct the problems or overcome weaknesses. If such differences do arise, you can apply the suggestions in Chapter 12 Conflict Avoidance and Resolution to overcome the disagreement or to reduce their impact on the success of your discussion.

ESTABLISHING AND GAINING AGREEMENT ON PRIORITIES

As part of your coaching and counseling interview, and in developing an improvement plan, it is essential to establish which competency weaknesses or which behavior changes deserve highest priority and which are lesser priority. Priorities then become the guides for setting up the sequence in which remedial activities are to take place and for the specific milestone.

EXPLORING ALTERNATIVE COURSES OF ACTION

Once there is agreement on priorities for the competency weaknesses and/or the performance problems, alternative courses of action can be identified from which the best one can then be selected. You may want to work on several of the deficiences that need to be eliminated. Or, the situation may not permit time to work on any but the one or two highest priority problems before proceeding to others. In any case, those alternative courses of action which deserve serious consideration have to be explored before agreement on the course of action is attempted.

SUMMARIZING

A supervisor who is a good coach or counselor will summarize from time to time, to ensure that the employee sees, in proper perspective, what the manager is saying. Even in a relatively short discussion, you should therefore summarize what you have said and what you have understood your employee to say.

Summarizing follows the view of many speakers and communicators who believe that messages are not likely to be thoroughly understood unless the sender has:

Told'em what they will be told,

Told'em, and

Told'em what they have been told.

OBTAINING AGREEMENT ON A COURSE OF ACTION AND ON FOLLOW-UP DATES

The next step in a coaching or counseling interview concerns agreement on the course and on the follow-up dates within that course of action. Just agreeing on the course of action will rarely achieve the deserved results. Agreement must also be reached on specific follow-up dates so that they become standards or goals with which progress on the agreed-on solution can be measured. When endeavoring to gain a common understanding, you may again find the approaches suggested under Chapter 12—Conflict Avoidance and Resolution to be useful.

CRITICAL OBSERVATION

Much information can be obtained about an employee's performance through critical observation. If you develop the habit of keeping your eyes on how your employees perform their work, as you move through the department, you will gain many valuable hints about the reasons for performance strengths and weaknesses. Obviously, to adhere to the principle of timeliness of feedback, you should discuss your findings with your employees as soon as you notice something that deserves recognition or requires corrections.

Work Sampling

Among the critical observations skills, are the skills of work sampling in an informal manner. Professionals in quality control understand informal and formal sampling procedures. Supervisors in other areas rarely appreciate the validity of repeated observations. As a result, *work sampling,* a venerable industrial engineering technique, has either become neglected or it degenerated into excessive monitoring—what employees sometimes call "Snoopervision." However, if it is used in a competent, fairly rigorous way to obtain data on various performance elements such as types of activity, neatness, pace (where applicable), atmosphere (friendly, unfriendly, humorous, etc.), then it can be a highly useful tool. With employees who report to you and with whom you have little contact, or in departments that are one or several levels below you, informal work sampling can provide indications of the reasons for performance difficulties.

Work sampling is not complicated. It consists of repeated random observations of what an individual or group is doing and *how* they are doing it. If a simple record is kept of individual observations, it can be a very useful tool in helping to establish the causes of performance problems or in providing a foundation for commendation. Intensive work sampling for one or two days can be useful when you are attemtping to assist a supervisor or professional employee in identifying knowledge or skill deficiencies so you can be more effective in coaching. Many managers believe that periods of close observation of this type are appropriate foundations for helping employees develop greater competence.

Several companies have recently adopted a procedure which requires field sales managers to perform such intensive, detailed competency reviews of all new sales representatives, usually about six months to a year after their starting date. These reviews use one or several knowledge/skill profiles.

Developing and Using Knowledge/Skill Profiles

Knowledge/skill profiles can be used to formalize the observation process as it pertains to the competence level of an employee. They apply to all types of positions. Because they can be difficult to prepare, they are used most frequently in those situations where they can bring the greatest benefits—where employees require knowledge in many subjects and high skill levels. Knowledge/skill profiles are especially valuable when managers have only occasional, though fairly intense personal contact with the people who report to them and where it is difficult to diagnose whether performance problems are due to inadequate competence or lack of effort.* Such is the situation which if faced by supervisors who are responsible for geographically dispersed salespeople or for offices in several locations. Where knowledge/skill profiles are used to determine personal development needs, they become highly useful coaching tools. Some organizations have detailed job descriptions from which the knowledge/skill profiles can be prepared. In others, supervisors have to prepare them. Preparation can best be done jointly with the employee.

A knowledge/skill profile is a list of topics which define the knowledge and skills, the competencies required by a *position.* Thus, it lists what the employee has to understand and the skills that he or she has to master to be effective on the job. Each line on the profile may represent a limited amount of knowledge that can be learned by studying a small book or manual, several chapters, or several articles. A line may also represent a skill that can be enhanced with a limited amount of practice. Most lines require both, some knowledge and a skill.

If a detailed job description exists, the knowledge/skill profile can be based on it, though it usually cannot match the job description exactly. For instance, two lines on the job description for a product manager may read: "Analyze competitive moves to determine probable market impact" and "Develop and evaluate alternative market strategies."

Analyzing competition and developing and evaluating strategies covers many similar topics and skills from the marketing through estimating and forecasting. Several lines of the knowledge/skill

---

* An excellent discussion of the distinction between cannot do and will not do can be found in Robert F. Mager and Peter Pipe, *Analyzing Performance Problems,* (Belmont, California: Fearon). Integration of the Mager Pipe Model with knowledge/skill profiles is discussed in Erwin Rausch, *Balancing Needs of People and Organizations,* originally published by BNA, Washington, D.C., 1978. Now published by Dictactic Systems, Cranford, N.J. 070160.

profile would apply to both job description lines because similar knowledge and skills are needed for analysis of competition as for evaluating marketing strategies.

On the other hand, the job-description line which reads, "Must be thoroughly familiar with the assigned product," could also be part of a knowledge/skill profile since it concerns a single topic which the product manager must know. It is also possible, of course, for several lines on the job description to converge on more than one knowledge/skill profile line. This is the case in parts of the marketing example, where some knowledge/skill lines apply to at least the two job description lines and possibly to more responsibilities.

A knowledge/skill profile provides a supervisor with a tool which can provide a step-by-step guidance in analyzing strengths and weaknesses of an employee's competence. Sometimes called a coaching guide, it can then help the employee and the supervisor decide on assignments which will sharpen knowledge and/or skills. Examples of a coaching guide for a salesperson and a knowledge/skill list for a machine shop supervisor are in Exhibit 10.1 and Exhibit 10.2.

EXHIBIT 10.1.   SAMPLE COACHING GUIDE

(For a sales person)

Name _____ Date of observation _____

How well CAN the representative (does the representative understand):   Competence
Level

1. Territory Planning
   Plan an efficient daily itinerary to achieve target call rate __   _____
   Follow itinerary   _____   _____
   Respond to obstacles by seeking other alternatives   ____   _____

2. Planning the Call
   After each call, record information which is important for the
      next call to that customer _____   _____
   Use information from customers and other sources to plan
      each call   _____   _____
   Set customer-action oriented objectives and action plans be-
      fore each call _____   _____

EXHIBIT 10.1. *(Continued)*

3. Getting In

Remember customer/customer staff member names ＿＿＿＿   ＿＿＿＿＿＿

Find ways to get in to see customers on itinerary ＿＿＿＿＿   ＿＿＿＿＿＿

4. Opening

Use opening statements/questions that start customer talking
on matter relevant to call objective   ＿＿＿＿＿＿＿＿＿＿   ＿＿＿＿＿＿

5. Identifying Needs

Probe to uncover the customer's needs ＿＿＿＿＿＿＿＿＿＿   ＿＿＿＿＿＿

Use open probing to encourage dialogue   ＿＿＿＿＿＿＿＿＿   ＿＿＿＿＿＿

Support uncovered customer need with a benefit statement   ＿＿＿＿＿＿

Change planned presentation in response to new need uncovered   ＿＿＿＿＿＿＿＿＿＿＿＿＿＿＿＿＿＿＿＿＿＿   ＿＿＿＿＿＿

6. Features and Benefits

Use information from past calls (and other sources) to include
assumed customer's needs in benefit statements   ＿＿＿＿   ＿＿＿＿＿＿

React to favorable comments about product with benefit
statements   ＿＿＿＿＿＿＿＿＿＿＿＿＿＿＿＿＿＿＿＿   ＿＿＿＿＿＿

7. Sales Aids

Put hands on what is needed without fumbling, during presentation   ＿＿＿＿＿＿＿＿＿＿＿＿＿＿＿＿＿＿＿＿＿＿   ＿＿＿＿＿＿

Control the sales aid ＿＿＿＿＿＿＿＿＿＿＿＿＿＿＿＿＿＿＿   ＿＿＿＿＿＿

Use sales aids properly ＿＿＿＿＿＿＿＿＿＿＿＿＿＿＿＿＿＿   ＿＿＿＿＿＿

8. Handling Objections

Offer proof when customer displays skepticism ＿＿＿＿＿＿＿   ＿＿＿＿＿＿

Continue probing when customer responds with stall   ＿＿   ＿＿＿＿＿＿

Answer objections directly to clear up misunderstanding and
stress benefit to minimize drawbacks ＿＿＿＿＿＿＿＿＿＿   ＿＿＿＿＿＿

Answer questions about product factually ＿＿＿＿＿＿＿＿＿   ＿＿＿＿＿＿

9. Closing

Respond to buying signals by closing   ＿＿＿＿＿＿＿＿＿＿   ＿＿＿＿＿＿

In closing statement include benefits previously accepted by
customer   ＿＿＿＿＿＿＿＿＿＿＿＿＿＿＿＿＿＿＿＿＿＿   ＿＿＿＿＿＿

Ask for specific action   ＿＿＿＿＿＿＿＿＿＿＿＿＿＿＿＿＿＿   ＿＿＿＿＿＿

Attempt to close more than once when first close does not
succeed ＿＿＿＿＿＿＿＿＿＿＿＿＿＿＿＿＿＿＿＿＿＿   ＿＿＿＿＿＿

At the moment, no books are available to provide guidance for
the development of knowledge/skill profiles. However, an excellent discussion of the coaching process can be found in *Coaching
for Improved Work Performance* by Ferdinand F. Fournies.

If you should decide to develop knowledge/skill profiles for one

EXHIBIT 10.2.   KNOWLEDGE/SKILL LIST—SUPERVISOR, MACHINE SHOP

Since successful performance as machinist or toolmaker, and in a first line supervisory assignment, are prerequisites for this position, the knowledge/skills required for the technical aspects of those positions are not covered here; by implication, the technical elements of the knowledge/skill lists for those positions are part of this section.

Knowledge/Skills:	Competence Level
Preparation of manpower plan	———
Preparation of budgets	———
Estimating costs and expenses	———
Equipment evaluation for purchase	———
Estimating capital investment requirements	———
Production forecasting	———
Equipment maintenance concepts/procedures	———
Interviewing	———
On-the-job training/procedures	———
Performance evaluation-and-review counseling	———
Time record keeping	———
EEO/AAP procedures	———
Company policies and programs (administrative)	———
Quality control concepts and procedures	———
Work methods concepts	———
Time standards concepts	———
Tool control procedures	———
Communications concepts	———
Leadership principles	———

or several positions reporting to you, keep the following points in mind:

1. The preparation of a profile is for the position—not for the person doing it.

2. A profile should list all important subjects which should be understood and all skills which should be practiced competently, though it is not necessary to have separate lines for knowledge and the related skill.

3. It is sometimes desirable not to lump all subjects and skills onto one profile, but to prepare several, such as one for each major responsibility or group of responsibilities. For instance, a sales representative's job might have separate profiles for each major product line or for each market seg-

ment, or types of customers, and another one for the common selling skills. Each product line might include several lines for the various aspects of underlying theoretic concepts for the product line and for competitive products.

Similarly, the complete profile of a machine shop supervisor's or a computer systems analyst's position may consist of two or more subprofiles. One or several would cover the underlying job of machinist or computer programmer, and one would list the higher level knowledge/skills of supervisor or system analysis.

4. Developing knowledge/skill profiles is not a one-time task. There is no need to agonize over validity, or accuracy of any line. Perfection or even excellence is not important initially, or even later on. The first time they are selected, the lines on the profile will not be adequate to cover all topics and skills, they are likely to be very uneven in the amount of knowledge they cover, or in relative importance to job performance. The lines can be sharpened during successive uses of the profile.

5. Lines should not be written to cover performance elements like: Does the employee *do* this or that. The profile line is concerned with what the employee should know or *be able to do,* not what he or she does. Hence, it could read: How thoroughly does the employee understand . . . or, how well can the employee . . ., or just: Product 736X, or Competitor ABC.

6. If the profile is for a position with only one incumbent, it is advisable to develop the profile *with* the employee. If the profile is for a position with several, or with many employees, designing the profile with a small committee of respected, competent people will pay big dividends. It will show better quality from the initial effort and easier acceptance of the concept as a valid, mutually helpful tool. For a discussion on the reasons why such participation will bring more cooperation with the concept see Decision Quality in Appendix B.

It is important that employees understand the purpose of the profile—to help identify knowledge/skill strengths and weaknesses. They should be aware that your function as supervisor, once these are identified, will be to help the employee learn—acquire the knowledge and skills for top notch performance. With all reasonable people, that is a very positive prospect.

Knowledge/skill profiles can be helpful tools during progress reviews and when developing the improvement plan. Using knowledge/skill profiles to obtain data on an employee's ability to perform can often be an important foundation for accurate, fair performance evaluation. The profiles can also provide essential data for an improvement plan that covers personal development as well as task requirements.

Employees are not often aware that knowledge/skill improvement would bring better performance or that their individual knowledge or skill is not up to that of more successful individuals. In these situations, the supervisor must provide perspective so the employee appreciates the need for learning. The supervisor then must help that person gain the knowledge and skill level for higher competence. This involves providing task assignments, study and practice assignments, and coaching support, that will enable the employee to acquire the highest competence level of which he or she is capable. Employees must be made aware, though, they cannot expect high level evaluation ratings for effort. The high ratings can be earned only when *both,* effort *and* competence were devoted to the task.

The use of knowledge/skill profiles is an observation technique. It is one of the supervisory skills which help to strengthen the relationship between supervisor and employee. Knowledge/skill profile use and development, and coaching during progress review sessions, help employees enhance their competence. When used skillfully, they can be important elements in bringing a positive attitude toward the performance management system.

PROCESS AND CONTENT

Process of work refers to the skill which is applied to an activity in which we may be engaged. A person who understands a process knows what is happening and why it is happening—whether a task is being performed well or not well.

Content merely concerns the steps in the task. This means, in a machining operation, the person who understands process knows *why* the result of a machining step is a good piece or a reject. He or she knows what makes a tool effective and what would make it more effective. Content refers merely to the steps such as inserting the tool, moving the wheels on the machine, and so forth.

In teaching or coaching—in helping someone learn, content is the subject matter; process is what is happening to learning. A process-minded teacher is a manager of learning who thinks about motivation to learn while lecturing and while working with students.

In performance management, process is an understanding of the principles that must be satisfied and the analysis of strengths and weaknesses of the performance management system. Content refers to the steps in the procedures that are to be followed.

In coaching or counseling, process stands for the way the message is transmitted, how well it is understood and for the techniques that can be used to attain even better understanding. It concerns when and where the discussion is held, how emphasis is placed, and techniques that the supervisor uses to motivate the employee. Content concerns the message itself, what it is that the supervisor wants to say or is saying.

There is another way of looking at process and content and this is through principles and action steps. Many skills can be considered as consisting of principles that have to be observed and action steps which are to be taken. While each action step is taken, principles are observed. A simple example is: during a selling presentation, the appropriate use of questions is a principle that has to be observed throughout. Action steps would involve greeting the customer, making an introductory statement, making the presentation, and closing. Obviously, asking appropriate questions applies to the greeting, to the opening, to the presentation, and to the close. Keeping in mind the principle of asking questions would help a salesperson be more effective during each element, each action step of the sales call.

Competence Types

Many a truth is spoken in jest—or with tongue-in-cheek remarks. Such is the case with a knowledgeable jester's words about competence. They separate four types of people in the work environment:

1. Knowing competents
2. Unknowing competents
3. Knowing incompetents or partially incompetents
4. Unknowing incompetents or partially incompetents

As you can see, they are aligned in order of overall competence.

The *knowing competent* is fully aware of what he or she is doing and how competent performance is on the particular task. In other words, the knowing competent understands both process and content. Content, in this sense, is the knowledge required for the task and process is the skill with which the knowledge is applied.

The *unknowing competent* is very capable with respect to a specific task but does not know why he or she performs it well. It is an intuitive type of competence—possibly a natural talent. The unknowing competent knows content but is only vaguely aware of process.

The *knowing incompetent or partially incompetent* understands what he or she is lacking that prevents high level competence in a specific task, but does not want to devote the effort to improve competence. Usually he or she is aware of the process but does not know the content.

Finally, the *unknowing incompetent or partially incompetent* is the person who can neither do nor knows why, or possibly thinks that he or she can do the tasks. Obviously, he or she neither knows process or content.

A supervisor who can keep process in mind—the principles and steps of performance management as well as the process of interaction with the employee, is likely to be a knowing competent and will achieve much more from a performance management system than one who cannot be as attentive to process.

As you have undoubtedly noticed, principles and action steps have been outlined to emphasize this need for attention to process as well as to content. The characteristics/principles of an ideal system represent the process of a performance management system which must guide all activities related to the system. In every aspect of performance management, some, or possibly all of these principles have to be kept in mind.

Chapter 11

TRANSACTIONAL ANALYSIS*

The term transactional analysis (T/A) develops from the concept that each communication between people is a "transaction." Therefore, Transactional analysis is a technique for analyzing human behavior and interpersonal communications. It is an excellent way to see the emotional involvement in the transmittal of messages and a good foundation for leading discussions toward a productive, mutually satisfying process. A brief overview is therefore provided here.

Transactional analysis emphasizes the psychological foundation of communications. It explains that an individual can speak from three different levels of psychological existence—parent, child, and adult ego states:

Parent ego state represents the things we are taught by our parents, teachers, and others we encounter in life. The goal of the parent is to be right and superior. The parent in us says, "work hard, stay pure, follow the rules." The parent is usually stuffy, self-righteous, a know-it-all who has an answer for everything.

---

* This brief synopsis is based on ideas contained in: Eric Berne, *Games People Play* (New York: Grove Press, 1964); Thomas Harris, *I'm OK—You're OK: A Practical Guide to Transactional Analysis* (New York: Harper & Row, 1969); Muriel James and Dorothy, Jongeward, *Born To Win: Transactional Analysis with Gestalt Experiments* (Reading, Massachusetts: Addison-Wesley, 1971).

The parent is easily aroused to strong emotions, especially protective feelings, and anger when challenged. The parent may, however, restrain the emotions and keep them inside so they are not easy to hear or see.

Child ego state represents pure emotion. Our child is almost the opposite of our parent—shows emotion easily, rushes into things, likes to play, explore, and create. The child part is relatively weak, insecure, and unsure of himself or herself.

Adult ego state acts as a data processing computer. Its function is to make decisions based on the data from the child, the parents, and what is happening now. The adult is logical, reasoning, helpful, understanding, and responsive—in a human way.

Figure 11.1 shows these three ego states as they are often depicted.

Though the adult state appears to be, and is, the more appropriate one for most work-related situations, to be "adult" at all times is not necessarily a desirable goal. A natural, open individual often displays the child, and even the parent, in his or her personality—because to be natural means to be one's self, and a complete self contains all three ego states.

The T/A approach starts be defining each communication between people as a transaction. If one person says hello to another person, that is a transaction. If the other person answers, that is

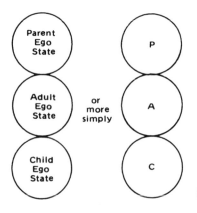

Figure 11.1. Three Ego States

another transactions. If a person responds to a greeting in a friendly way, that is a positive transaction, just as a greeting usually is. Failure to respond to a greeting is also a transaction; However, it is a negative transaction.

Transactions have to start from some ego state. If at any one moment the parent ego state is dominant in you, then, when you speak, it is the parent ego state that other people hear; or, if the child ego state is dominant at the moment, it is the child that is speaking when you say something.

COMPLEMENTARY TRANSACTIONS

Complementary transactions occur when a message from an ego state of one person is responded to be a message from the ego state which it addressed in the other person. An example of this transaction is shown a left in Figure 11.2. It could depict a supervisor saying, jokingly, to someone who is struggling to carry a heavy package: "Hey, Joe, can I give you this package to take along?" (Parent-Child statement (PC)) The reply might be, "By all means, please do; that'll make it more fun." (Child-Parent statement (C-P))

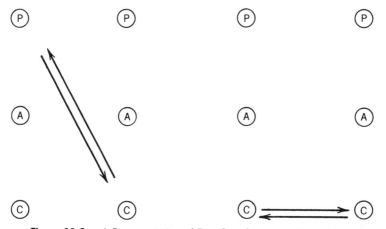

Figure 11.2. A Representation of Two Complementary Transactions

Complementary transactions are usually quite satisfying. They need not be between different ego states. "Come on, let's go out and have a beer. What do you say?" and a response of "Okay, that sounds like a great idea," are complementary Child-Child transactions, for instance (right side of Figure 11.2). At work, the most effective transactions are complementary Adult-Adult, though there are appropriate times when it is desirable for the Child or the Parent to be dominant.

CROSSED TRANSACTIONS

Crossed transactions are the result of an unexpected response made to a statement. For example, take the following exchange, represented at left in Figure 11.3

Supervisor: "Did you shut the machine off?" (Adult addressing Adult)

Employee: "If you want it shut off, you do it." (Parent addressing Child)

It is obvious that a crossed transaction does not lead to easier and friendlier communications. At the extreme, this kind of transaction could almost immediately lead to a heated exchange, as in the right side of Figure 11.3.

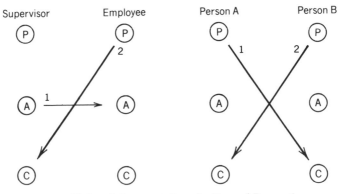

Figure 11.3. A Representation of a Crossed Transaction

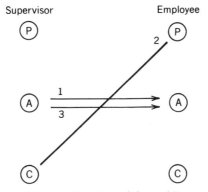

Figure 11.4.   Another Type of Crossed Transaction

Person A to Person B: "Stop smoking; Can't you see that the smoke is drifting to my side?" (Parent-Child)

Person B to Person A: "Who gave you the right to tell me when to smoke?" (Parent-Child)

Please note that from the parent ego state you can only address the child or possibly the parent in the other person. You cannot address the adult. Such is the nature of the parent ego state. The same is true of the child. It can address the other person's child or parent, but not the adult. Only the adult can address all three ego states. When Parent B responds to a statement from Adult A, he or she either shifts to the adult, or answers by addressing the child or parent in Person A. In turn, Person A can refuse to accept this position, and again respond from the adult ego state.

Crossed transactions can occur easily because often either the child or parent ego state is dominant in a person. The supervisor who must get something done, starts a conversation from the adult state and receives a reply from either the child or the parent in the other person. The result is a minor crossing of transactions; if this crossing is recognized, it is generally not difficult to switch to a complementary transaction. Obviously, most work will be accomplished if complementary transactions are adult to adult because then the facts of the situation can be reviewed and the actions that should be taken can be discussed in a calm and factual way (see Figure 11.4).

HIDDEN TRANSACTIONS

Hidden Transactions are more complicated than the other types. They have an unspoken meaning, somewhat like a double message. When such a message is sent, it is usually disguised behind a socially acceptable transaction. One that is well-known, and depicted in Figure 11.5, is the old cliche, "Would you like to come up and see my etchings?" Obviously, the person is speaking out loud from the adult ego state. The purpose of the invitation, however, is not to see etchings. If no etchings exist, then it is really the child inviting the other person's child; and the response can be, "Yes, I would love to see your etchings, but let's have dinner first." Or it could be a cold, adult, "No, thank you."

In the first example of a complementary transaction (Figure 11.2) there may also be a hidden meaning if the supervisor feels that the employee should have gotten help rather than take safety chances. The hidden meaning (Adult-Adult) might be, "Don't lift heavy loads alone."

Recognizing ego states and understanding transactions are the most important aspects of T/A and can help you maintain calmness when another person is temporarily dominated by the child or parent. Remaining in the adult state is the more mature course of action, and the satisfaction of knowing that you are in control and aware of the process of the transaction can help you to gradually bring the other person to the same adult ego state.

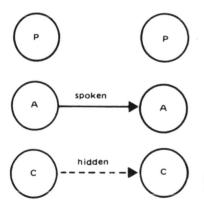

Figure 11.5. A Representation of a Hidden Transaction

OTHER TRANSACTIONAL ANALYSIS CONCEPTS

In addition to the ideas just discussed, there are other concepts in transactional analysis that are not needed for a better understanding of the process of communications and conflicts in the performance management function.* They are life positions, strokes, stamp collecting, games, and life scripts.†

* Transactional analysis is a fascinating subject, for further information, you might read Eric Berne, *Games People Play* (New York: Grove Press, 1964); Thomas Harris, *I'm OK—You're OK: A Practical Guide to Transactional Analysis* (New York: Harper & Row, 1969); Muriel James and Dorothy Jongeward, *Born to Win: Transactional Analysis with Gestalt Experiments* (Reading, Massachusetts: Addison-Wesley, 1971).

† Life scripts according to Transactional Analysts (mostly psychiatrists) refer to the unconscious, early decisions as to how life shall be lived.

Chapter 12

CONFLICT AVOIDANCE AND RESOLUTION

Conflict will exist in any organization and might originate from one or several of many sources. Not all such conflict is damaging. Some, such as constructive competition, can even be beneficial. This chapter addresses a supervisor's* role in managing undesirable conflict, especially as it relates to conflict that emerges in the course of performance management activities.

In perhaps its most basic form, conflict is the result of differences in ideological or philosophical outlook between people or between groups, or in the benefits which different courses of action bring to each of them. For example, it is not uncommon for an employee to be in conflict with the supervisor on interpretation of performance results. The employee's economic and career interests are that he or she wants to obtain as favorable an evaluation as possible. In addition, the employee may place emphasis on his or her loyalty and reliability, and consider the effort devoted to work as being significantly higher than those employees who are at the low end of the performance scale. On the other hand, the supervisor compares the employee's performance against reason-

---

* Please note that the word supervisor is used for all levels of management. The word employee includes employees at all professional, supervisory, and managerial levels (see Preface).

221

able standards and therefore makes comparisons with other employees who achieve the standards or exceed them.

Interpersonal conflict also can result from personality differences between individuals or from clashing of emotional needs. Still other instances of conflict stem from differences in perception. People see problems in different lights, and their responses are conditioned by their viewpoints. For instance, the employee and the supervisor may have widely different views on the fairness of the evaluation which the supervisor assigned to the employee's performance. More serious problems of this nature occur when the goals of an organization and the characteristics and needs of the individuals in that organization point in different directions.

Then, too, there are status differences. A supervisor may resent it if an employee does not respect his or her opinion during an evaluation. When this happens, problems may well develop between the individuals that might lead to serious conflict. For any conflict to be reduced and resolved, someone has to assume responsibility and leadership in moving away from the problem toward a more constructive relationship. This responsibility falls on the shoulders of the supervisor—you. Your objective in any conflict is to prevent lose-lose situations and, as much as possible turn win-lose situations into win-win outcomes.

Most behavioral scientists believe that conflict situations are best reconciled when a climate of open communications is established. The following step-by-step procedure helps to bring such open communications and thus leads toward a satisfactory outcome to a conflict situation:

1. Reduce the emotional level. The skills discussed in transactional analysis, in counseling, and the Johari window can be very useful here. Remain in the adult ego state, in T/A language or, if you have slipped into the parent state, return to the adult as quickly as possible.

2. If you are attempting to resolve the conflict, you will seek to clarify where the real *conflicts of interest* lie. In many instances, this identifies misunderstandings or misconceptions that can be removed in discussion. Conflict is often resolved at this stage entirely.

3. This step concerns the identification of alternatives that can be considered for resolution of the conflict. These range from severe win-lose situations, in which one party wins significantly while the other takes extensive losses, to the far more desirable win-win situation, in which both parties gain something from the resolution of the conflict. The possibilities (alternatives) include:

   a. Postponement of the conflict. This may be excellent strategy when the possibility exists that unfolding events will either remove the source of the conflict, or change conditions so that the conflict will be in a different environment where it may be easier to resolve. Postponement, therefore, sometimes can lead to a win-win situation. In performance evaluation/appraisal sessions, in progress review interviews, and during development of the improvement plan postponement can sometimes be an excellent strategy for preventing serious conflict. If agreement appears difficult to achieve because the differences of opinion are too wide, you can postpone the remainder of the session and suggest that the employee think about the situation, or that he or she look at some additional data, or possibly even give an assignment that would help clarify the issue. You would, of course, also offer to think about the situation or to investigate something yourself.

      This technique can easily bridge much of the opinion gap, especially if the assignment is appropriate and if the employee really obtains better perspective from it, or if you uncover new relevant information that throws a different light on the situation.

   b. Use of authority. This generally is a win-lose situation, except in the rare instances when all parties who are involved desire such a resolution. This is usually the case when a decision by an authority figure is preferred to the continuation of the conflict, or when exceptionally enlightened decisions are often made by a highly respected authority figure. Use of authority by the manager is also desirable in rare instances such as severe violation of rules by one party or behavior detrimental to health and safety.

Use of authority is not limited to the supervisor. In any coaching or counseling situation, the employee can refuse to agree to a course of action, or just refuse to cooperate with some or all of the discussion. This too is use of authority and the employee "wins," for the moment at least. Lower ratings or disciplinary action may even the score, from the supervisor's point of view, but in reality it does not improve the situation. It just brings a second win-lose resolution of a second conflict—the one that concerns the response to the employee's inappropriate use of authority during the previous discussion.

c. At the other extreme use of authority is full concession to the other party, which also is a win-lose situation. However, there are useful applications when the conflict involves matters of relatively low importance. Concessions to the other side may have long-run benefits that outweigh the disadvantages of the concession. In this case, what is a win-lose situation for the short run turns into an ultimate win-win situation.

d. In addition to these alternatives, compromises can be used to resolve conflict. A compromise generally produces a lose-lose situation. Each party, however, loses less than it would if it conceded or if authority were used. In compromises, the parties to a conflict accept less than what they are seeking, but do attain something that improves their positions when compared to what they might lose in the continuation of the conflict.

e. There may be other alternatives which careful discussion can sometimes uncover. These are what are frequently referred to as "creative solutions." In such a solution each party gains over the preconflict situation and therefore can consider itself to have won something from the conflict. Solutions of this type are the most desirable ones, and individuals skilled in conflict resolution, such as mediators and competent managers will always attempt to continue discussions until such a solution has been found, or it becomes clear that none exists.

UNDERSTANDING THE JOHARI WINDOW

Figure 12.1 depicts the Johari window, a most useful tool for understanding the process of any discussion, including those in a conflict, whether it is a part of a selection interview, a coaching interview, a counseling interview, a progress review, or a performance evaluation session. The Johari window continues, and parallels, our discussion on the use of questions and provides further practical guidelines for leading any discussion toward a satisfactory conclusion. If you can get to see its benefits, the Johari window can help you create and maintain an open communications climate in any discussion, not only in the more formal interview situations we just mentioned.

You may have run across the Johari window before in management training sessions, in college, or in a book. If you did, you may have seen it as shown in Figure 12.1 a pseudo-psychological picture which dealt with highly personal matters. Yet, this is not the purpose for which the Johari window can be most useful. In the expanded version presented here, it is a much more practical useful concept.

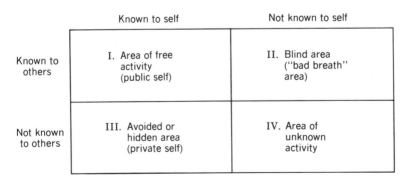

	Known to self	Not known to self
Known to others	I. Area of free activity (public self)	II. Blind area ("bad breath" area)
Not known to others	III. Avoided or hidden area (private self)	IV. Area of unknown activity

Figure 12.1. Early Version of Johari Window

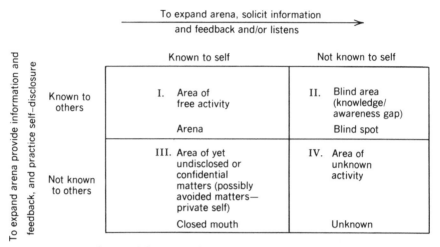

Figure 12.2. Expanded Version of Johari Window

The name of the diagram comes from developers, Joseph Luft and Harry Ingham. As developed by Luft and Ingham, its primary purpose was for use in counseling on personal characteristics. It has gradually been broadened, particularly as a result of Didactic Systems' work with linking elements,* the skills of a manager. An early version of the Johari window appears in figure 12.1. It refers to matters one knows about oneself and matters one does not know about oneself.

The more comprehensive Johari window is shown in Figure 12.2. It is expanded to include *all* matters known and not known, to oneself, that are relevant to the particular discussion to which the diagram applies.

Both figures show four areas that are created if you consider:

There are some things that you know, and some things that you do not know

There are some things that another person, or other people, know, and there are some things that this other person or the other people do not know.

* See, Erwin Rausch, *Balancing Needs of People and Organizations,* originally published by BNA, Washington, D.C., 1978. Now published by Didactic Systems, Cranford N.J. 07016.

The four areas in Figure 12.2 are:

1. The area of free activity, the arena represents those infor-
    mation items, topics, and other aspects of your discussion,
    that are known to you and to others. If you know that a
    member of your staff is knowledgeable with respect to these
    matters, and the staff member is equally aware of your
    knowledge of these matters, you can discuss the topic with
    the employee freely. Similarly, when both you and the em-
    ployee know that he or she must learn about a particular
    subject, you can talk openly about *how* he or she can learn
    that subject and how you can help. The learning gap is in-
    formation which you both are aware of and therefore, it is
    part of the arena. Opening the arena is a primary objective
    of the person whose function it is to lead the discussion to a
    satisfactory conclusion.

2. The area on the lower left represents information known to
    you but not known to the other(s). It can be called the area
    of yet undisclosed or confidential matters. Previously it was
    considered the area of the private self but, in the broader
    use of the concept, it consists primarily of information or
    ideas that have not been discussed as yet, or will not be dis-
    cussed. We can call this close-mouth area. It includes all
    those matters which are known to you but not known to the
    other person or persons. Opening the arena in this direction
    merely requires that you identify these elements that are
    relevant to the discussion, but are not known to others, and
    then provide as much of that information as you can pro-
    vide. You can also open the area downward if you provide
    some self-disclosure.

    The word self-disclosure as used here is not meant to
    suggest that you should bare your soul. Rather, the self-dis-
    closure that is most useful, involves describing particular
    experiences from your past which illustrate a point, or ex-
    plain more clearly why you take the position you are taking.

3. The area in the upper right is the blind area or the knowl-
    edge awareness gap. This is the area which represents what
    you do not know that the other(s) may know. To enlarge

the arena and to achieve the best mutual understanding, you need to reduce this area. You can do so by requesting feedback, by asking questions and sometimes by merely remaining silent.

4. The area in the lower right represents information and knowledge known neither to you or to the other(s). This area is totally hidden and becomes apparent only if events bring new awareness. For instance, if a discussion is ended to obtain more information, when you reconvene, a totally new diagram is required for the next discussion. It starts again with the vertical and the horizontal divider lines in the middle. However, more is now known, and the unknown area in relation to the previous unknown area, contains less. Therefore, at least theoretically, there is a better foundation for mutual understanding possible.

Looking at *a* in Figure 12.3, you can see how the Johari window concept can be used to keep track of process during a discussion. Obviously, if you seek information and feedback, by asking questions, keeping silent at times, and by listening carefully, you will find out a great deal about the things that you do not yet know. The arena will open up to the right as shown in *b* of the figure. On the other hand, if you provide information, feedback, and self disclosure, you will enlarge the arena downward (this is shown in *b*).

As *c* in Figure 12.3 shows, to take full command of the in-

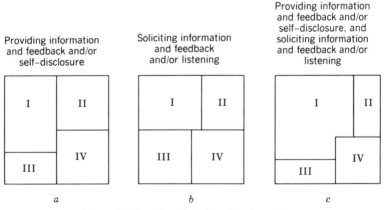

Figure 12.3.   How the Johari Window Changes

terview and to guide it toward the most successful possibile conclusion, you have to: seek information and feedback, ask questions and listen, and at the same time, provide information, feedback, and self-disclosure.

It is important to note that, in a discussion between two people, one could really look at two separate Johari windows. In the section entitled Example of Counseling Discussion and Analysis we will analyze a brief counseling discussion between Bill, the supervisor, and Sharon, the employee. To illustrate how the two possible Johari windows are really equivalent, Figure 12.4 and Figure 12.5 both for the Bill/Sharon discussion. The left Johari window is drawn for Bill and the right one for Sharon.

If Bill provides information, then the arena in Bill's window opens downward, by reducing what Sharon does not know. In Sharon's diagram, the arena opens to the right because it is enlarged by something Sharon did not know before. Since the amounts of enlargement downward, or to the right respectively, are the same because the same information was exposed, it really doesn't matter which diagram is used.

This may seem somewhat confusing at first but it will undoubtedly clarify itself during the analysis of the counseling discussion discussed in the section entitled Example of a Counseling Discussion and Analysis.

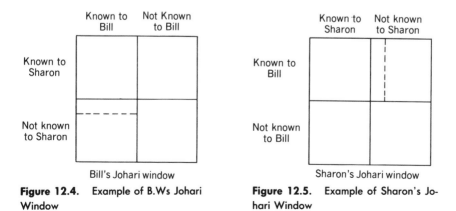

Figure 12.4. Example of B.Ws Johari Window

Figure 12.5. Example of Sharon's Johari Window

USING QUESTIONS APPROPRIATELY

The use of questions is an important topic in one-on-one discussions such as coaching and counseling interviews. Questions can be used to solicit feedback to ensure that your employee really understands what it is that you are saying. They can also be used as you provide feedback so you can obtain clarification of what is on his or her mind. You are using questions to confirm that your employee has thoroughly understood your message and also to confirm that you really know what he or she has said.

Questions can also be powerful tools in obtaining agreement. They can help to develop to see how things look to other people, to learn their likes, needs, wants, views, and attitudes. They can sometimes be the best road to securing voluntary and willing acceptance.

Questions have the purpose of:

"Drawing-out" the other person to obtain an understanding of his or her viewpoint

Directing thought toward agreement in ways which are acceptable to the other person

Showing acceptance of the other person's right to an objection and minimizing objections rather than fighting them

Encouraging the other person to continue to express doubts and objection until all have been aired

Focusing in on the areas of agreement so that a mutually acceptable approach can emerge

There are four ways to ask a question: (1) using an open question, (2) using a closed question, such as a directive question or statement, (3) using a reflective question or statement, and (4) using a moment of silence.

1. Open questions. An open question:

1. Cannot be answered yes or no, 173 degrees, blue, too hot, or with a brief sentence.
2. Invites a true expression of opinion and feelings regardless of whether they are favorable or unfavorable to your point

of view. For example, How do you feel about ... What do you think of....

There are several advantages to using open questions, including:

Open questions promote involvement in the discussion.

They show your interest in the other person. We are all flattered when others are interested in us and in what we think.

They make the other person more comfortable and secure because they allow the other person to say as much or as little as he or she chooses.

They can get the other person to think about what you are saying.

They draw people out, letting you learn more about them, and what is on their minds. Their answers can tell you what their needs are or where the real blocks to acceptance of your viewpoint are, so that you can design your approach accordingly.

2. Closed questions, including directive questions.

Closed questions seek specific, brief answers. Usually closed questions can be answered with yes, no, a specific number, date or time, or with a very brief sentence. They can help to set direction for further probing such as in:

Do you agree that ...?

Do you mind if ...?

There are several advantages to using closed questions, including the following:

Closed questions do not interrupt your momentum during a presentation.

They can provide a quick indication of agreement or disagreement with a statement.

They may allow you to regain control of a presentation.

Questions or statements which request expansion or further explanation at one particular point are *directive questions or state-*

ments. They can be answered with a single word or short phrase. Generally speaking, directive questions or statements should be held off until you have had a complete expression of feelings and opinions so that you understand the other person's point of view as much as possible. Some examples are: You said that you like . . . and Then do you agree that . . .?

Directive questions or statements clarify areas of agreement and keep two-way communication going, but they also accomplish other things in which you are directly interested:

> They bring more information about the other person's thinking on points where you need such information

> They tend to make other people more favorable to your position because "the more you get them to explore the area of agreement, the less important the area of disagreement will seem"

> They give other people the opportunity to convince themselves, by getting them to concentrate on the positive factors, they often realize that it is to their advantage to find a common ground.

3. Reflective questions or statements.

Reflective questions or statements are repetition or rephrasing, in your own words, of what the other person is trying to say, or seems to feel. The most essential ingredient to reflection is careful *listening,* followed by *selectivity.* To properly reflect feelings, you must really *listen,* rather than be thinking about your own plan or what you are going to say next. It is important, then, to select the most important idea or feeling from what has been said, and put it into your own words. An example would be: I think it is an ineffective approach. . . . The reflective question is: You don't think it will work?

Reflective questions or statements can be helpful in several ways:

> They are a good way of avoiding arguments because they enable you to respond without either rejecting or accepting what has been said

They show that you understand what has been said. If your reflection is erroneous, the other person will correct you. This, in itself, can go a long way toward creating mutual understanding

The sharing of feelings tends to create a "climate for agreement"

If the other person has been illogical or irrational (basing ideas on false concerns), he or she will very often be able to see the error better when it is expressed by you. If he or she corrects the mistaken impression, you are relieved of this responsibility without creating friction

Reflection enables the other person to pick up the main idea after you have repeated it so that there is a logical progression to thinking

Reflection encourages people to express themselves further or to clarify something they said.

As you will find out when you seriously try to improve your own use of questions, using questions appropriately is not easy. The techniques discussed here can help you establish a dialogue with the respective employee, during the various types of interviews which an effective performance management approach requires. Success in using questions depends on a genuine interest and concern for the person whose agreement you are trying to obtain. As useful as good questions can be, like all good things, they can be overused or misused. (See the section entitled Leading a Discussion Toward Agreement.)

PROVIDING INFORMATION AND FEEDBACK

One skill that is implied in the effective use of the Johari window is the skill of providing information and feedback effectively. To be effective, feedback must be relevant, timely, and factual and specific.

Feedback in coaching or counseling is:

Relevant when you are suggesting that someone do something that he or she considers to be a *worthwhile* topic to study, a *useful* skill to sharpen, or a *desirable* change to implement

Timely when you refer to situations which have occured recently

Factual (nonjudgmental) and *specific* when the other person can clearly understand what specific events or observations give you the impression that a knowledge/skill deficiency exists or that a behavior change might be advisable.

Two other aspects of feedback that deserve mention are: (1) feedbacks should concern only those matters that are under the control of the other person and (2) feedback should be given calmly.

Clearly required by one of the basic principles of fairness of a performance management system is that feedback should concern only matters that are *under the control of the employee*. Telling a young man that he is not smart enough is not going to help him very much. There is nothng he can do about it, if it s true, nor can he do anything with the feedback if it is not true. On the other hand, suggesting that he could improve his competence by studying some specific subject or specific chapter in a book, or practice a specific way of doing something, could be very helpful to him. The feedback addresses actions he can take. Furthermore, it is factual and specific and therefore not likely to be reserved.

Similarly, feedback given *calmly* will be less likely to be perceived as a reprimand or as criticism. In a discussion, particularly during a coaching interview, criticism will put an employee on the defensive and thus make him or her less willing to share thoughts or feelings.

LISTENING

Some people do not consider listening to be a skill. Possibly they feel that ears always listen, even when they do not hear. Listening to understand, sensitive listening, is nevertheless a difficult skill for most people. Some of us are born with natural sensitivity to others, however, most of us have to devote conscientious effort to listen *effectively*.

Listening is needed when we are speaking, as well as when we are quiet. While we are speaking to someone else, our eyes and ears can receive messages from the other person if we are tuned in to them. These messages give us feedback on how the other person listens and perceives what we are saying. They can also tell us how well our thoughts our ideas are accepted.

To be an effective listener, you have to:

Be empathetic (you have to put yourself into the speaker's shoes).

Concentrate. Signal your attention with eye contact. If the conversation is face-to-face, get close enough to observe nonverbal clues to the speaker's meaning.

Then, organize and evaluate the message, by asking yourself:

What is the speaker's purpose? What are the main points? How are they organized? Are they supporting what is being said?

Is the speaker consistent? How does what is being said relate to what was said before?

Is the message complete? If information has been omitted, why?

Does the speaker use words like embarrassed, cheated, fearful, frustrated, enjoyed, and glad which may indicate hidden feelings?

Do the nonverbal clues (eye-contact, tone of voice, attention to your explanations) match the speaker's words or do they appear to contradict him or her?

Finally, ask yourself questions that try to relate the message to your own needs.

How are you going to use this information?

How does it relate to what you know about the other person or how does it affect your purposes in speaking with him or her?

Is there anything that you do not fully understand and should have clarified?

How could you paraphrase the speaker's main points so that he or she knows that you understand?

Passive Listening

In passive listening, we are hearing what the other person is saying. We can listen intently, but we have little need to dig in and fully understand what the other person is saying. We listen passively when we give someone a chance to get something "off his or her chest." Sometimes passive listening is useful in social relationships where we provide an opportunity for the other person to tell a story, uninterruptedly. If we appear to be fully attentive during passive listening, we are showing respect for the other person and we are providing a useful service to him or her. Sometimes we find it very enjoyable to listen passively particularly when the story or the message is an interesting one.

Active Listening

In the work environment and particularly in coaching and counseling active listening is required. Active listening is a much more demandng skill. During active listening we make effective use of many techniques that help us ensure that we fully understand the message that the other person is sending. This message comes to us only in the words he or she is speaking but also through the nonverbal overtones which the message carries.

In active listening, we are attempting to obtain clarification of the message which the other person verbalizes. Possibly even more important, though, we are searching for the real meaning of what the other person is saying. In coaching and counseling situations, very often the employee will not tell us directly what is on his or her mind. There may be concerns about being misunderstood, about being perceived as inadequately knowledgeable or about divulging highly personal matters.

The key to active listening is what the other person is really saying not just the words which he or she uses. We can do this by using:

Silence

Questions

Nonverbal signals

Giving direct feedback by assisting, interpreting, and reflecting

During active listening we participate in the transmittal of the message by providing feedback to the sender of the message. Sometimes we use questions to clarify aspects of the message. While we are speaking to give feedback, and while we are attempting to clarify, we are tuning in on the nonverbal signals as much as we are during the time the other person is speaking. We are interpreting the words the other person has used and the nonverbal messages, to obtain a full picture of the entire message. Very often when the other person is not speaking, we may allow a moment of silence, to see whether he or she wished to clarify or expand on what was said.

Throughout the entire process, of course, we are attempting to apply as much empathy (putting ourselves in the other person's shoes) as we can. When we listen, we have to remember that our reception of the message is very often strongly colored by our perception of the other person—what we think of him or her and how we feel about our relationship. Active listening and empathy require that we separate ourselves from these feelings while we are listening and devote ourselves entirely to obtaining a complete understanding of what the other person is trying to say. After we have obtained the full meaning of the message, it is time to decide what we will do about it. In those decisions, the relationship and what we think of the other person may influence us. If we want to be competent as active listeners, though, we should resist the temptations to allow these influences to affect us, *while* we are listening.

Though they were presented as separate and different, active and passive listening are actually closely related. They are part of the same process. In the most active extreme, we do all the things we have discussed. During passive listening, we do the least. In between are all the gradations of more or less active listening.

Silence and Questions

We can obtain direct cues to the message which the other person is sending to us even if it is a complicated message, with several layers of meaning, by asking for information such as who, what, when, why, and how. We can get that information, sometimes with silence, usually with questions.

When we use silence effectively, we obtain more information from the person who is sending the message and we get the person to clarify his or her thoughts. Sometimes our silence, as listeners, will indicate that we are thinking about the message, or that we have understood and accepted the message. At other times a period of silence may tell the other person that we are neither confused or need more information. In a way, silence can serve as a question.

Nonverbal Communications

When a person is sending a message, he or she also provides cues of thoughts that are not expressed in words. The observant listener can pick up these cues as an indication of how the person sending the message feels about what he or she is saying. This information gives the active listener an important insight into the total meaning of the message. Facial expressions, body posture, hand movement, breathing, tone of voice, all contribute to the meaning. As listeners, we also send nonverbal messages which affect the person sending the message.

When we are in the sender's role, we notice these messages of listeners and very often adapt our message accordingly. When listening to someone we are, of course, looking to see whether the words and the nonverbal-communication are sending coordinated messages. Similarly, when we are sending messages, listeners cannot help but obtain indications that they interpret about our character trait such as honesty, sincerity, and enthusiasm.

Assisting

When we attempt to obtain clarification of a message, and while we are listening, we provide feedback in three major ways:

By assisting the person who is speaking express thoughts when he or she has difficulty finding the appropriate words. Under those situations, we reach out to grasp the facts and feelings and respond in a way that will help the other person express the entire message.

By interpreting our impression of what the other person is attempting to say. By listening to the words, the tone, and by being sensitive to the nonverbal cues, we can get a picture of the total meaning of the message.

Once we have that total picture of a portion of a message, or of the entire message, we can *reflect* our interpretation back to the speaker. We can tell the sender of the message, in our own words, what we believe he or she means to say. This provides feedback on the accuracy with which the viewpoint has been understood. Usually, the person sending the message will let us know whether or not our interpretation, as reflected, is correct, or where it might be incorrect.

These steps allow us to get deeper meaning of the message to which we are listening.

There are two types of questions which we may want to ask ourselves to determine how good we are as listeners. One set of questions applies everytime we are listening to someone and the other set concerns our general listening skills. Two lists are provided as examples of these sets of questions. There is some overlap, but they are provided merely as suggestions for a list or lists that you may want to use.

The first set of questions is:

What did the speaker say?

Why is he or she telling me this?

What is there in his or her words, tone, or gestures that tells me about his or her attitude?

How can I use what I am hearing?

What response is needed from me?

Does the speaker know how I am interpreting his or her message?

The second set of questions is:

Do I look the speaker in the eye while I am receiving a message?

Do I look for nonverbal signs with which the speaker communicates?

Do I concentrate on ideas when you listen?

Do I determine, while I am listening, whether I agree or disagree?

Do I begin to phrase responses while I am listening?

Do I accept the responsibility for making certain that I have received the message correctly and completely?

Do I listen while I am speaking?

Do I try to summarize, in my mind what the speaker has said, before I shape my responses?

Do I concentrate on feelings when listening?

Am I affected in the way I am listening, by the relationship with the speaker?

LEADING A DISCUSSION TOWARD AGREEMENT

There is another way to look at the process of a discussion or interview, and the use of questions to achieve agreement. In Figure 12.6, the horizontal axis shows the other person's knowledge about

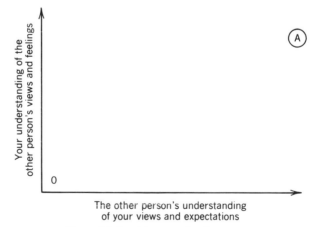

Figure 12.6. Diagram of a Discussion

your point of view—how you see the situation, what you hope to achieve, and so forth. A point to the left would mean that the other person knows very little about your views and a point at the right indicates that he or she knows a great deal about these matters.

Similarly, points near the bottom of the diagram represent very little knowledge, on your part, about the other person's needs and views—his or her apprehensions and feelings about the matter you are discussing. A point high up on the diagram represents extensive awareness by you, and thus a good foundation for a high level of empathy.

You will undoubtedly agree that point A represents a high level of understanding and thus the greatest likelihood of a satisfactory outcome of any discussion. If, during your coaching or counseling interview, point A is reached, then there exists the best possible environment for a course of action that is satisfactory to both sides.

Now look at Figure 12.7. It depicts the situation of a supervisor who represents his or her view almost without interruption, from beginning to end, as the line from 0 to X shows. This supervisor talks a lot but allows very little opportunity for the employee to ask questions or to express his or her views.

Obviously, such a "discussion" is highly unsatisfactory and will

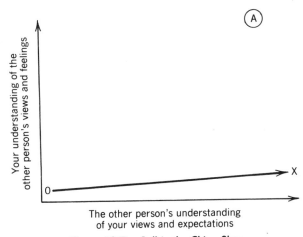

Figure 12.7. Bull in the China Shop

never bring a high level of mutual understanding. If you wanted to hang a label on such a supervisor you might find "Bull in the China Shop" appropriate.

Similarly, Figure 12.8 shows another approach that some supervisors use. It represents a serious misuse of the questioning technique and also does not lead to a high level of mutual understanding. In this approach, as the line 0 to Y shows, the supervisor asks many questions and spends very little time providing information or explaining his or her own viewpoint. This type of supervisor is not open, is seen "holding cards close to the vest," as manipulative. He or she is likely to be viewed with even more suspicion than the supervisor depicted in Figure 12.7. An appropriate label for such a supervisor might be "Interrogator."

The approach which is most likely to lead to the desired high level of mutual understanding is one that attempts to reach point A through open discussion, with sharing of information and feelings, with careful listening, and with mature exploration of alternatives that deserve consideration. Such a discussion would start with a brief statement by the supervisor which ends either in silence of in a question. Next, it is the employee's turn to speak. When the supervisor again picks up the discussion, he or she might answer the employee or immediately provide some further information and again end either with silence or with another

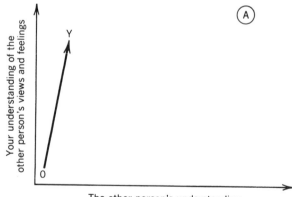

Figure 12.8.   Interrogator

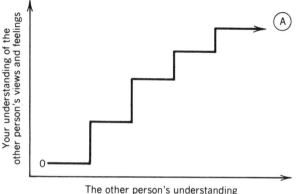

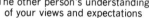

Figure 12.9 Diagram of a Discussion Between Two People in Which a High Level of Mutual Understanding Was Reached

question. The discussion thus proceeds in a step-wise fashion toward point A as shown in Figure 12.9.

PROVIDING RECOGNITION AND EVIDENCE OF CONFIDENCE AND SUPPORT

This last item is certainly not the least important. It affects all the other items because, if you hope to help your employees gain higher levels of motivation, then you must provide more satisfying moments for them. *Sincere* recognition and praise bring pleasant moments. Recognition and praise, of course, also show that you have confidence, this brings even stronger satisfaction as does evidence of support from you, the supervisor.

Even more important is the actual support you provide, in coaching, in counseling, in assisting with resources when needed, and acceptance of your *appropriate* share of the responsibility when standards or goals are not met. It goes without saying that, if this last item is taken seriously it will avoid the feeling which is common among many employees and which is best expressed with a simple ditty by an unknown poet:

> It's not my place
> To run the train

> The whistle I can't blow
> It's not my place
> To say how far
> The train's allowed to go
> It's not my place
> To shoot off steam
> Or even clang the bell
> But let the bloody thing
> Jump the track—
> And see who catches . . .
>
> Anonymous

EXAMPLE OF A COUNSELING DISCUSSION AND ANALYSIS

The following example is given of a counseling discussion between Bill, the supervisor and Sharon, the employee. As you read this discussion, comment on a separate piece of paper, about the process, the use of T/A and Johari window concepts, and conflict resolution techniques where applicable. Writing out these comments will give you a chance to see, for yourself, how thoroughly you have absorbed these concepts and how well you can apply them to a specific situation. Examples of comments have been provided under the first statement by Bill and by Sharon to provide ideas for your notes.

1. Bill: "Good morning, Sharon. Thanks very much for coming in; please have a seat and make yourself comfortable. How has everything been going during the last few weeks?"

   Comment: Sets stage; asks question; opens arena to right.

2. Sharon: "Well, pretty good. I've got no major complaints."

3. Bill: "That's good to hear, but there is one problem that I would like to discuss with you which is apparently affecting your work and the relationship you have with others in our department."

	Comment:	Provides information; opens arena downward.
4.	Sharon:	"Oh, yeah? What's that?"
5.	Bill:	"Sharon, the other day I couldn't help but over-hear your conversations on the telephone and, to be quite frank, I don't think you were handling them as politely as you could have. I'm not particularly happy with what I heard."
6.	Sharon:	"I'm sorry to hear that, Bill. I do my best, but as you know, I don't like handling the telephone calls on the days Norma is out. Maybe I just had a bad day."
7.	Bill:	"No, I don't think so Sharon, because I have noticed this attitude in other things that you do in the office. For example, your contacts with other employees and even with physicians and nurses are not always the best; you seem to irritate other people and give them the impression, at least from what I can see, that you are unwilling to listen to their point of view and to cooperate with them."
8.	Sharon:	"Well, that might be true; but I don't think they have done much to cooperate with me either. You know they have made some comments about me behind my back which I've overheard and I'm not sure that I want to work closely with people like that in our department."
9.	Bill:	"Well, Sharon, that's my problem and I will find out about it, if it exists, and do whatever I can. But, in the meantime, you still have some obligation to accept your share of the responsibility. And that's what I think we should be discussing. What do you think can be done about this matter?"
10.	Sharon:	"Well, I'm really not sure what can be done. This is a tough thing to find a solution to."
11.	Bill:	"That's true, Sharon, but I would appreciate it if you would give it some thought, because it is af-

fecting your work. Why don't we close this discussion now, and what I would like to ask you to do is to think about this for the next few days. Try to prepare some specific steps for improvement. Let's meet again next Monday morning at 10:00 and we can review the things that you have decided to do; at the same time, I'll give some thought to what I can do to help correct the situation and we can compare notes. How does that sound to you?"

12. Sharon: "Okay, I'll try, but I'm not sure if I know what you're looking for."

13. Bill: "Please try, Sharon. Do the best you can. Let's plan on getting together again next week."

In the following, the discussion Bill and Sharon is reproduced with annotations.

1. Bill: "Good morning, Sharon. Thanks very much for coming in; please have a seat and make yourself comfortable. How has everything been going during the last few weeks?"

   Comment: Sets stage; asks question; opens arena to right.

2. Sharon: "Well, pretty good. I've got no major complaints."

3. Bill: "That's good to hear, but there is one problem that I would like to discuss with you which is apparently affecting your work and the relationship you have with others in our department."

   Comment: Provides information; opens arena downward.

4. Sharon: "Oh, yeah? What's that?"

5. Bill: "Sharon, the other day I couldn't help but overhear your conversations on the telephone and, to be quite frank, I don't think you were handling them as politely as you could have. I'm not particularly happy with what I heard."

   Comment: Provides information; opens arena downward;

		feedback not very precise, somewhat judgmental.
6.	Sharon:	"I'm sorry to hear that, Bill. I do my best, but as you know, I don't like handling the telephone calls on the days Norma is out. Maybe I just had a bad day."
	Comment:	Opens arena to the right.
7.	Bill:	"No, I don't think so, Sharon, because I have noticed this attitude in other things that you do in the office. For example, your contacts with other employees and even with physicians and nurses are not always the best; you seem to irritate other people and give them the impression, at least from what I see, that you are unwilling to listen to their point of view and to cooperate with them."
	Comment:	Judgmental nonspecific feedback; potentially troublesome; opens arena only slightly downward by revealing his feelings.
8.	Sharon:	"Well, that might be true; but I don't think they have much to cooperate with me either. You know they have made some comments about me behind my back which I've overheard and I'm not sure that I want to work closely with people like that in our department."
	Comment:	Defensive reaction; Sharon moves toward child ego state; enlarges arena only slightly to right by revealing her feelings.
9.	Bill:	"Well, Sharon, that's my problem and I will find out about it if it exists and do whatever I can. But in the meantime, you still have some obligation to accept your share of the responsiblity. And that's what I think we should be discussing. What do you think can be done about this matter?"
	Comment:	Supportive, at first, opens arena downward; asks question to open arena further to right and to

		help Sharon move to adult ego state; assertive but attempts to seek a win-win solution.
10.	Sharon:	"Well, I'm really not sure what can be done. This is a tough thing to find a solution to."
	Comment:	Sharon refuses to further open the arena or move closer to Point A in Figure 12.9.
11.	Bill:	"That's true, Sharon, but I would appreciate it if you would give it some thought, because it is affecting your work. Why don't we close this discussion now, and what I would like to ask you to do is to think about this for the next few days. Try to prepare some specific steps for improvement. Let's meet again next Monday morning at 10:00 and we can review the things that you have decided to do; at the same time, I'll give some thought to what I can do to help correct the situation and we can compare notes. How does that sound to you?"
	Comment:	Postpones, to avoid conflicts and to provide opportunity to obtain additional information which might help to reduce the unknown area in the Johari window; solicits feedback with closed question.
12.	Sharon:	"Okay, I'll try, but I'm not sure if I know what you're looking for."
	Comment:	Attempts to open the arena to the right.
13.	Bill:	"Please try, Sharon. Do the best you can. Let's plan on getting together again next week."
	Comment:	Fails to listen, possibly on purpose, since at this time, opening the arena further may not serve any useful purpose.

A FEW CONCLUDING THOUGHTS

In this chapter, a number of concepts have been covered which are closely related to each other. In some ways they overlap but in other ways they expand on each other.

During any discussion between two individuals, or one person and a group, the person who accepts the responsibility for leading the discussion to a successful conclusion, applies a series of skills:

1. Keeping process in mind. Here thinking of the Johari window as well as appropriate use of the various types of questions, the use of silence, the principles of providing feedback and of transactional analysis are all relevant.

2. Avoiding conflict by following the steps for preventing or reducing the impact of conflict while, at the same time, keeping in mind the process elements previously discussed.

3. Coaching, by following the series of steps previously discussed, keeping in mind the same process concepts apply.

4. Thinking of the Johari window to become aware of the need to seek information and feedback, to listen actively, to apply silence where it might be appropriate and to provide information and feedback.

5. Using of questions approximately to seek feedback and to broaden the area of mutual understanding.

6. Applying transactional analysis concepts to reduce undesirable emotional involvement and maintain the discussion at the "adult" level.

7. Counseling, by following the series of steps previously discussed while keeping in mind the same process elements.

APPENDICES

THEORETICAL FOUNDATIONS

APPROPRIATE APPROACHES TO PARTICIPATION BY EMPLOYEES IN PERFORMANCE MANAGEMENT DECISIONS

Extensive research by many investigators, especially since the 1950s has shown time and again that the most effective leadership style in any situation is one that allows appropriate participation by employees.

The decision on participation is particularly important in performance management because credibility is of such great importance to the continued success of the system.

What is *appropriate* participation? During the early years of the behavorial sciences, it was believed that greater participation is appropriate participation. It was felt that the more participation in decision making which a supervisor allows, the more receptive employees will be to serious discussions of performance and how performance can be improved. In those days, there was a lot to that point of view. Supervisors made most decisions, even those which greatly affected the quality of work life of employees, without discussion or consultation. In today's world a leadership style that is as autocratic as was accepted then, is unthinkable. Appropriate participation is not a luxury today, or a practice which is restricted to enlightened supervisors—it is a necessity. Still, a few supervisors are really good at it.

Extent of Participation—Continuum of Leadership Behavior

Figure A.1 originally published in the *Harvard Business Review** has been revised for use in this book, it is a widely used diagram which can provide a framework for a discussion of the extent of participation.

You can see in Figure A.1 that the horizontal line shows various points that depict different levels of participation which the manager† allows in a specific decision. At the very right, the supervisor retains a great deal of authority, as is shown by the vertical distance between the top of the box and the diagonal line. As a result, there is a very little freedom for employees to make decisions. At the other extreme, at the left side of the figure, the supervisor used very little organizational authority and therefore allows extensive freedom for subordinates to make decisions. The major conclusion of the diagram is that managers have available to them an almost infinite variety of styles.

It is important to keep in mind that, by choosing the level of participation which a supervisor allows, he or she has made a critical decision, which by itself exercises considerable control over the outcome of the decision. For instance, if a supervisor is working with a subordinate on a matter with respect to which the subordinate has relatively little experience, the supervisor can choose to restrict participation to only certain aspects of the decision or to obtaining the employee's suggestions. On the other hand, on matters where the supervisor has great confidence in the employee, the supervisor can allow a vastly higher level of participation. By making this choice of participation level correctly a supervisor actually enhances the control which he or she exercises. A supervisor who understands his or her people, can be fairly certain of the

---

* Modified from: Robert Tannenbaum and Warren H. Schmidt, *How to Choose a Leadership Pattern,* Harvard Business Review, March-April 1958. Copyright 1981, Didactic Systems, Cranford, New Jersey. All Rights reserved.

† The word manager is used here and in the diagram synonymously with the word supervisor in earlier segments of the book.

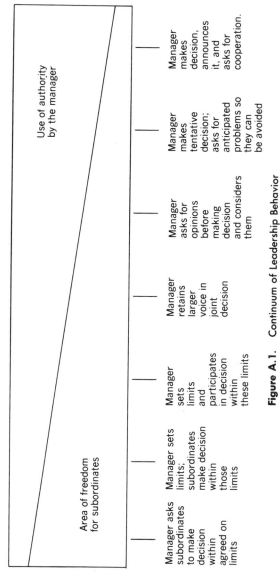

Figure A.1. Continuum of Leadership Behavior

255

outcome which can be expected while, at the same time, stimulating maximum creativity and commitment on the part of the employee.

Influences on the Extent and Timing of Participation

Decisions on the extent and timing of participation depend on three factors. They are (1) the competence and professional maturity of the employee, (2) the demands of the situation, and (3) the normal leadership style of the supervisor.

COMPETENCE AND PROFESSIONAL MATURITY OF THE EMPLOYEE

The more competent and professionally mature an employee is, the greater the extent of participation that can be allowed. A competent employee understands the job, knows what needs to be done, and therefore can be given considerable freedom if he or she has, what can be termed as professional maturity. The level of professional maturity is meant to describe the extent to which an employee is willing to assume responsibility for defining and working toward challenging job requirements such as goals or results oriented standards.

And then, of course, there are situations when the employee would prefer the supervisor to set a standard, accepting the fact that the supervisor is much more knowledgeable about what is realistic and appropriate. This is particularly true when there is considerable trust between employee and supervisor. It can also be true, of course, in the opposite situation, when there is very little or no trust. The employee may not want to accept responsibility for a standard and remain in a position where he or she can always claim that it is unfair and inappropriate.

THE SITUATION

The situation can present many considerations which affect the selection of appropriate participation level. These include (1) the extent of structure of the job, (2) the potential risk of erros or inadequate performance to the supervisor, and (3) the urgency.

The more structured the job, and the greater the risk to the supervisor, the more direct control will any sensible supervisor retain over job procedures and over the way the job is performed.

In highly structured tasks where many employees perform the same or similar work, the employee obviously cannot participate extensively in decisions or standards. Very often even the individual supervisor may have only limited voice in these decisions.

When there is considerable stress in the organization for output, the supervisor may have to tighten standards without the willing, full consent of the employees. The same may be true in crisis situations and in matters affecting health, safety, and sometimes quality. The standards may have to be set in a fairly autocratic manner even with more competent employees.

In performance management, both in the review of job responsibilities and in the development of the improvement plan, there is either less structure or no more structure than on the job itself. At the same time, the risks to the supervisor from decisions that are not excellent, are certainly not great. Participation levels equal to, or higher than those normal for the job itself, therefore would seem to be appropriate.

Supervisor's Leadership Style

The supervisor's personal style, and behavior that would be appropriate and consistant with that style, is important to the selection of paticipation level. Within the limits of personal or preferences, competent managers will, of course, allow much greater freedom to capable and experienced employees than they will to those with lower competencies.

A supervisor who is generally rather controlling, obviously should not step out of this normal role and suddenly be exceedingly participative in any one decision, or group of decisions. To do so would puzzle employees and, in all probability would reduce the supervisor's credibility or the confidence that the employees have in his or her stability.

Timing of Participation

Besides the level or extent of participation, a second aspect concerns the timing. By controlling the time when a subordinate is brought into a decision, the supervisor also exercises extensive control over the limits within which the employee may participate in the decision itself.

An example will illustrate this point. As supervisor, you have a wide range of possible ways in which you can update the list of responsibilities on any specific job. You can review the responsibilities of the job, decide what you feel has changed and/or what the job function and responsibilities should be. You can then present this picture to the employee, pointing out, clearly that this is what the job is all about and that these are the responsibilities on which you will evaluate the employee's performance. You can do this politely, and ask for comments which will reveal the employee's feelings about your decision, without changing your decision, even if the employee objects. If you then conclude by asking for cooperation, you will have practiced a leadership style that allows a minimum of participation and which involves the employee at a very late stage.

You have the choice, of course, to involve the employee much earlier, especially if you intend to grant the employee more participation. However, even with minimal participation, you can inform the employee a week or several days before you meet with him or her to discuss changes or revisions in job responsibilities. You could ask the employee to prepare some thoughts on what these changes have been and what the job responsibilities now are. You could point out that you are requesting this preparation primarily to ensure that the employee sees these responsibilities primarily to ensure that the employee sees these responsibilities essentially in the same manner as you.

Your primary purpose in this situation might have been to make a developmental assignment so that you could better evaluate how clearly the employee understands the responsibilities. Nevertheless, you would have brought him or her into the decision at a much earlier stage. Your purpose also could have been to check your own perceptions and to possibly modify your list on the basis of the employee's input. Very often, bringing employees in early on a decision automatically results in a higher level of participation. Sometimes, though, as the example indicates, that may not be the case. The point is that timing decisions are not entirely the same as level (or extent) decisions and should also be given appropriate thought by a supervisor who endeavors to achieve high competence.

Sometimes employees can be brought into a decision at a later time and still be given a major voice. This situation can occur when higher levels in an organization first have to set policy or when outside developments have to be awaited.

In general though, for the type of decisions which performance management requires, it is usually advisable to bring employees in at an early stage.

Participation extent must be selected for many decisions in a performance management system. An example is the setting of standards or goals. The more competent, experienced, and mature a subordinate is, the greater is his or her ability likely to be, to set challenging and appropriate goals or performance standards. There is little need for the supervisor to be involved with standards/goals of such an employee, except to provide the necessary support, advice, and consultation when requested. The supervisor might briefly review the standards with the employee to ensure that all aspects of the project or responsibility have been considered, and might sometimes suggest modifications from the broader perspective which the supervisor's postion provides. At the other extreme is the employee who either has very little experience or who works in a highly structured job along with many other people, or who is personally not sufficiently mature to demand high level performance from himself or herself. With such employees a far more authoritarian position has to be taken. However, authoritarian does not mean dictatorial. With these employees, detailed explanation is still required, of the reasons for decisions about standards.

Concepts Which Can Help to Select Appropriate Level and Timing of Participation

In light of the complexity of decisions on how much participation is appropriate, it is clearly impossible to be close to perfect every time. What makes for reliable, good leadership, is a high batting average of appropriate selection of participation levels. The important point is that the supervisors do and can apply a variety of styles. The challenge to supervisors is to be *perceived* as consistent despite the different styles and, of course, to apply them appropriately.

To help guide in participation decisions, two concepts can be very useful. They are:

1. The life cycle concept
2. The quality of a decision

Life Cycle Concept*

The life cycle concept provides indications of the level of competence and maturity of an employee, and thereby to the most appropriate participation level. It compares the job/competence maturity of an employee with the life maturity of a person. It points out that, as individuals, we obviously begin life in a most immature form. At that point, the parent, who is our leader, will be fairly authoritarian, telling us what we should do and what we should not do, without particular concern about how we like the decision. In infancy, for instance, a child is told not to cross the street and if it does, it may receive a spanking. The parent, though showing great warmth, affection, and love for the child at other times, pays little attention to how well the child likes being told what to do and what not to do, or enjoys the punishment which accompanies disobedience.

The whole concept of obedience/disobedience is an important one at an immature level of development. It is stressed to children that they must be obedient or else they will suffer the consequences. As a child grows and matures, parents must relax this unilateral decision making, particularly in evaluating what is the appropriate behavior for the child and what is not appropriate. The limits expand for the child to act without restriction by the parent, and without reproof. Furthermore, those restrictions that do remain, are explained in greater detail, as the child matures. The peak of this detailed explanation and also of fairly high involvement by the parent occurs sometime during the later high school years, when the maturing offspring must understand and

* The Life Cycle Concept is based on the work of Paul Hersey and Kenneth Blanchard, *Training and Development Journal,* February 1974 reprinted for *Balancing Needs of People and Organizations,* Didactic Systems.

accept, the standards set by parents or they will be disobeyed surreptitiously or possibly even openly.

Once the child has left home to go to work or college, obviously parents can provide far less guidance. They set only very few standards/limits and rarely administer negative consequences for what they consider to be inappropriate behavior. Less explanation is also required because there is less opportunity and less contact.

Finally, when the offspring is settled in career and family, the relationship is reversed. Often the offspring sets standards, not only for his or her behavior, but also for the behavior of parents who wish to continue a close relationship with the offspring.

A similar development occurs with an employee in an organization. When the new employee starts work, he or she is told where the office or workplace is, what the work hours are, and all the other rules and procedures of the organization. The new employee is not asked how he or she likes these basic work conditions, but is merely asked to comply with them.

Depending on the experience and competence of a new employee, he or she will progress rapidly toward greater self-sufficiency and greater participation in decisions. Those employees who have limited competence, initially, will progress only slowly. Those who have high level professional competence, will progress very rapidly and will quickly be treated by the supervisor the same way as experienced employees who are mature and have been in their respective professional positions for a considerable period of time.

Some employees, however, do not progress very far toward the position where extensive participation is possible. These are employees who either work in highly structured positions and, having accepted them, must also accept the fact that tasks will be assigned to them and that they will have relatively little voice in such assignment. Similarly, employees with very low level of competence, will also receive work assignments, and decisions will be made that effect them, with relatively little participation. At the extreme, a retarded employee who works as a sweeper may require regular reminders of the routine and will be asked very few questions about how well he or she likes the particular sequence of work.

At the professional extreme, the best participation style is likely to be very high. For instance, consider that you are in charge of a basic research laboratory of such stature that an "Albert Einstein" might be working for you. The supervisory function and the relationship would be similar to that of a parent to a grown, competent, established offspring. Probably the most appropriate style would be to say to "Albert Einstein," in the morning, good morning, "Albert," I am glad you came to work. Is there anything I can do for you?

This life cycle concept of leadership suggests a range of styles that are more appropriate for the various types of employees. It does not precisely pinpoint which specifies spot on the leadership continuum, for instance, would be appropriate. It does provide some proof why the left side of the continuum is the more appropriate one for those employees who are highly professional, competent, and mature while the right side is appropriate for those who are neither experienced nor professional nor mature. If you were to rank all employees in your organization on a scale based on life cycle concept maturity, the ranking would then help you to decide, under normal conditions, which narrow range of points on the leadership continuum would be the most appropriate range for any one employee.

Please remember, though, that the situation might dramatically change the amount of participation which you could or would allow. In a crisis situation, even the most experienced employees might receive only limited freedom to participate in decisions.

Decision Quality

One other concept that can help with deciding what level of participation to use is based on the work by Norman Maier.* As Figure A.2 shows, Maier points to two dimensions of the quality of decisions, (1) technical quality and (2) acceptance quality.

As you can see in this figure, the further to the left a decision belongs, the lower the technical expertise that is required for a

---

* Assets and Liabilities in Group Problem Solving: The Need for an Integrative Function, *Psychological Review,* Vol. 74 April 1967 reprinted for *Balancing Needs of People and Organizations,* Didactic Systems.

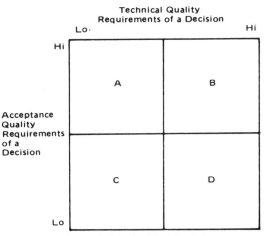

Figure A.2.   Decision Quality

high quality decision. Points on the right side of the figure require high technical expertise. Similarly, the lower a point on the diagram, the less acceptance is needed for a decision to be implemented effectively. Points high on the diagram require extensive acceptance so that there will not be obstacles to the implementation of the decisions.

With technical quality, Maier means the extent of technical knowledge that is required to make a high quality decision. Some decisions require extensive knowledge in a particular field. For instance, designs require knowledge of the discipline which applies to a particular design.

On the other hand, acceptance quality does not require any specific knowledge. A decision has high acceptance quality if it satisfies the needs of the people who are affected by the decision. In other words, a decision has high acceptance quality, if most people who are affected by it believe it has been made correctly.

To achieve high technical quality, the greatest possible expertise should be applied to the making of that decision. To obtain high acceptance quality, it is usually best to obtain input from all those who feel that they are affected and should be involved with the decision, or at least obtain input from a representative group of these people.

With respect to performance management, setting results

oriented standards in highly technical fields would therefore require experts in those fields. To obtain acceptance of such standards would require a detailed explanation of how they were set and why they were decided at that particular level, and/or a high level of participation by all those who are affected by the standards.

Goals and standards are usually in quadrant B, the quadrant where supervisors fail most often to act competently. Decisions in this quadrant require participation of all those who are involved, as well as of the best technical experts that can be found. They could also be made by the technical experts and then be carefully explained to all those who are affected so that a high degree of acceptance is obtained—if that is possible.

For completeness, the other quadrants are briefly discussed:

Quadrant A—Decisions in this quadrant require high participation by all who are affected.

Quadrant C—Decisions in this quadrant can and should be made by the supervisor or manager. If a supervisor or manager fails to make the decision, and seeks high level participation, that supervisor will be seen as indecisive or as vascillating.

Quadrant D—decisions can generally be made by the supervisor in conjunction with technical experts. By definition, very little explanation is required to gain acceptance from those who are affected.

Errors in identifying where in the figure a decision belongs can be very costly. For example, the general manager of a fairly large organization in a metropolitan location treated a change in work hours as though it were a decision in quadrant D rather than in quadrant A or B. As a result, he announced the new hours and within weeks the employees who had previously rejected union organization, accepted it overwhelmingly.

The decision quality figure serves as another guide in selecting the extent, and even the timing of participation. It helps to identify the point on the leadership behavior continuum which is most appropriate for a specific situation. Please note that this figure does not address the competence or maturity of subordinates but rather addresses how the situation might affect the selection of the best participation level.

A FEW CONCLUDING THOUGHTS

A competent supervisor will achieve a high batting average in the selection of the appropriate point on the leadership behavior continuum and in the selection of the time at which to involve subordinates.

If you wish to improve your own competence in selecting appropriate level and timing of participation, you might keep in mind that:

The entire leadership behavior continuum is available to you.

Ranking your employees in terms of their maturity and competence in relation to all other employees would provide one indication of a narrow range of points on the leadership continuum.

Looking at the situation and applying the thinking suggested by the Maier figure to that situation would further narrow the range.

Jointly, the life cycle concept and the Maier figure can thus help you zero in on a relatively small range of participation extent/levels (and timing) that would be most appropriate for the decision you are planning to make.

Most important, of course, is to practice the application of these concepts and develop the habit of adding this step (of selecting appropriate level and timing of participation). Just thinking more frequently about this selection will, by itself, help you to improve in performance management.

LAWS AND REGULATIONS WHICH AFFECT PERSONNEL ACTIONS

This Appendix contains highlights from major federal laws which have an impact on labor-management relations. Only sketches of these laws are provided; if you require more detailed information, check with your personnel and industrial relations department to see if copies of the actual statute are available for review.

As you review these thumbnail sketches, keep in mind that the purpose of most of these laws is to create an environment in which employees can choose their own direction and have the freedom to organize without threat of reprisal or other influences from management.

NATIONAL LABOR RELATIONS ACT OF 1935 (WAGNER ACT)

In 1935, a federal law was passed which had the effect of strengthening the general position of organized labor. This act came at a time when employees were being exploited by management and its primary purpose was to protect the rights of employees. It defines and protects the rights of employees and employers to encourage

267

collective bargaining, and it reduces the impact of certain practices on the part of labor and management that could be harmful to the general welfare.

The Wagner Act provides considerable detail on the rights of employees to organize and to bargain collectively with their employers with representatives of their own choice. To insure that employees can freely choose their own representatives for the purpose of collective bargaining, the Wagner Act establishes a framework whereby employees can exercise their choice by secret ballot election conducted by a National Labor Relations Board (NLRB) representative. Furthermore, in order to protect the rights of employees and employers, the act defines certain practices of employers as unfair labor practices. Included in this category are management support of company unions, interference with employees' rights to organize, discharge of workers for union activities, discrimination against workers for making complaints to the NLRB, and refusal to bargain collectively with employee representatives.

The law is administered and enforced principally through the NLRB, acting through regional and field offices located throughout the country. The NLRBs major concern is to assure that the act is adhered to, particularly with respect to those portions that allow employees a "free choice" and prevent employers from interfering with that choice. The five-member board decides on cases involving charges of unfair labor practices and determines representation election questions that come to it from its regional offices.

Specifically, among other rights, the act allows employees to:

Form or attempt to form a union

Join a union whether the union is recognized by the employer or not

Assist the union in organizing the employees of an employer

Go on strike to secure better working conditions

Refrain from activity in behalf of a union

Employers are prevented from interfering, coercing, or restraining employees in the exercise of their rights. For example, employers may not:

Threaten employees with loss of jobs or benefits if they should join a union or vote for one

Threaten to close down an office if a union should organize in the office

Question employees about their union activities or membership under circumstances which will tend to restrain to coerce the employees

Spy on union gatherings

Grant wage increases which are deliberately timed to discourage employees from forming or joining a union

Further restraints are placed on employers; the specific act should be read if more detailed information is required.

LABOR MANAGEMENT RELATIONS ACT OF 1947 (TAFT-HARTLEY ACT)

This is a federal statute passed in 1947 which amends the National Labor Relations Act of 1935. The law is sweeping in its content and repeats practically all the protection to organizing that was covered in the Wagner Act. It also provides substantial limitations on union activity. Generally, the Taft-Hartley Act (1) puts a ban on the closed shop, (2) withdraws from forepeople federal protection with regard to the right to organize, (3) guarantees more freedom of speech to employers than was allowed under the Wagner Act, (4) establishes a number of unfair labor practices of unions, (5) puts limitations on strikes and lockouts resulting from termination or modification of contracts, (6) bans certain types of boycotts and jurisdictional strikes, and (7) establishes new rules for board certification of unions.

As is stated in the act itself, its purpose is "to promote the full flow of commerce, to prescribe the legitimate rights of employees and employers . . . and to provide orderly and peaceful procedures for preventing the interference by either with the legitimate rights of the other."

Certain unfair labor practices of unions were outlawed in the Taft-Hartley Act; it prohibited unions from:

Restraining or coercing either employees in exercising their right to join or not to join a union or an employer in the selection of representatives for collective bargaining

Inducing an employer to discriminate against an employee because of nonmembership in the union, except for nonpayment of dues

Refusing to bargain collectively with an employer

Engaging in secondary boycotts and jurisdictional strikes

Requiring workers to pay exorbitant membership dues

Engaging in any act that would cause an employer to pay money for services not performed

The Taft-Hartley Act included many other sections; in short, many have said that this act did for management what the Wagner Act did for unions. Collective bargaining under the law was now accompanied by legal rights and responsibiities of both management and labor.

LABOR MANAGEMENT REPORTING AND DISCLOSURE ACT OF 1959 (LANDRUM-GRIFFIN ACT)

A federal statute, passed in 1959, designed to rid unions of corruption and to ensure internal union democracy, it contains a "bill of rights" for union members, regulations concerning trusteeships, conditions to be observed in election of union officers, and a definition of the fiduciary obligations of union officers. The law also forbids hot cargo clauses, tightens the Taft-Hartley Act restrictions against secondary boycotts, outlaws certain types of picketing, gives state agencies jurisdiction over disputes the NLRB has declined to handle, drops the noncommunist affidavit provisions of the Taft-Hartley Act, and substitutes a provision that communists cannot hold union office and that former communists must be out of the party for at least five years before holding office. Convicted felons are also banned from holding union office within five years after serving a prison term.

EQUAL PAY ACT OF 1963

The purpose of this act was to prohibit discrimination by employers, because of sex, in the payment of wages to employees engaged in commerce or in the production of goods for commerce.

This act states that

> No employer having employees subject to any provisions of this section shall discriminate, within any establishment in which such employees are employed, between employees, on the basis of sex, by paying wages to employees in such establishment at a rate less than the rate at which he pays wages to employees of the opposite sex in such establishment for equal work on jobs, the performance of which requires equal skill, effort, and responsibility, and which are performed under similar working conditions except where such payment is made pursuant to (i) a seniority system; (ii) a merit system; (iii) a system which measures earnings by quantity or quality of production; (iv) a differential based on any factor other than sex: provided, that the employer who is paying a wage rate differential in violation of this subject shall not, in order to comply with the provisions of this subsection, reduce the wage rate of any employee.

TITLE VII, CIVIL RIGHTS ACT OF 1964

Title VII is part of a very broad act of Congress that is intended to eliminate any form of discrimination from various aspects of national life. Specifically, Title VII states that

It shall be an unlawful employment practice for an employer:

1. to fail or refuse to hire, or to discharge any individual, or otherwise to discriminate against any individual with respect to his compensation, terms, conditions, or privileges of employment because of such an individual's race, color, religion, sex, or national origin; or

2. to limit, segregate or classify his employees (or applicants for employment) in any way which would deprive or tend to deprive any individual of employment opportunities or otherwise adversely affect his status as an employee because

of such individual's race, color, religion, sex, or national origin.

Title VII is administered by the Equal Employment Opportunity Commission (EEOC) which is an independent agency of the federal government.

AGE DISCRIMINATION IN EMPLOYMENT ACT OF 1967

As amended, the Age Discrimination Employment Act prohibits job discrimination against workers between 40 and 70 years of age. It is similar to Title VII. Employers are forbidden to fail or refuse to hire, to discharge, or otherwise discriminate against any person with respect to compensation, terms, conditions, or privileges of employment because of that person's age.

The Act forbids an employer to operate a seniority system or employment benefit plan that requires or permits the involuntary retirement of an employee under age 70.

EQUAL EMPLOYMENT OPPORTUNITY ACT OF 1972

This act is an amendment of Title VII of the Civil Rights Act of 1964. Under this amendment, the EEOC was given the right to file suits in federal courts against those who violate the provisions of the Civil Rights Act.

The 1972 law also states that employers who are following affirmative action plans accepted by the federal government for a 12-month period, cannot be denied or suspended on a government contract without a special hearing. Finally, the 1972 amendment extends the coverage of Title VII to the employment relationship in most government activities.

CIVIL SERVICE REFORM ACT OF 1978 (CSRA)

The Civil Service Reform Act of 1978 brought about major changes in the performance appraisal systems and processes used by agencies of the federal government, and in the calculation of pay for federal workes in executive agencies and departments.

Background

Until the implementation of CSRA provisions, performance appraisal systems in the executive branch of the federal government had based merit promotions on the provisions of the Civil Service Act of 1883. Appraisal systems varied widely but usually called for rather subjective judgments in such areas as "demonstrates initiative" and "exhibits leadership abilities." Written standards were not required. In many instances, the performance appraisal process was no more than a once-a-year perfunctory interview between supervisor and employee where the supervisor informed the employee of his or her judgment of the employee's performance.

Pay increases were tied to longevity of service and were automatic as long as performance was rated "satisfactory" or higher. Nonmonetary, and monetary awards and quality-step-increases* were tools at the disposal of the supervisor to reward an employee who performed at a level higher than satisfactory. Among the tools for disciplining the less-than-satisfactory employee were a number of corrective and disciplinary actions including dismissal. However, supervisors were reluctant to use any of these, since they required extensive effort and paperwork. The performance appraisal process in the federal government had deteriorated to the point where 98 percent of *all* career federal employees in the executive branch were rated satisfactory, 1.5 percent oustanding, and .5 percent unsatisfactory.

In his message on civil service reform to the Congress on March 2, 1978, then President Carter explained his proposals by stating:

> Under the civil service system ... (the 9200 top administrators) lack the incentives for first rate performance that managers in private industry have. The Civil Service System treats top managers just like the 2.1 million employees whose activities they di-

---

* Salary increase which are given sooner than at the end of the otherwise mandatory 12, 24, or 36 months waiting period, based on a higher than satisfactory rating.

rect. They are equally insulated from the risks of poor performance, and equally deprived of tangible rewards for excellence.*

The current Federal pay system provides virtually automatic
"step" pay increases as well as further increases to keep Federal
salaries comparable to those in private business. This may be appropriate for Federal employees, but performance—not merely
endurance—should determine the compensation of Federal managers and supervisors. . . .

The simple concept of a "merit system" has grown into a tangled
web of complicated rules and regulations.

Managers are weakened in their ability to reward the best and
most talented people—and to fire those few who are unwilling to
work.

The sad fact is that it is easier to promote and transfer incompetent employees than to get rid of them.

It may take as long as three years merely to fire someone for just
cause, and at the same time the protection of legitimate rights is a
costly and time consuming process for the employee." [sic]†

In addition to these failings, provisions of other laws and regulations were hard to fulfill under the old Civil Service regulations.
For instance, the Equal Employment Opportunity Act of 1972 can
be viewed as a culmination of Title VII of the Civil Rights Act of
1964. It strengthened that segment of the Act to the federal sector by executive orders. The Equal Employment Opportunity Act
requires that all personnel actions affecting employees and applicants for employment in departments and agencies of the federal
government be made without discriminations based on race, color,
religion, sex, or national origin.

The Uniform Guidelines on Employee Selection Procedures of
1978 were designed to give a simple set of principles to aid compliance with "requirements of federal law which prohibits employment practices which discriminate on grounds of race, color,
religion, sex and national origin."‡

---

* "Civil Service Reform Act of 1978," *Report of the Committee on Post Office and Civil
Service on H.R. 11280 to reform the Civil Service Laws* (Washington: 1978), p. 100.
†*Ibid.*, p. 101.
‡ "Adoption by Four Agencies of Uniform Guidelines on Employee Selection Proce-
dures (178), *Federal Register*, August 25, 1978, Part IV.

The Uniform Guidelines define employment decisions as "hiring, promotion, demotion, membership (for example, in a labor organization), referral, retention. . . . Other selection decisions, such as selection for training or transfer may also be considered employment decision if they lead to any of the decisions listed above."*

Clearly, the demands of these laws and regulations could not be met as long as the practices of appraising and rating employees were unrealistic. As a result of these circumstances, then President Carter meant to make Civil Service reform "the centerpiece of government reorganization" in his term of office.† His objectives for the reform were:

To strengthen the protection of legitimate employee rights

To provide incentives and opportunities for managers to improve the efficiency and responsiveness of the federal government

To reduce the red tape and costly delay in the present personnel system

To promote equal employment opportunity

To improve labor-management relations

These principles were echoed by the Controller General of the United States in his letter to Robert N.C. Nix, Chairman of the Committee on Post Office and Civil Service where the Comptroller wrote:

We believe the current system of performance appraisals should be improved. We recommended that performance appraisal system should include four basic principles.

First that work objectives be clearly spelled out at the beginning of the appraisal period so that employees will know what is expected of them.

Second, that employees participate in the process of establishing work objectives thereby taking advantage of their job knowledge as well as reenforcing the understanding of what is expected, and

* *Ibid.*
† *Ibid.*, p. 3.

Third that there be clear feedback on employee performance against the present objectives.

Fourth that the results of performance appraisals be linked to such personnel actions as promotion, assignment, reassignment, and to discipline.*

Provisions of the Law

Overview

The principle provisions of the law are:

Merit principles are established on which recruitment to and retention in the federal workforce is determined. (Title I)

Based on these principles, executive agencies and departments establish new performance appraisal systems, subject to review by the new Office of Personnel Management. (Title I)

Agency and department heads are responsible for carrying out and enforcing civil service laws, rules, and regulations (Title I)

Protection is given all employees against discrimination, political coercion, and unfair, arbitrary, and illegal actions in the appointment to and advancement within the civil service. (Title I)

The Civil Service Commission is replaced by the Office of Personnel Management. Many of the Commission's functions transferred to the Merit System Protection Board and the EEOC. The Office of Personnel Management serves as the central personnel Office. (Title II)

The senior Executive Service is established for the management positions of grades GS-16, GS-17, and GS-18 under the General Schedule in Title 5, U.S. Code, to give greater flexibility and mobility to top federal managers. (Title IV)

Pay increases based on longevity are eliminated. While there are comparability adjustments (to keep government salaries competitive with those in private organizations) to pay on an annual basis, *other increases are to be made based* on merit, with a strong provision that bonuses be given for sustained superior performance. (Title IV)

A merit pay system is established for management employees

---

* *Ibid.,* p. 3 and 99.

in the grades GS-13, GS-14, and GS-15. *Automatic pay increases are eliminated.* Besides periodic comparability increases, pay adjustments are based solely on performance. (Title V).

MERIT PRINCIPLES

Title I of the Civil Service Reform act establishes in law the general principles of the merit system principles as they apply to the competitive civil service and the executive branch. The major ones which affect performance appraisal are:

Recruitment of qualified individuals reflecting all segments of the national population: recruitment and advancement will be based solely on relative ability, knowledge, and skills under a system designed to ensure open competition and equal opportunity.

Discrimination on account of political affiliation race, color, religion, national origin, sex, marital status, age, or handicapping condition should not be a factor in federal employment.

The principle of equal pay for equal work shall be continued as a basic pay policy

Employees should maintain high standards of integrity, conduct, and concern for the public interest

The federal workforce should be used efficiently and effectively

Employees whose performance is inadequate should be encouraged to improve and employees who cannot and will not improve their performance to meet established standards should be separated from the federal service

Employee should receive education and trainng to improve agency and individual performance

Employees should be protected against arbitrary actions, personnel favoritism, or partisan political coercion

Employees who disclose information which they believe evidences violations of law, misuse of funds, or other wrongful actions should be protected from reprisals for such disclosure

Thus, the CSRA confirms the Civil Rights Act and the Uniform Guidelines on Employee Selection. By stressing education and training as a means to improve agency and individual performance, the new law also reaffirmed the Government Employee Training Act of 1959 and ties selection for education and training to performance.

With these requirements and the relative autonomy given to departments and agencies to design and implement their own performance appraisal system, the government accomplished four things. It:

1. Created the basis for the use of the most advanced thinking in performance appraisal
2. Allowed for sufficient adaptation of performance appraisal systems to a specific environment or culture
3. Demanded that a new management style be used where supervisor and employee entered a quasi-contractual agreement at the beginning of the performance appraisal cycle
4. Demanded that more communication take place between supervisor and employee in regard to both laying out expectations and giving feedback

One could make a case that the CSRA thus established a true system of evaluations based on performance. Under it, most federal employees in the executive branch have the right:

To know what is expected of them

To know where they stand

To be treated objectively and fairly

To get timely feedback on their performance

To get hired based on merit

To get assigned, detailed, promoted, retained, demoted, and fired based on merit, that is, performance

To get paid based on performance

To get selected for education and training based on a demonstrated need of their employer and themselves

Results

First Reactions

How much supervisors and employees were or are aware of this new system is not clear. Certain is the fact that the CSRA caused great excitement, at least in Washington. Agencies and departments delighted at the relative autonomy given them in designing their own performance appraisals and influencing pay.

Senior executives and managers in GM-13, GM-14, and GM-15 positions anticipated greater involvement in shaping their work and greater rewards for their efforts.* Employees in positions GS-12 and below were not paid much attention and did not become deeply concerned since their longevity-based step increases would not be abolished. There was a small minority, but a very vocal one, who voiced objections to the Act, to the new pay arrangements and to the performance appraisal systems. Some who had seen systems come and go, resolved to sit back and watch this one come and go as well.

Some employees were plainly apprehensive. The security of their pay and their very job were threatened, but they received little attention, since they were a small minority with many low-rated employees. Some seriously feared the political corruption of the Senior Executive Service which they envisioned to become the captive of politicos and thus the haven of incompetent political contributors at best. This possibility was pointed to by Herbert E. Harris II in his dissent to the proposed CSRA calling it an "Open Door for Political Manipulation.†

IMPLEMENTATION

The administration meant business. Scores of high ranking officials appeared at panels, luncheons, and dinners selling the CSRA. The Office of Personnel Management, though shorn of much of its powers, leaped to the task. The Office established an agency consultant group which answered inquiries, furnished consultants for the design of agency performance appraisals, designed and delivered training at their own sites for all (federal) comers and at requesting agency sites.

Top government officials were taken to Ocean City, Maryland, to an elaborate, intensive, and exhaustive campaign-workshop-panel discussion with high-ranking Carter administration officials and a large Office of Personnel Management representation led by

---

* GM positions are successors to the GS positions in these grades.
† *Ibid.* pp. 394–398.

Alan Campbell, then director, and Jules Sugarman, the second in command. A second such effort closer to Washington was less impressive and less well received. Scores of explanatiory issue papers were produced and widely circulated. Attractive booklets appeared which described principles and procedures and extolled the virtues of the new system.

Still, agency reaction was mixed. Some quasi-executive agencies took a wait-and-see attitude in which some still persist. Some agencies sought help from the Office of Personnel Management and—getting no clear answer—waited, or struggled on their own. Some judged the CSRA to be the way to go and earnestly tried to install their performance appraisal systems not only as a guage of success but as a management tool.

As a result of these diverse efforts, some reasonably good performance management systems were developed in federal agencies. However, most suffered from their "immaturity" and from lack of full support. Pay increments were small because of the difficult economic conditions and the pressure of the budget squeeze. President Carter left office before or soon after most systems began operating.

The final tally is not in yet, but it appears likely that merit/performance will become an increasingly more important factor in personnel decisions in the federal government. It is reasonable to assume that, given the trend in society toward closer ties between performance and reward, the same will occur in government service. The basic guidelines of the regulations governing performance evaluations are sound when compared to the characteristics of an ideal system. Little change is therefore likely in the foundation of the CSRA—established system. Specific future regulations, in all probability, will be geared to spread the features of those systems which are working well.

Appendix C

PERFORMANCE MANAGEMENT FORMS AND PROCEDURES*

EXHIBIT C.1. PERFORMANCE REVIEW PROCEDURE

Introduction

Evaluation is an important element in good personnel management. It provides the feedback which tells people where they stand and, at the same time, is a step in helping them improve their capabilities and performance. Evaluation of performance should be an ongoing process. A performance review, culminating in a conference between staff member and supervisor, shall be conducted periodically but at least annually. This review gives both staff member and supervisor an opportunity to review performance and to look at the future together. It is also an appropriate time to clarify work plans and other working conditions which might affect job performance.

A performance review should usually take place just prior to a staff member's salary review. A review should also be held, if one has not taken place within six months, when either supervisor or staff member is changing assignment or terminating. Any review should be a give-and-take situation, with both supervisor and staff member providing input.

---

* The forms and memos in this appendix are provided solely as examples to illustrate some of the points raised in this book. Since they are taken from actual situations, none satisfy all the criteria and principles which were covered. They should not be seen as models to be adopted without questions, or revisions. Nor should they be regarded as a shortcut to the Implementation Considerations, Chapter 5.

Procedure

1. Department of Personnel shall maintain records and notify the supervisor when regular performance reviews are due (salary review, transfer, promotion, or termination). Either supervisor or staff member may request a review at any other time.

2. Department of Personnel shall send appropriate materials to staff member's immediate supervisor sufficiently in advance of the review so that there is ample time to schedule the following outlined procedure.

3. On receipt of the materials, the supervisor shall notify the staff member of the forthcoming review and arrange a definite time for a performance review conference. Sufficient time should be allowed and arrangements should include complete privacy with no interruptions.

4. The staff member shall receive and review a copy of the Performance Review Summary in preparation for the performance review conference. Exempt staff should also be given a Performance Review Worksheet. This worksheet may be completed independently or, at staff member's request, with the help from the supervisor.

5. The supervisor shall complete the Performance Review Summary prior to the conference. For exempt staff, the supervisor shall complete pages 1 and 2; page 3 shall be completed jointly during the conference, and after discussion of the summary and worksheet.

6. Signatures shall be obtained as called for on the forms and all forms returned to Department of Personnel for the staff member's file. A copy of the summary will be provided to the staff member, on request; it should be kept confidential. Department of Personnel will return copies of the Action Plan to the staff member and the supervisor for periodic review of progress.

EXHIBIT C.2.   MEMORANDUM

To: (Supervisors of exempt staff)   Date: _____

From: DEPARTMENT OF PERSONNEL   Return to

Personnel by:_____

Re: Performance review for (Name of exempt staff)

The exempt staff member identified above is scheduled for performance review.

Attached are materials you will need:

    Job Description—Two copies of most recent

    Performance Review Worksheet for Exempt Staff—One copy

    Performance Review Summary for Exempt Staff—Two copies

Please follow the instructions below and return the completed forms to the Department of Personnel.

Review one job description and give one to the staff member for review.

Give the worksheet to staff member and set a date by which you want it returned, allowing about a week for completion. It may be completed independently or, at staff member's request, with your help.

Give staff member a blank copy of the summary for review in preparation for the conference.

Set a mutually convenient date for a conference, allowing sufficient time for the session and arranging for complete privacy with no interruptions.

Once you have received the completed Worksheet, fill out pages 1 and 2 of the summary.

During the conference discuss pages 1 and 2 of the summary with the staff member. Then complete page 3 by developing action plans *together*.

Sign the summary and have staff member make any desired comments before signing.

Following the conference, forward completed summary to your immediate supervisor for review and signature. The signed summary and worksheet shall be sent to the Department of Personnel for the staff member's file. Copies of the action plans will be returned to you and to the staff member.

In evaluation the staff member, consider:

Specific instances that can serve as examples to support your rating

Each responsibility independently

The need to be fair, honest, impartial, and objective. There is a tendency on the part of some supervisors to give a high rating when it is not justified. To obtain greater objectivity, it may be worthwhile to fill out the form on one day and review it another, which will help reduce any halo effect.

EXHIBIT C.3. PERFORMANCE MANAGEMENT SYSTEM—RESPONSIBILITY REVIEW WORKSHEET—EXEMPT STAFF

Name: _____ Job Title: _____

The performance review is intended to help both you and our organization. In preparation, complete this worksheet and return it to your supervisor. This will ensure inclusion of your viewpoint and make the review more meaningful. (Use additional paper if more space is needed).

Major Responsibilities: Describe the major responsibilities of our job *as you see them*. Use your job description as a guide if you wish, but don't be limited by it. To help identify these major responsibilities, consider the following: Results that are expected of others; improving operations; and responding to change. In addition, if you have supervisory responsibilities, think about developing staff and delegating authority.

Significant Accomplishments: List any of your significant accomplishments during the past year. Among those might be the solution of a problem, implementation of an idea, improvement of a procedure, accomplishment of a goal, or successful solution of a complex assignment. Reviewing the major responsibilities you have identified may be helpful.

Difficulties: List any trouble spots—things that made you less effective than you could be. Note any support you need to remove these difficulties.

Comments: Make any other comments that will assist in the performance review:

Signature _____ Date _____

EXHIBIT C.4.   PERFORMANCE REVIEW SUMMARY—EXEMPT STAFF

Name: _____   Job Title: _____

Reason for Review: __Salary Review __Promotion or Transfer __Termination __Departure of Supervisor __Other (Explain)

General Major Responsibilities of all Exempt Positions	Performance consistently beyond requirement; a level attained by few	Performance beyond requirements, outstanding in some respects	Competent performance	Performance below requirements; could be rated competent with expected improvement	Performance greatly limited; improvement to competent rating not expected
Review each major responsibility and note significant contributions. Also note where effectiveness could be increased or where improvements are needed. Then place a check (√) in column on the right which best describes the employee's performance on each of the major responsibilities listed in the first column. (You may prefer to complete page 2 before page 1)					
Improving Operations: Seeks opportunities for improvement; approaches them imaginatively; persists in implementation.					
Planning and Organizing: Seeks realistic and challenging goals; prepares plans for achieving them; arranges for appropriate evaluation of progress; follows up.					
Responding to Change: Adapts to necessary changes in job responsibility and requirements; obtains knowledge and skills needed and desirable; controls emotional responses to change.					
Communicating: Communicates all matters where others need information where needed and desirable; skilled in verbal and written expression; gives and seeks timely and factual feedback.					

285

EXHIBIT C.4. CONTINUED

Name: _____ Job Title: _____

Reason for Review: __ Salary Review __ Promotion or Transfer __ Termination __ Departure of Supervisor __ Other (Explain)

	Performance consistently beyond requirement; a level attained by few	Performance beyond requirements, outstanding in some respects	Competent performance	Performance below requirements; could be rated competent with expected improvement	Performance greatly limited; improvement to competent rating not expected
Working With Others: Sensitive to needs of others; anticipates conflicts and seeks mutually acceptable solutions; meets commitments.					
Specific Major Responsibilities of Staff Member's Position. Review each major responsibility and note significant contributions. Also note where effectiveness could be increased or where improvements are needed. Then place a check (√) in column on the right which best describes the employee's performance on each of the major responsibilities listed in the first column. (You may prefer to complete page 2 before page 1)					
List below major responsibilities. Use worksheet and job description as a guide, but don't be limited by them.					

Check the Description Which Best Matches Your Estimate of the Staff Member's *Overall Performance.*

Comments:

Staff Member: Make Any Comments You Wish About Your Performance Review.

Were you given an opportunity to complete the performance review worksheet? __ Yes __ No

Did you complete it? __ Yes __ No

If yes, __ Alone __ With your Supervisor

Staff Member _____ Date _____   Immediate Supervisor _____ Date _____

Your signature does not necessarily signify your agreement with the review; it simply means the summary has been discussed with you.   Next Level Supervisor _____

EXHIBIT C.5. PERFORMANCE REVIEW SUMMARY—EXEMPT STAFF

Name: _____   Job Title: _____

Action Plans: Using as guides the performance review worksheet and Page 1 and 2 of the summary, identify ways and develop plans which staff member and supervisor will implement to help staff member become more effective.

List specific actions to be taken by staff member to make needed improvements and increase effectiveness. Consider such things as knowledge and/or skills to acquire, things to do differently.	List specific actions to be taken by management to support the staff member's efforts to improve and increase effectiveness, such as procedural changes, method of supervision.

Staff
Member _____ Date _____

Immediate
Supervisor _____ Date _____

Next Level
Supervision _____ Date _____

EXHIBIT C.6.   MEMORANDUM REGARDING PERFORMANCE REVIEW

To: (Supervisors of nonexempt staff) _____   Date: _____

From: Department of Personnel

Return to
Personnel by: _____

Re: Performance review for (name of nonexempt staff) _____

The nonexempt staff member identified above is scheduled for performance review. Attached are materials you will need:

Job Description—Two copies of most recent

Performance Review Summary for Nonexempt Staff—Two copies (Form P-4)

Please follow the instructions below and return the completed forms to the Department of Personnel.

Review one job description and give one to staff member for review.

Give staff member a blank copy of the summary for review in preparation for the conference

Set a mutually convenient date for a conference, allowing sufficient time for the session and arranging for complete privacy with no interruptions.

Complete the summary before the session, then discuss with staff member.

Sign the summary and have staff member make any desired comments before signing.

Following the conference, forward completed summary to your immediate supervisor for review and signature. The signed summary shall be sent to the Department of Personnel for the staff member's file.

In evaluating the staff member, consider:

Specific instances that can serve as examples to support your rating.

Each factor or responsibility independently.

The need to be fair, honest, impartial, and objective. There is a tendency on the part of some supervisors to give a high rating when it is not justified. To obtain greater objectivity, it may be worthwhile to fill out the form one day and review it another, which will help reduce any halo effect.

288

EXHIBIT C.7. PERFORMANCE REVIEW SUMMARY—NONEXEMPT STAFF

Name: _____ Division/Department/Unit _____

Reason for evaluation: __ Salary Review __ Transfer or Promotion __ Termination __ Departure of Supervisor __ Other (Explain)

For each factor being rated, place a check (√) at any point on the line, at or between arrows, which best describes the staff member's performance.

Quality of Work	Rarely makes errors	Few errors; neat work	Frequently careless; many errors; sloppy work	Comments:
Quantity of Work	Exceptionally fast and productive	Volume is satisfactory	Exceptionally slow	Comments:
Willingness to improve:	Takes initiative in seeking ways to improve	Takes steps to improve when opportunities are clearly evident or suggested	Never seeks ways to improve; rejects suggestions for improvement	Comments:
Dependability	Exceptionally good attendance and always meets deadlines	Good attendance; usually meets deadlines	Poor attendance; frequently misses deadlines	Comments:

EXHIBIT C.7. CONTINUED

Name: _____   Division/Department/Unit _____

Reason for evaluation: __ Salary Review __ Transfer or Promotion __ Termintion __ Departure of Supervisor __ Other (Explain)

For each factor being rated, place a check (√) at any point on the line, at or between arrows, which best describes the staff member's performance.

Cooperation with Procedures and Supervisor	Thoroughly understands procedures; makes exceptional effort to achieve best results	Understands procedures; devotes effort to follow through	Frequently fails to follow procedures
			Comments:
Working with others	Almost always cooperative	Usually cooperative; rarely fails to consider needs of others	Frequently abrasive
			Comments:
Self-Sufficient	Has mastered all phases of work	Works independently most of the time	Frequently needs instruction and checking
			Comments:
Work Organization:	Work is exceptionally well organized	Reasonably well organized	Frequently needs help in organizing work

Overall Performance

Performance consistently beyond requirements; a level attained by few	Performance beyond requirements; outstanding in some respects	Competent performance	Performance below requirements; could be rated competent with expected improvements	Performance greatly limited; improvement to competent rating not expected

Comments Pertaining to Overall Performance

Staff Member _____ Date _____

Your signature does not necessarily signify your agreement with the review; it simply means the summary has been discussed with you.

Immediate Supervisor _____ Date _____

Next Level Supervision _____ Date _____

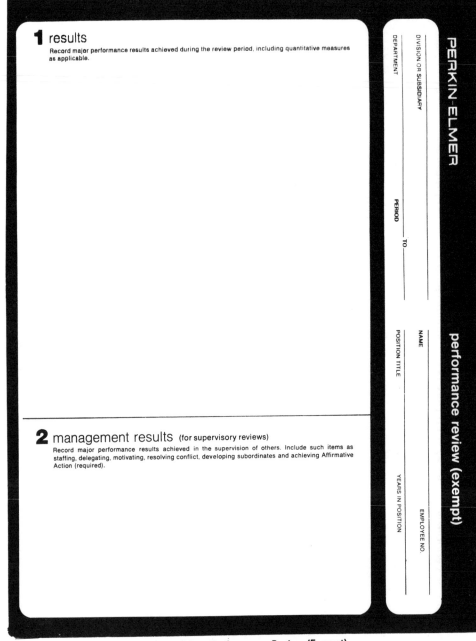

Figure C.1. Performance Review (Exempt)

3 comments on results

Describe how well performance results were achieved compared to position standards and specific performance requirements. Also comment on planned results not completed.

The way an employee works on and/or achieves results often positively or negatively affects the employee's performance or the performance of others. Comment on the methods and approach used by the employee in performing his/her job.

Figure C.1. (*Continued*)

Employee performance is often beneficially or adversely influenced by conditions beyond his/her control. Comment on any circumstances which should be considered in reviewing employee performance results for this period. How did the employee handle these conditions?

4 overall performance rating _____

Choose a rating from the definitions below which most accurately describes the employee's performance during the review period and record in the space provided above.

EXCEPTIONAL: Performance consistently exceeds all position requirements and standards, showing that significant effort was expended to achieve a total contribution far above expectation.

OUTSTANDING: Performance frequently exceeds position requirements and standards, showing that additional effort was expended to achieve results above expectation.

COMMENDABLE: Performance fully and consistently meets position requirements and standards.

CONTRIBUTING: Performance meets several important position standards, but overall results are not fully up to standard. Improvement will be planned to meet standard completely.

CHANGE REQUIRED: Performance is below standard. Significant improvement must be planned to achieve assigned position standards.

5 recommendations

Comment on performance areas in which improvement or development is indicated.

Figure C.1. (*Continued*)

6 development plans

After a discussion with the employee, record any specific self-development plans which will improve performance in the current job and/or prepare for future advancement.

7 employee comments

Employee is requested to sign this form acknowledging that its contents have been discussed. This does not necessarily indicate agreement with the review. Employee is invited to make comments below or on an additional sheet if required.

EMPLOYEE SIGNATURE   DATE

8 supervisor comments

Record results of the performance interview and any subsequent discussion of employee comments and reactions. Indicate what action is planned to resolve open questions.

SUPERVISOR SIGNATURE   DATE

reviewed by   title   date

NEXT LEVEL(S) OF SUPERVISION

INDUSTRIAL RELATIONS REPRESENTATIVE

Figure C.1. (*Continued*)

HIERARCHIES OF GOALS AND OBJECTIVES

Everybody has goals, even people who do not realize that they set them. Some take their goals seriously; others do not. But almost everybody, even most people who lead very simple lives, have some vague, general idea about where they would like to be sometime in the future.

For people who think seriously about the future, though, and who expect to accomplish something in life, goals are not merely guesses about the future; they are real and meaningful targets to strive for. Some of these goals are complex and distant in the future. Others are simple and short term. For instance, if you have decided to go on a vacation in three months, you have set a goal. It is a very clear and direct goal, and you probably see clearly what steps you must take to accomplish it. Obviously, you have to decide on destination or itinerary. You must arrange for tickets and for money, possibly for traveler's cheques, and for the clothing and sports gear you may need. If no emergency arises, you will then be able to leave on your vacation as intended.

Not all goals are as easily accomplished. Many goals are not as specific. They may not have a date when they should be accomplished, and even the goal itself may be somewhat vague. For instance, consider the example of a college graduate with a degree in management whose career goal is to become a top-level manager, possibly the president of some organization. This goal, of course, is clear but nowhere near as specific as the one in the preceding example. It does not state the exact position or the size of the company or the industry, or a date by which it will be accomplished.

There are some fundamental differences between the two types of goals just described, differences which significantly affect planning. Taking a vacation is a short-term goal, which can be achieved easily unless an emergency or really unusual circumstances interfere. Becoming a high-level manager is a long-range objective. It usually would not be very productive to tie it down with specifics such as the company and executive level or the date by which it is to be achieved. It is clearly important to distinguish between long-term and short-term goals and to work with them differently.

Most organizations working with goals have therefore tried to identify different kinds of goals. Some talk about objectives as being long range, general targets, while they view goals as specific, relatively short-range targets. Other organizations reverse these definitions of goals and objectives. As has already been pointed out, the words "objective" and "goal" will be used interchangeably. The distinction between long and short-term goals is fundamental; but beyond this there is a need to further identify the various types of goals. Thus, goals may be arranged in two hierarchies, one in time, and one in scope, as shown in Figure D.1.

Each hierarchy rests on *action steps*, the specific tasks that have to be accomplished so that the goals will be reached. Action

*Action steps are not goals. Their significance is explained in this and later chapters.

Figure D.1.   Hierarchies of Goals

steps are not goals. While the distinctions between the various levels of goals are not of great significance, the distinction between goals and action steps has broad implications. From the point of view of making a goals program successful, the distinction between action steps and goals is of crucial importance. Whereas goals are ends to be reached, action steps are the means to these ends.

PHILOSOPHICAL GOALS/ MISSION STATEMENTS

Philosophical goals are not meant to be achieved. They include such qualifying words as "best," "fastest," and "most." They aim towards the future. For instance, one philosophical goal for an organization could be to provide the best service for its public or to provide the best product of a certain kind to its customers. Some could refer to the public or to customers, others to the interests of employees, shareholders, the community, and so on.

Philosophical goals exist for organizational units as well as for the entire organization. For example, an engineering department could have as its philosophical goal the objective of designing better quality, less costly products than those of any competitor. Philosophical goals describe in the broadest possible terms the overall aims of an organization or a subunit. Thus, the term "mission statement" is often considered an accurate definition of philosophical goals. The individual members of an organization seldom are directly concerned with achieving the organization's philosophical goals because these merely define the environment within which more specific goals should be set. People work primarily on operational levels; and, as the goals at these levels are being achieved, the entire organization also achieves strategic goals, and thus moves in the direction of its mission statements.

Although philosophical goals are rarely guides for action, they do offer a sense of direction and purpose. Frequently they are not in writing and exist only as a consensus within the organization. Individuals, of course, often have mission statements for which they strive. "To be an excellent manager" is such a statement. Individuals also work toward achieving their own personal philosophical goals, in their careers and in their lives, by setting their own strategic and operational goals. For instance, in order to achieve the philosophical goal of becoming an excellent manager, a high school graduate would have to set strategic goals such as obtaining appropriate degrees, serving an internship in an appropriate discipline, being successful in a series of positions with increasing responsibilities, and so forth. Operational goals within these strategic goals would concern taking specific courses, obtaining good grades, establishing good performance records in respective positions, and so forth.

STRATEGIC GOALS

Strategic goals are the big goals, usually fairly long range, which help to move the organization in the direction of one of its mission statements (see Figure D.2).

As Figure D.3 shows, the organization's strategic goals are specific enough so that departments, divisions, bureaus, or offices can set strategic goals for their respective units to support organizational strategic goals. For instance, in the example, Unit A could be the Merchandising Department, Unit B could be the Personnel Department, and Unit C could be the Quality Assurance Department. Each of these departments has strategic goals supporting all the strategic goals of the organization that are relevant to its function.

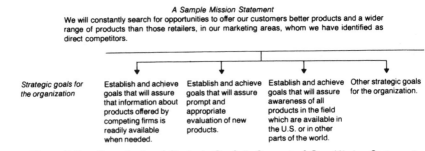

A Sample Mission Statement
We will constantly search for opportunities to offer our customers better products and a wider range of products than those retailers, in our marketing areas, whom we have identified as direct competitors.

| *Strategic goals for the organization* | Establish and achieve goals that will assure that information about products offered by competing firms is readily available when needed. | Establish and achieve goals that will assure prompt and appropriate evaluation of new products. | Establish and achieve goals that will assure awareness of all products in the field which are available in the U.S. or in other parts of the world. | Other strategic goals for the organization. |

Figure D.2. Organizational Strategic Goals in Support of One Mission Statement

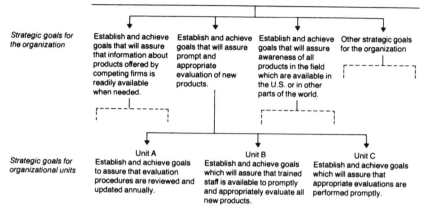

A Sample Mission Statement
We will constantly search for opportunities to offer our customers better products and a wider range of products than those retailers, in our marketing areas, whom we have identified as direct competitors.

Strategic goals for the organization

Establish and achieve goals that will assure that information about products offered by competing firms is readily available when needed.

Establish and achieve goals that will assure prompt and appropriate evaluation of new products.

Establish and achieve goals that will assure awareness of all products in the field which are available in the U.S. or in other parts of the world.

Other strategic goals for the organization

Strategic goals for organizational units

Unit A
Establish and achieve goals to assure that evaluation procedures are reviewed and updated annually.

Unit B
Establish and achieve goals which will assure that trained staff is available to promptly and appropriately evaluate all new products.

Unit C
Establish and achieve goals which will assure that appropriate evaluations are performed promptly.

Figure D.3. Unit Strategic Goals in Support of One Organizational Strategic Goal

Note that in this example all strategic goals merely specify requirements for operational goals. Such goals are very common because they, in effect, define the areas in which operational goals could, and often should, be set regularly. Strategic goals can be of a different nature, though, pertaining to results that are to be achieved only once. Here are some examples:

Develop and market a new product line or a new line of services

Penetrate a new geographic market

Achieve industry agreement on a new set of standards

Solve a major scientific problem

Mount an expedition to explore....

A unit's strategic goals can then be allocated to the various subunits (or managers) in such a way (see Figure D.4) that they will be accomplished if every subunit achieves its own. How this allocation of goals takes place and how the decisions are made concerning who gets what are discussed in Chapter 5. If all subunits achieve their strategic goals, then larger organizational units will achieve theirs all the way up the entire organizational structure.

It is important to keep in mind, as this picture becomes more

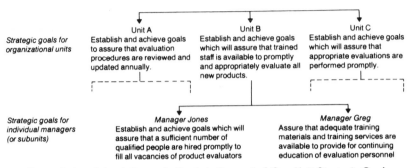

Figure D.4. Subunit Strategic Goals in Support of One Unit Strategic Goal

complicated, that the organization referred to here can be a corporation, an institution, one government agency, or an entire government; but it can also be a division, a department, or even a single office. Wherever a goals program originates, mission statements, expressed or implied, exist; and strategic goals should be prepared in a more or less formal way if people are to communicate effectively with higher and lower levels, as well as the same level, of an organization hierarchy. Each strategic goal, then, should be supported by strategic goals of the various lower organizational units, or managers; and these managers must accept their share of the particular goal. Please note that this discussion is intended only to assure a common viewpoint on the structure of the goals hierarchy. In no way does it suggest how many goals should be set, or how formally they should be expressed. The point here is that for a goals system to work properly everyone should understand how the various goals in different levels relate to each other.

Very often an organizational unit's strategic goal is simply parceled out among the submits of the organizational unit. This is especially true of those functional units where each subunit assumes a proportionate share of the organizational unit's strategic goal. Goals which specify at what rate sales should grow, for instance, would be divided among the various regionals or functional sections of the sales department.

Some strategic goals are not parceled out though, but apply only to one individual or one organizational unit. This is the case with Manager Greg in Figure D.4.

OPERATIONAL GOALS

Supporting each strategic goal are operational goals. The dividing line between operational and strategic goals is not very sharp, nor is it necessary to have a sharp one. While everyone should be aware of strategic goals which are relevant to his or her work, most of the time activities of individuals are concerned with the operational goals designed to achieve the strategic goals.

If all the individuals in an operational unit achieve the unit's operational goals, then they will either achieve the unit's strategic goals or else they will be as close to achieving them as they can possibly come. This is true, of course, only if the goals were set properly in the first place.

Operational goals are more specific than strategic ones. As a matter of fact, much that is being taught about the importance of goals being stated properly and measurably, with specific completion dates, applies primarily to operational goals. It does apply, to some extent, to strategic goals; but if those are not as specific, it is not likely that problems will arise as long as the operational goals supporting a strategic goal are clarified quantitatively, qualitatively, and in time.

Operational goals are different for different functions but can be quite similar for people in the same function. For example, sales representatives could all have sales goals for the same products or services, but with respective dollar amounts of sales determined by each of the territories. Similarly, production goals could be almost identical for different units and people performing the same kind of work. There would still be some operational goals that would be different, however; and these would pertain to the development of individuals or to correcting specific problems unique to certain individuals or organizational subunits. Examples of operational goals are given in Figure D.5, which shows at least one goal at each level of the entire hierarchy.

Operational goals as well as strategic goals can be long range and short range. For instance, the operational goal of achieving a certain production level by a certain date can be a shortrange goal, but there could be the longer operational goal of achieving an even higher production level—a record level—by a later date. There is,

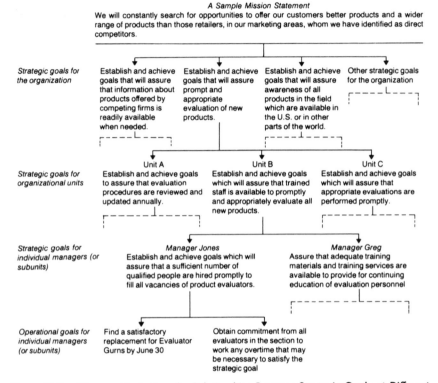

A Sample Mission Statement
We will constantly search for opportunities to offer our customers better products and a wider range of products than those retailers, in our marketing areas, whom we have identified as direct competitors.

Strategic goals for the organization	Establish and achieve goals that will assure that information about products offered by competing firms is readily available when needed.	Establish and achieve goals that will assure prompt and appropriate evaluation of new products.	Establish and achieve goals that will assure awareness of all products in the field which are available in the U.S. or in other parts of the world.	Other strategic goals for the organization

	Unit A	Unit B	Unit C
Strategic goals for organizational units	Establish and achieve goals to assure that evaluation procedures are reviewed and updated annually.	Establish and achieve goals which will assure that trained staff is available to promptly and appropriately evaluate all new products.	Establish and achieve goals which will assure that appropriate evaluations are performed promptly.

	Manager Jones	Manager Greg
Strategic goals for individual managers (or subunits)	Establish and achieve goals which will assure that a sufficient number of qualified people are hired promptly to fill all vacancies of product evaluators.	Assure that adequate training materials and training services are available to provide for continuing education of evaluation personnel

Operational goals for individual managers (or subunits)	Find a satisfactory replacement for Evaluator Gurns by June 30	Obtain commitment from all evaluators in the section to work any overtime that may be necessary to satisfy the strategic goal

Figure D.5. Diagram Illustrating the Relationships Between Strategic Goals at Different Organizational Levels, and Operational Goals at the Lowest Level. (At each level only a few goals are shown in support of only one of the goals at the next higher level. Many others, of course, could exist at each level.)

of course, nothing wrong with considering the record goal as a strategic one or with calling all goals which are supported by operational goals strategic goals.

Usually it is not necessary to have a clear picture of the line that separates strategic goals from operational goals. Sometimes that line is quite fuzzy and at other times it is unimportant. What is important, though, is that all operational goals be clearly measurable.

One other point deserves mention here. Many managers consider all short targets as goals, and, of course, they are. Even the daily, almost routine tasks of completing a specific project: shipping a specific order; or processing a "normal" number of forms, reports, inquiries, etc., are goals, although extremely short-term ones. But as far as the managerial work of the unit is concerned, these are rotine tasks and should not be included in a goals program. Major problems or opportunities concerning them, on the other hand, may properly be treated as goals. For instance, increasing the level of "normal" activity, reducing the number of "normal" errors, or introducing new methods—are meaningful goals. They may deserve the priority which inclusion in the goals program will give them.

ACTION STEPS—THE WORKING ENDS OF A GOALS PROGRAM

Although the distinction between goals and action steps might seem to be of no greater consequence than the distinction between strategic and operational goals, this really is not the case. There are major differences in the way managers should look at action steps, and these differences have implications of great significance to the success or failure of a goals program.

As previously explained, goals are statements that describe ends to be achieved. At the operational level, goals should always be measurable, significant, and attainable—but also challenging. *Action steps,* the specific steps that are necessary and desirable in order to come closer to accomplishing a goal, are not ends to be reached; but, rather, they are the steps necessary to achieve the end results.

Action steps must also be measurable, of course, but it does not matter whether they are challenging. Action steps by definition are achievable. Examples of action steps for the goal of assuring that a qualified person will be found by the end of June to replace Evaluator Gurns who is retiring include placing of advertisements and other specific recruiting and selecting activities.* Action steps

---

* Note that many such steps could possibly be taken—without finding a qualified replacement for Evaluator Gurns by June 30, at the salary which can be offered. That is why the distinction between a goal and an action step is so important.

for the goal of providing adequate training on a specific topic to current employees include such items as searching for and purchasing training materials, scheduling specific seminars, conducting the seminars, etc.

The most important characteristics of action steps is that they are generally *under the control* of the person or group which has been assigned and/or has accpeted the responsibility for carrying them out. Thus, the individual or group can properly be held responsible for the completion of action steps.

Goals, because they are also subject to external and uncontrollable events and circumstances, may never be achieved even if all appropriate action steps have been taken. The goal of having adequate personnel available at a specific salary scale can be achieved only if enough qualified people are available and willing to accept positions at the specified salary scale.

Action steps can be large or small, short term or long term. The length of time or the size of task is not the key factor. The only thing that is of importance is that an action step is essentially under full control of the person or people responsible for it.

Sometimes what appears to be an action step prior to its completion may turn out in retrospect to be a goal. The action step of driving to a certain place and arriving there at a certain time can turn out to be a goal if exceptionally inclement weather or a major, sudden obstruction prevents the trip from being completed on time. As a rule, it is fairly easy to tell whether someone can be held accountable for completing an action step because only unusual and unexpected events will prevent its achievement.

INDEX